A Handbook on Accession to the WTO

Peter John Williams

This guide has been prepared to assist public understanding of the process of accession to the WTO. The WTO Ministerial Conference and the General Council have the exclusive right to adopt interpretations of the Marrakesh Agreement Establishing the WTO and its Multilateral Trade Agreements. This guide is not intended to, and does not provide, a legal interpretation of WTO provisions.

A WTO Secretariat Publication

With a foreword by Arif Hussain

CAMBRIDGE
UNIVERSITY PRESS

CAMBRIDGE UNIVERSITY PRESS
Cambridge, New York, Melbourne, Madrid, Cape Town, Singapore, São Paulo, Delhi

Cambridge University Press
The Edinburgh Building, Cambridge CB2 8RU, UK

Published in the United States of America by Cambridge University Press, New York

www.cambridge.org
Information on this title: www.cambridge.org/9780521728683

First published 2008

Printed in the United Kingdom at the University Press, Cambridge

A catalogue record for this book is available from the British Library

ISBN 978-0-521-42594-0 hardback
ISBN 978-0-521-72868-3 paperback

CONTENTS

LIST OF BOXES AND TABLES

BOXES

TABLES

FOREWORD

Since the establishment of the WTO on 1 January 1995, no less than 23 States and separate customs territories have joined the multilateral trading system through the procedures of Article XII of the Marrakesh Agreement. These represent a range of economies, from global players to important emerging and transition economies and least-developed countries. A relatively large number are at various stages of the accession process. A certain limited number have still to take the decision to seek WTO membership.

Accession to the WTO is complex, multifaceted, and demanding. The nature of the WTO's contractually binding system of rules and disciplines makes this inevitable. Each accession is a negotiation between the acceding government and WTO Members and it is conducted multilaterally and bilaterally. In each case, the essential issue is the same: to attain a workable balance between the special needs of the acceding government on the one hand and the credibility and viability of the rules-based WTO system on the other. The accession process is designed to ensure that new Members emerge as full and effective players from their date of membership. It is a process of learning and preparation for WTO membership. For the same reason, each accession is conducted and completed on its own merits.

For a variety of reasons, the accessions dossier has acquired a high profile in the WTO's activities. This has resulted in an increasing demand for information on the dynamics of the accession negotiations based on experience gathered to date. The Handbook is aimed at satisfying this demand. The purpose is to explain how the WTO accession process functions and to provide some insights into the commitments undertaken by States and separate customs territories who have joined the Organization since the establishment of the WTO.

The Handbook contains a detailed analysis of the accessions conducted so far and tries to draw genuine, meaningful patterns – where they exist – it being understood that each accession is conducted on its own merit, with its own pace, and is therefore unique. This analysis takes us up to the present situation. It goes without saying that the picture will evolve as countries currently in the negotiation phase become Members of the WTO. The WTO's Accessions Division keeps developments up-to-date through regular revisions of its WT/ACC/10 document. In the years to come, this Handbook would therefore need to be read together with the updates provided and circulated by the Accessions Division.

Credit for this publication must go first and foremost to Mr. Peter Williams who worked in close collaboration with the Accessions Division, as well as with other Divisions of the WTO Secretariat. We should also express appreciation for the support provided by the Information and Media Relations Division in making this publication possible.

We hope the Handbook will serve as a useful source of reference for officials from acceding governments, WTO Members, the academia, and the general public.

Arif Hussain
Director, Accessions Division
WTO Secretariat
August 2007

LIST OF ABBREVIATIONS AND ACRONYMS

AMS	Aggregate measure of support
BIS	Bank for International Settlements
DTIS	Diagnostic Trade Integration Study
EBRD	European Bank for Reconstruction and Development
FAO	UN Food and Agriculture Organization
GATS	General Agreement on Trade in Services
GATT	General Agreement on Tariffs and Trade
GDP	Gross domestic product
IF	Integrated Framework for Trade-Related Technical Assistance for Least-Developed Countries
IGO	Intergovernmental organization
IMF	International Monetary Fund
LDCs	Least-developed countries
MFN	Most-favoured nation
MTAs	Multilateral Trade Agreements
NGO	Non-governmental organization
OECD	Organisation for Economic Cooperation and Development
OIE	World Organization for Animal Health
PSI	Preshipment inspection
SCM	Subsidies and Countervailing Measures
SPS	Sanitary and phytosanitary measures
SSGs	Special safeguard provisions
STDF	Standards and Trade Development Facility
TBT	Technical barriers to trade
TRIMs	Trade-Related Investment Measures
TRIPS	Trade-Related Aspects of Intellectual Property Rights
TRQs	Tariff rate quotas
UNCTAD	United Nations Conference on Trade and Development
UNDP	United Nations Development Programme
WTO	World Trade Organization

INTRODUCTION AND SUMMARY

This Handbook is intended for readers wanting detailed information on the process of accession to the World Trade Organization (WTO). It will be of practical use to people involved in one way or another with the process and with the negotiations on accession to the World Trade Organization. The Handbook provides the general reader with a basis for informed discussion and analysis of the WTO's membership process. It first places accession in the context of the WTO. It then sets out the basic provisions governing accession before going on to look at the standard procedures followed and then at the terms on which applicants have acceded to the Organization. Finally, its annexes bring together the main documents used in the accession process.

The primary source used in its preparation is the documentation of the WTO[1] itself. It is therefore beyond the scope of this publication to examine the preparations that take place in each acceding country or in each of the participating WTO Members, even though these are crucial parts of the process.

ACCESSION IN PERSPECTIVE

The WTO is an intergovernmental organization that provides the multilateral framework for the conduct of world trade. The WTO Agreement establishes the Organization and provides the institutional framework for its administration. The individual agreements annexed to the WTO Agreement contain detailed obligations relating to: trade in goods, trade in services and trade-related intellectual property measures (TRIPS) and the settlement of disputes concerning WTO provisions. This package, and agreements reached after the WTO Agreement came into force in 1995, are accepted by all WTO Members as a single undertaking, and as a basic condition of membership in the Organization.

WTO agreements on goods, services, and TRIPS contain rules that discipline the adoption and application of measures relating to international trade. These provide a measure of special and differential treatment for developing countries and least-developed countries (LDCs). Each WTO Member has also negotiated lists of detailed market access commitments setting maximum levels for its customs tariffs

[1] All official WTO documents listed in this Handbook are available as free downloads from the Documents Online section of the WTO website www.wto.org.

on imports of goods, restrictions on trade, and limitations on national treatment in particular categories of services.

Twenty-three new Members have acceded to the WTO since 1995, bringing its membership to 151.[2] The WTO membership accounts for 96 percent of world trade and, in this respect, the Organization is close to achieving its aim of becoming a truly universal body. A further 32 governments have applied for membership. Only 13 members of the United Nations have not yet taken this step. While many of the 45 non-Members are small, they are home to some 580 million people. Many of them are in the early stages of economic development and 18 of them are LDCs. All countries with large economies which are still outside the multilateral trade system are either applicants for membership in the WTO or are currently in the process of negotiating accession.

The basic WTO provision governing accession to the Organization (Article XII of the Marrakesh Agreement Establishing the WTO) states simply that "any State or separate customs territory possessing full autonomy in the conduct of its external commercial relations and of the other matters provided for in this Agreement and the Multilateral Trade Agreements may accede to this Agreement, on terms to be agreed between it and the WTO". While the terms of accession are decided on a case-by-case basis and are different for each applicant, accessions are similar enough for patterns to emerge. The main aim of this Handbook is to uncover these patterns where they exist and to identify exceptions to these. This provides an indication of what is generally expected of acceding countries. It must be stressed, however, that WTO Members are not bound by precedent, that practice has evolved over the life of the WTO and that it is likely to evolve further in future.

Because they stand outside the system, all applicants need expert advice on the complexities of the WTO and the demands of the accession process. The provision of trade-related technical assistance and training (TRTA) does not form part of the accession process proper but the WTO Secretariat provides TRTA at all stages of the accession process to LDCs, developing countries and low income countries in transition to a market economy, with priority being given to LDCs. The WTO programme of TRTA focuses on providing information on WTO agreements and developments in the Organization. Funding for WTO TRTA has increased significantly in recent years, largely thanks to voluntary contributions made by some individual WTO Members. However, some form of prioritization is necessary to ensure that all eligible recipients benefit and acceding countries need to keep this in mind when making their requests. It should also be recognized that the WTO cannot by itself meet all needs. Cooperation with other agencies that supply TRTA relevant to accession and individual WTO Members providing technical assistance and training to acceding countries is both welcome and essential.

The procedures governing the conduct of the negotiations for accession are, in practice, based on proposals made by the Secretariat very soon after the creation of

[2] August 2007.

the Organization in 1995. These have provided a framework for negotiations and have on the whole ensured transparency and predictability while allowing accession working parties to adapt to individual cases where necessary. More recently, the WTO has adopted a specific set of Guidelines on the Accession of LDCs, designed to simplify and streamline procedures for these countries.

The first step in the process of becoming a Member of the WTO is for the applicant government to send a communication to the Director-General of the WTO. This must state that the applicant wishes to accede under Article XII. The WTO General Council considers the request and establishes a Working Party mandated to examine the application and to report back with recommendations, which may include a draft Protocol of Accession. Membership of the Working Party is open to all interested WTO Members. In the great majority of cases, Working Parties are set up rapidly. Once a Working Party is established, all applicant governments become observers to the General Council with the rights and obligations that this entails, including the obligation to pay a financial contribution. All matters relevant to an accession are dealt with in its Working Party and the General Council is not usually called upon to consider such matters until it receives the final Report of the Working Party which also concludes the Working Party's mandate.

The Working Party begins its work with an examination of factual information on the trade regime of the applicant. This is based on a Memorandum supplied by the applicant on all aspects of its trade regime, supporting documentation containing more detailed information on its trade measures and written answers to questions addressed to it by members of the Working Party. The Working Party continues its factual examination of the trade regime till all relevant aspects of the applicants' trade and economic regime have been satisfactorily clarified and documented. When enough progress has been made, Working Party members often ask the Secretariat to prepare and circulate a Factual Summary of Points Raised. This document eventually forms the basis of the Working Party's Report.

Once a sound factual basis has been established, negotiations on the terms of accession are initiated under the aegis of the Working Party. The basic pattern is that commitments on rules are negotiated *multilaterally* in the Working Party itself; that its agricultural support and export subsidy commitments, which are also systemic, are discussed and negotiated *plurilaterally* in an informal group of interested Working Party members and then brought to the Working Party for approval; and that its concessions on customs tariffs and its specific commitments on services are negotiated *bilaterally* with interested Working Party members. However, bilateral negotiations with individual WTO Members may also take up issues normally dealt with in the multilateral context.

Acceders must be prepared to accept all the rules contained in the WTO Agreement. Their obligations on rules are contained in their Protocol commitments – so called because they are either contained in the relevant paragraphs of the Working Party's Report and incorporated by reference in the Protocol setting out the terms of accession or, in some cases, in the text of the Protocol itself. These commitments would, for instance, identify the relevant WTO provisions and record the steps that the applicant has taken, or is committed to take to bring its laws, regulations and practices into line with these provisions. Commitments may also contain other provisions considered appropriate to a particular accession.

The negotiations for tariff bindings and specific commitments on services are based on a detailed offer from the applicant. Requests are then made by interested Members. When the bilateral negotiations are concluded, bilateral agreements are signed by both parties and passed to the Secretariat which consolidates these in draft multilateral Schedules. The results of the plurilateral discussions on agricultural support and export subsidies are contained in Part IV of the Goods Schedule. When the Schedules are ready, they are presented to the Working Party to review and ensure that bilateral agreements are correctly transposed and that they conform to WTO rules.

The results of the negotiations are all brought together in a draft Protocol setting out the terms on which the applicant is to be invited to accede. The Protocol is annexed to the Report of the Working Party. The Working Party also annexes a draft Decision for the General Council inviting the applicant to accede on the terms set out in the draft Protocol. The General Council/Ministerial Conference adopts Working Party Reports in accordance with the relevant WTO decision-making procedures. When they adopt the Decision, WTO Members offer terms of accession to the acceder. When it accepts the Protocol, by signature or otherwise, the acceder also accepts those terms and becomes a Member of the WTO thirty days after notifying acceptance of the Protocol.

While the rules of the WTO provide for voting, it is a well-established practice for all decisions to be taken by consensus. The practice is deeply rooted in the culture of the WTO, as it was in its predecessor the General Agreement on Tariffs and Trade (GATT). Members strive, wherever possible, to achieve consensus. While an objection by one Member can prevent decisions from being taken at each step of the accession process, the WTO has also been successful in containing the impact of political issues on its work. Only in rare cases have procedural decisions been delayed until a consensus has been reached.

After describing the procedures followed for accession, this Handbook focuses on the terms on which applicants have acceded to WTO. Each new Member of WTO undertakes to abide by the provisions of the WTO Agreement and its annexed Multilateral Trade Agreements and by the provisions in its Protocol commitments on (i) rules, (ii) customs tariffs, (iii) agricultural support and export subsidies, and (iv) services. Because the provisions of the WTO are dealt with in other Handbooks in this series and in many other publications, this Handbook concentrates on the Protocol commitments.

It first examines a number of general points: requests that applicants observe a standstill and do not introduce new restrictive measures for the duration of the accession negotiations; the oft-heard view that commitments accepted by new Members can be more stringent than those of original WTO Members at similar levels of economic development (sometimes referred to as WTO-plus commitments); special and differential treatment for developing countries; legislative action plans outlining the action being taken by applicants to achieve conformity with WTO requirements; transitional periods; and the implementation of the Guidelines governing the accession process for LDCs.

It then examines the rules accepted by new Members in their Protocol.[3] An examination of some 40 different subjects shows that these rules may:

- confirm that the acceding country will impose the measures in question only in conformity with the relevant WTO provisions by the date of accession and give examples of the main provisions concerned, either by referring to them or quoting from them;
- specify the way in which the new Member will interpret and implement a WTO provision;
- create an obligation accepted by the new Member without referring to WTO provisions;
- provide that the new Member will ensure that its measures are transparent by publishing them, by providing notifications and by providing information and consulting on request;
- specify the steps that the new Member will take to bring its existing laws, practices and administrative arrangements into conformity with the Protocol commitment;
- grant transitional periods, in particular to LDCs;
- contain factual statements describing the existing laws and enforcement mechanisms related to the implementation of specific WTO rules. In such cases, the intention of the commitment would presumably be to make these contractually binding.

Analysis of the Tariff Schedules of new Members shows that applicants are expected to bind all tariff lines in the Goods Schedule.

The earliest accessions do not reflect present practice and the LDCs are in a category of their own. These aside, the simple average of the final *ad valorem* tariff bindings of new Members has been somewhere between 6 percent and 16 percent. *Ad valorem* tariffs on agricultural products tend to be bound at higher rates (simple averages varying from a low of 9 percent to a high of 42 percent) than on non-agricultural products (5 percent to 24 percent). Although the correlation is not strong, the average of bindings is somewhat higher for developing countries than for other new Members. That some of the new Members have a flatter tariff structure than others is demonstrated by the fact that the highest final *ad valorem* bound rates in different acceders varies from 15 percent to 500 percent in the agricultural sector and from 20 percent to 55 percent in the non-agricultural sector. All these new (non LDCs) Members bar one,[4] participated, either wholly or partially, in at least some of the sectoral initiatives negotiated during the Uruguay Round and since. The share

[3] A tabular presentation listing these subjects and showing the relative frequency of these commitments is at Annex 12.

[4] A small, vulnerable, isolated developing country.

of non-*ad valorem* bound rates is typically low. They are, however, somewhat more common in the agricultural sector than in the non-agricultural sector.

The average of the final bound rates of the two LDCs that have already acceded is 19 percent and 26 percent respectively. They were not expected to participate in sectoral initiatives and did not do so.

When tariffs were bound below the level of the rates actually applied, transitional periods of up to ten years were often negotiated in order to allow reductions to be phased in gradually.

WTO Members are reluctant to allow new Members to use tariff rate quotas (TRQ) and special safeguards (SSG) that are a feature of the Agreement on Agriculture. Only a minority of more recent acceders has negotiated the right to use a limited number of TRQs and only one of these the right to use SSGs. TRQs are very uncommon in the non-agricultural sector.

Part IV of the Goods Schedule sets out levels of support in favour of agricultural producers that are not subject to reduction commitments: "green box" measures that have no, or at most minimal, trade-distorting effects; certain support measures maintained by developing countries; and "blue box" payments under certain production-limiting programmes. Measures subject to reduction commitments are said to be in the "amber box". Fourteen of the new Members did not provide amber box support above the *de minimis* level in the base period and were not obliged to reduce the level of domestic support on accession. The Schedules of the other new Members specify maximum permitted levels of amber box support and reduction commitments. The norm was for the developing countries to reduce the level of their amber box support by some 13 percent and the other new Members by some 20 percent. It appears that ten of the new Members have a *de minimis* level of 10 percent, i.e. were treated as developing countries in this respect. Only one had claimed a *de minimis* level of 10 percent but this was reduced to 8.5 percent in negotiations. The remainder have a *de minimis* level of 5 percent.

Acceders are expected to bind their agricultural export subsidies at zero whether or not they granted such subsidies in the base period.

The complexity of the Services Schedules makes them difficult to summarize but it is clear that the new Members have generally accepted a large number of specific commitments. The high level of commitment is confirmed by an analysis at the sub-sectoral level, although there is a wider spread in the number of commitments made at this level.

Recent practice has been for new Members, including LDCs, to make specific commitments in key sectors: professional services (legal, accountancy, architectural and engineering); computer and related services; other business services, courier services; telecommunications (value-added and basic); construction, distribution, educational, environmental, financial (insurance, banking and other); tourism; and air transport. Fewer commitments were made in other sectors such as: postal, audio-visual, marine transport, and rail transport. Some of these were full commitments and some were partial commitments. While many restrictions on market access and limitations on national treatment were scheduled, some of these partial commitments simply provided specified periods of time for these restrictions and limitations to be phased out. LDCs made commitments in nearly as many sectors as some of the other acceders.

Some observations

The procedures for accession to the WTO have, in general, worked smoothly. There are a number of reasons for this. These procedures are based on decades of experience in the GATT 1947. They do not restrict the freedom of Members or foreclose any options. There have, for instance, been no debates about terms of reference for individual Working Parties which are as open-ended as WTO Article XII itself and no differences of opinion about their composition, as all interested WTO Members are free to join.

The WTO is a multilateral organization but has important bilateral elements. The same is true of the accession procedures. These are multilateral in the sense that all WTO Members have the right to participate in the General Council/Ministerial Conference and in accession Working Parties. However, in practice, only some WTO Members have the resources necessary to participate actively in the details of all the individual accession processes. Parts of the accession negotiations are conducted bilaterally and in private and the results of these are subject to multilateral review only after bilateral agreements are signed with each of the Members requesting such negotiations.

The WTO Agreement is a complex legally-binding instrument dealing with a wide variety of subjects. Applicants must prepare detailed technical documentation. Typically, these run into hundreds of pages. This places a significant administrative burden on the limited resources of their administrations. In addition, applicants need to prepare the substantive offers on which negotiations are based, to negotiate the whole range of basic obligations and to satisfy WTO Members that they will have the necessary legislation and administrative arrangements in place to implement their obligations when they become Members. The busy WTO calendar and preoccupation with other on-going negotiations oblige WTO Members to assign priorities and to concentrate on those acceders that respond most effectively to the challenges of accession. The rules and procedures do not limit the requests that WTO Members may make of applicants (with certain exceptions for LDCs). Members take final decisions on the terms of accession and decisions are taken by consensus. These features contribute to the special character of the accession negotiations. It is perhaps not surprising that the period of time between the filing of an application and accession is counted in years, and that the shortest completed accession process lasted almost three years and the longest more than 15 years.

For all these reasons, applicants need to possess a firm conviction that WTO membership is in their national interest, if they are to fulfil the demands of the accession process. Invariably, a large number of different government agencies are responsible for the range of subjects dealt with in these negotiations and a strong lead needs to be given from the highest levels of government in each acceding country. It is not an accident that almost all governments that have acceded see WTO membership as reinforcing and consolidating a national reform process on which they were already embarked for their own reasons.

Article XII sets no limits to the terms that may be agreed and the terms of accession are different for each new Member. However, the factual analysis presented in this Handbook shows some patterns emerging that enable conclusions to be drawn about the terms likely to be asked of acceding governments. By identifying exceptions that have been made, the analysis also highlights some unique features of each accession. The terms of accession have evolved in some respects since the entry into force of the WTO in 1995 and there has been something of a "ratchet effect" – a novel commitment, once accepted, tends to be asked of other acceders.

The accession process is flexible and continues to evolve. It is likely to be further adapted to the needs of each case.

1

ACCESSION IN PERSPECTIVE

The multilateral trading system came into being on 1 January 1948 when the General Agreement on Tariffs and Trade (GATT 1947) was signed by its 23 founding members.[1] The GATT's membership expanded considerably in the following decades as many countries gained their independence and took over the rights and obligations of membership that metropolitan powers had accepted on their behalf, and others negotiated their accession to the treaty. All the Members of GATT 1947 decided by the end of the Uruguay Round of trade negotiations (1986–1994) to take on the greatly enlarged rights and obligations of the new organization they had negotiated – the World Trade Organization (WTO), which came into force on 1 January 1995 with 128 original Members.[2] While these accounted for an extremely large percentage of world trade, many economies remained outside the multilateral system. Since its inception, WTO Members have repeatedly stressed their commitment to making the WTO universal in scope and coverage – an ambition shared by a large number of governments outside the system.

Since 1995 another 23 governments have negotiated their accession to the WTO, which now has 151 Members.[3] This is an endorsement of the principles on which the Organization is based and the validity of its disciplines. The new Members are, in the order in which they acceded:

1. Ecuador
2. Bulgaria
3. Mongolia
4. Panama
5. Kyrgyz Republic
6. Latvia
7. Estonia
8. Jordan
9. Georgia
10. Albania
11. Oman
12. Croatia
13. Lithuania
14. Moldova
15. China
16. Separate Customs Territory of Taiwan, Penghu, Kinmen, and Matsu (Chinese Taipei)

[1] "Contracting Parties."

[2] See Marrakesh Agreement Establishing the World Trade Organization, Article XI, Original Membership. The original Members included the member States of the European Communities (EC) and the EC themselves. The WTO legal texts refer to the EC not the European Union as the Union does not have a legal personality. Though not original Members, the General Council gave Granada, Papua New Guinea, Qatar, St. Kitts and Nevis, and the United Arab Emirates additional time to complete the negotiation of their Schedules. These countries acceded to the WTO after 1 January 1995 under the special procedures established by the General Council (WTO document WT/L/30).

[3] August 2007.

17. Armenia
18. Former Yugoslav Republic of Macedonia (FYROM)
19. Nepal (LDC)
20. Cambodia (LDC)
21. Saudi Arabia
22. Viet Nam
23. Tonga

The detailed statistics contained in Annex 1 demonstrate that these new Members have made a significant contribution to the WTO's goal of becoming a truly universal body. Based on these statistics, the percentage of world trade accounted for by Members of the Organization has risen from 86.8 percent to 96.4 percent and the percentage of GDP from 89.4 percent to 96.7 percent. Population figures are equally relevant and important. Whereas original Members accounted for only 66.0 percent of the world's population, the accession of the new Members has brought this figure up to 90.1 percent.

The WTO has shown itself flexible enough to accommodate Members of very different economic sizes, at all stages of economic development. The five that are largest in trade terms (EC, USA, China, Japan and Canada) account for as much as 68 percent of the trade of all WTO Members and the five smallest for less than 0.01 percent of that trade. Its membership includes not only all the wealthiest countries in the world but also 32 of the 50 LDCs.[4]

There are at present another 32 governments which have applied to accede to the WTO (in alphabetical order):

1. Afghanistan (LDC)
2. Algeria
3. Andorra
4. Azerbaijan
5. Bahamas
6. Belarus
7. Bhutan (LDC)
8. Bosnia and Herzegovina
9. Cape Verde (LDC)
10. Comoros (LDC)
11. Equatorial Guinea (LDC)
12. Ethiopia (LDC)
13. Iran
14. Iraq
15. Kazakhstan
16. Lao People's Democratic Republic (LDC)
17. Lebanon
18. Liberia (LDC)
19. Libyan Arab Jamahiriya
20. Montenegro
21. Russian Federation
22. Samoa (LDC)
23. Sao Tomé and Principe (LDC)
24. Serbia
25. Seychelles
26. Sudan (LDC)
27. Syria
28. Tajikistan
29. Ukraine
30. Uzbekistan
31. Vanuatu (LDC)
32. Yemen (LDC)

The above account for 4 percent of world trade, 3.3 percent of world GDP, but as much as 8.4 percent of world population. Their membership of the WTO would bring the coverage of the Organization to 99.95 percent of world trade,

[4] As defined by the United Nations (UN).

99.98 percent of world GDP, and 99.35 percent of world population. Thirteen of these applicants are LDCs.

To date, only 13 member States of the United Nations have not applied to accede to the WTO. They are, in alphabetical order:

1. Eritrea (LDC)
2. Kiribati (LDC)
3. People's Democratic Republic of Korea
4. Marshall Islands
5. Micronesia
6. Monaco
7. Nauru
8. Palau
9. San Marino
10. Somalia (LDC)
11. Timor-Leste (LDC)
12. Turkmenistan
13. Tuvalu (LDC)

Together, these States account for 0.05 percent of total world trade, 0.03 percent of world GDP, and 0.70 percent of world population. Five are LDCs.

These statistics give a good idea of the remaining scope for accession to the WTO.[5] About a quarter of UN members are still not Members of the Organization. Most of these are small in economic terms, but they are home to some 580 million people – 18 are LDCs. Only one, the Russian Federation, has more than 1 percent of world trade.

Annex 1 contains an overview of these findings and the detailed statistics on which they are based.

[5] As noted below, some separate customs territories may also accede to the WTO.

2

THE BASIC RULES

1 BASIC WTO PROVISION

The fundamental provision governing accession to the WTO is Article XII of the Marrakesh Agreement Establishing the World Trade Organization.

> **Box 1: Article XII – Accession**
>
> 1. Any State or separate customs territory possessing full autonomy in the conduct of its external commercial relations and of the other matters provided for in this Agreement and the Multilateral Trade Agreements may accede to this Agreement, on terms to be agreed between it and the WTO. Such accession shall apply to this Agreement and the Multilateral Trade Agreements annexed thereto.
>
> 2. Decisions on accession shall be taken by the Ministerial Conference. The Ministerial Conference shall approve the agreement on the terms of accession by a two-thirds majority of the Members of the WTO.
>
> 3. Accession to a Plurilateral Trade Agreement shall be governed by the provisions of that Agreement.

Article XII was modelled on the corresponding clause in the GATT 1947, the forerunner of the WTO, which governed accessions to the GATT for more than 40 years, from 1947 to 1995.[1] One striking feature of this provision is its brevity. Anyone coming new to the subject might ask why applicants cannot become Members of the Organization simply by notifying their acceptance of the obligations of membership and, if negotiations are necessary, why this basic provision does not provide them with more information about what "terms to be agreed" with WTO Members will determine their accession. The primary reason why the drafters did not attempt to prescribe universally applicable terms of accession was that the terms are to a large extent decided in negotiations on a case-by-case basis, in relation to each applicant's national measures. In each negotiation, the challenge is to arrive at an appropriate balance between preserving and applying the rules and disciplines of

[1] Article XXXIII of GATT 1947. The text of the General Agreement is now incorporated into the WTO Agreement as one of its multilateral trade agreements. It is known as "GATT 1994" to make clear that it is legally distinct from the GATT set up in 1947 ("GATT 1947") which ceased to have effect after the WTO came into force on 1 January 1995. While the text of GATT 1994 still contains Article XXXIII, it is no longer operative as it is not possible to accede to GATT 1994 without acceding to the WTO as a whole.

the Organization and accommodating them, to the extent possible, to the individual circumstances of the acceding government.

Although Article XII itself does not prescribe procedural rules to be followed in the course of the accession process, a fairly well-defined set of procedures based on those used in GATT 1947 has been developed by the WTO Secretariat in consultation with Members and through customary practice.

2 OTHER RELEVANT WTO PROVISIONS

Article XVI:1 of the WTO Agreement states that, except as provided for elsewhere in the Agreement or the Multilateral Trade Agreements, the WTO shall be guided by the decisions, procedures and customary practices of GATT 1947.

Articles XII:2 and IV:2 provide that decisions on accession are taken by the Ministerial Conference (which meets at least once every two years) or, in the intervening period, by the General Council (which meets much more frequently, usually once every six to eight weeks). Also relevant is Article IX, whose relationship with Article XII was clarified by the General Council in 1995. Whereas Article XII:2 provides that decisions on the terms of individual accessions are to be approved by a two-thirds majority of the WTO Members, Article IX:1 states that the WTO practice is to arrive at decisions by consensus; that, except as otherwise provided, a vote is only taken when it has not been possible to reach a consensus; and that a consensus is reached if no Member, present at the meeting when the decision is taken, formally objects to the proposed decision.[2]

The parallel existence of these two provisions raised the question of which one would take precedence, and under which conditions. Moreover, the absence of smaller delegations from the General Council meetings made it difficult to secure a two-thirds majority necessary for an affirmative decision in that forum. These issues were resolved in November 1995 when the General Council agreed that consensus-based decision-making would apply to WTO accessions—unless a Member requested a vote or consensus could not be reached.[3] For the text of these provisions and the Decision, see Annex 2.

3 MINISTERIAL DECLARATIONS

The WTO has held six Ministerial Conferences, in Singapore (December 1996), Geneva (May 1998), Seattle (November-December 1999), Doha (November 2001),

[2] Marrakesh Agreement Establishing the WTO, Articles IX:1 (and footnote 1) and XII:2.

[3] WTO documents WT/GC/M/8, p. 6, 15 Nov 1995, and WT/L/93, 24 November 1995, "Decision-making procedures under Articles IX and XII of the WTO Agreement." The General Council also took note of the understanding that non-Geneva-based delegations would be given sufficient time to attend the meeting in question and that they would be provided with the opportunity to vote in absentia where a vote became unavoidable.

Cancún (September 2003), and Hong Kong (December 2005). Five of these adopted Ministerial Declarations, all of which addressed the subject of the accession of new Members to the Organization.[4] The relevant texts are reproduced in Annex 3.

These Declarations welcomed the accessions that had taken place and the progress made in ongoing accessions. Ministers resolved to bring applicants into the system as rapidly as possible and recalled that accession to the WTO required full respect of its rules and disciplines as well as "meaningful market-access commitments."[5]

By the time of the second Ministerial Conference in Geneva although a large number of applications for membership had been received, only four new Members had actually joined. Discussion of the issues raised led to the adoption of a set of Guidelines on the Accession of LDCs dealt with below.

The Doha Ministerial Conference which launched a new WTO Work Programme decided that negotiations under this Programme would be open to States and separate customs territories currently in the process of accession but that decisions on the outcomes of the negotiations would be taken only by WTO Members.[6] At Doha, Ministers also committed themselves to facilitating and accelerating the accession of LDCs.[7]

4 GUIDELINES ON THE ACCESSION OF LEAST-DEVELOPED COUNTRIES

The WTO accepts the UN classification of LDCs and therefore currently recognizes 50 countries as falling into that category.[8] Thirty of these were original Members of the WTO and two have since acceded (Cambodia and Nepal). These 32 comprise over one-fifth of the WTO's membership. A further 13 (Afghanistan, Bhutan, Cape Verde, Comoros, Equatorial Guinea, Ethiopia, Lao PDR, Liberia, Samoa, Sao Tomé and Principe, Sudan, Vanuatu and Yemen) are currently in the process of accession. The other five remain outside the system (Eritrea, Kiribati, Somalia, Timor-Leste, and Tuvalu).

Following the Doha Ministerial, a WTO Work Programme for LDCs was launched.[9] The implementation of this Programme led to the adoption by the General Council of the Guidelines for the Accession of LDCs in December 2002. In the Guidelines, Members decided that negotiations for the accession of LDCs to the WTO should be facilitated and accelerated through simplified and streamlined

[4] WTO documents WT/MIN(96)/DEC, para, 8; WT/MIN(98)/DEC/1, para, 7; WT/MIN(01)/DEC/1, paras 9, 42 and 48; WT/MIN(03)/20, para. 2; WT/MIN(05)/DEC para 54.

[5] E.g. 1996 Singapore Ministerial Declaration, para. 8; 1998 Geneva Ministerial Declaration, para 7; 2001 Doha Ministerial Declaration, paras 9 and 42.

[6] WTO document WT/MIN(01)/DEC/1, para 48.

[7] Doha Ministerial Declaration, paras 9 and 42.

[8] www.unohrlls.org/en/ldc/related/62.

[9] WTO document WT/COMTD/LDC/11.

accession procedures, with a view to concluding these negotiations as quickly as possible. The full text of the Guidelines is reproduced in Annex 4.[10]

In the area of *market access*, WTO Members are to "exercise restraint in seeking concessions and commitments on trade in goods and services from acceding LDCs, taking into account the levels of concessions and commitments undertaken by existing WTO LDCs' Members." For their part, acceding LDCs are expected to offer "reasonable market access concessions and commitments on goods and services commensurate with their individual development, financial and trade needs", in line with relevant WTO provisions on goods and services.

In the area of *WTO Rules*, the Guidelines state that special and differential treatment, as set out in the Multilateral Trade Agreements, Ministerial Decisions, and other relevant WTO legal instruments, shall be applicable to all acceding LDCs, from the date of entry into force of their respective Protocols of Accession. The Guidelines provide that "transitional periods/transitional arrangements foreseen under specific WTO agreements, to enable acceding LDCs to effectively implement commitments and obligations, shall be granted in accession negotiations taking into account individual development, financial and trade needs" and that "these transitional periods/arrangements shall be accompanied by Action Plans for compliance with WTO rules, . . . supported by Technical Assistance and Capacity Building measures for the acceding LDCs." Finally under this heading, the Guidelines make clear that "commitments to accede to any of the WTO plurilateral trade agreements or to participate in other optional sectoral market access initiatives shall not be a precondition for accession to the Multilateral Trade Agreements of the WTO" but "WTO Members may seek to ascertain acceding LDCs interests in the plurilateral trade agreements".

With regard to the "process of accession", the Guidelines state that the good offices of the Director-General shall be available to assist acceding LDCs and chairpersons of the LDCs' accession Working Parties in implementing this decision and call for continued efforts to expedite and streamline the process of accession.

The Guidelines then go on to lay down that targeted and coordinated technical assistance and capacity building shall be provided by the WTO and other relevant multilateral, regional and bilateral development partners, on a priority basis, to assist acceding LDCs. Assistance shall be accorded with the objective of effectively integrating the acceding LDC into the multilateral trading system. Technical assistance and capacity building is to cover all stages of the accession process, i.e. from the preparation of documentation to the setting up of the legislative infrastructure and enforcement mechanisms.

The implementation of these Guidelines is reviewed regularly and the results of these reviews are included in the Annual Report of the Committee on Trade and Development to the WTO General Council.

[10] WTO document WT/L/508.

3

TECHNICAL ASSISTANCE AND TRAINING FOR ACCEDING COUNTRIES

Accession to the WTO is a complex process and all acceding governments need expert advice to master the WTO rules and obligations, the procedures governing the accession negotiations, the demands that the process makes of them and how to respond to these demands. Applicants are also *ipso facto* participants in the negotiations under the Doha Development Agenda[1] and need to keep abreast of the issues being dealt with there, as they will be expected to accept the results of these negotiations when they become WTO Members.

The WTO provides trade-related technical assistance and training to acceding LDCs, developing countries and low-income countries in transition within its area of competence.[2] Its main purpose has been to assist these applicants to better understand and implement WTO obligations and to exercise their rights under the WTO agreements once they become Members of the Organization. The system recognizes the special needs of least-developed countries. The priority accorded to TRTA for acceding LDCs was made explicit in the Doha Declaration, where Ministers "instruct the Secretariat to reflect the priority that [they] attach to LDC accession in the annual plans for technical assistance"[3] and in the Guidelines for the Accession of LDCs.

WTO agreements are designed to make a substantial contribution to economic development[4] but it is up to traders to translate the opportunities created by these agreements into increased trade. The WTO does not itself provide TRTA to address supply-side issues, such as the difficulties that new Members may have in producing goods and services of exportable quality and getting them to export markets, but cooperates with other providers of TRTA active in this area. The WTO has emphasized the necessity for the effective coordinated delivery of technical assistance with bilateral donors and relevant international and regional intergovernmental institutions.[5] The WTO Secretariat coordinates its TA Plans, to the extent possible, in an informal, *ad hoc* way.[6] It has also joined with OECD to establish the Doha Development Agenda Trade-Related Technical Assistance and Capacity Building Data

[1] However, decisions on the outcomes of the negotiations are taken only by WTO Members. Doha Ministerial Declaration, WTO document WT/MIN(03)/20, para 2.

[2] Marrakesh Ministerial Declaration of 15 April 1994, para 5.

[3] Ministerial Declaration, para 42.

[4] Marrakesh Agreement Establishing the WTO, Preamble.

[5] Doha Declaration, para 39.

[6] WTO document WT/ACC/10/Rev. 3, p. 35.

Base (TCBDB) to bring together information on the assistance being provided to beneficiaries by donor countries and agencies.[7]

The provision of TRTA is dealt with separately from the WTO's formal accession process outlined above. In particular, WTO Members have not agreed to allow applicants to make the implementation of WTO commitments conditional on the receipt of TRTA.

The following paragraphs deal with relevant TRTA available from the WTO Secretariat and from other organizations.

WTO SECRETARIAT

Applicants benefit from WTO TRTA in two ways. On the one hand, Secretariat officials provide technical assistance to their delegations at all stages of the accession process. On the other, they also benefit from the regular WTO programme of TRTA organized by the WTO Institute for Training and Technical Cooperation (ITTC).

Funding for WTO TRTA has increased considerably since the adoption of the Ministerial Declaration launching the Doha Development Agenda (DDA) and a new round of negotiations.[8] Total funds available for 2006 were SFr. 28 million. Of this, nearly SFr. 6 million (21 percent) was included in the regular budget of the WTO, the remainder coming from voluntary contributions and funds rolled over from the previous year. This figure is roughly comparable to funds available in 2004 and 2005, which were SFr 27 million and 22 million respectively. A total of 28 WTO Members donated funds during that three-year period. Seven donors gave SFR 1 million or more in 2006 – in alphabetical order, these were France, Germany, Netherlands, Norway, Sweden, United Kingdom, USA. The present level of activity is linked to the implementation of the DDA and, at Doha, Ministers agreed that "there is a need for technical assistance to benefit from secure and predictable funding".[9] This notwithstanding, only monies included in advance in the regular budget can be regarded as truly secure. Securing adequate funding presents a continuing challenge.

ACCESSIONS-RELATED ASSISTANCE

The Accessions Division of the Secretariat[10] assists acceding governments to prepare documents required for the accession process (Memorandum on the Foreign

[7] Ibid, p. 34. http://tcbdb.wto.org/index.asp?lang=ENG: shows beneficiary countries, donor countries, donor agencies and trade category.

[8] This paragraph is largely based on Annual Report on Technical Assistance and Training, 2006, WTO document WT/COMTD/W/157. See also Plan for 2007, WTO document WT/COMTD/W/151 and Corr.1.

[9] Doha Ministerial Declaration, para 40. TRTA is dealt with in no fewer than 12 paragraphs of the Doha Ministerial Declaration, 14 November 2001, paras 16, 21, 24, 26, 27, 33, 38–40, 42, and 43.

[10] WTO document WT/COMTD/W/157, paras 121–124.

Trade Regime, replies to Members' questions, initial and revised offers, as well as other technical documents) and responds to their questions regarding WTO rules and enforcement requirements. The bulk of this technical assistance is provided from Geneva, and missions to the acceding country are a complementary tool used as appropriate. Follow-up is systematic and carried out from Geneva. Policy level missions, which also have a technical assistance component, have had an increasingly critical role to play in advancing accessions in terms of creating awareness and commitment at high levels of government, Parliament, media, and in the public and private sectors. These missions are often undertaken with the Chair of the Working Party. Progress achieved by acceding governments in moving their accession process forward is direct evidence of the impact and sustainability of technical assistance activities. In order to better respond to acceding governments' needs, in 2005, the Accession Division developed a simulation exercise on market access negotiations on goods, and several of these exercises have been carried out since then, upon request of acceding governments. Complementary and coordinated support is also provided by other Divisions of the Secretariat in their specific areas of expertise.

WTO PROGRAMME OF TRADE-RELATED TECHNICAL ASSISTANCE

WTO TRTA is demand-driven, the onus being on the acceding governments themselves to formulate their requests for assistance. The Organization must deal with a demand that has increased over the past few years within the constraints of the human and financial resources available. It tackles this in a number of ways.

On the demand side, efforts have recently been made to see that requests from governments for technical assistance and training are based on needs assessments that reflect their overall priorities rather than on *ad hoc* requests from different government agencies. Applicants therefore need to assess their needs, assign priorities and coordinate requests made by their different government agencies involved in the accession process before forwarding their request to the WTO Secretariat. These consolidated requests are sent both to the Director of the Accessions Division and the Director of the Institute for Training and Technical Cooperation at WTO.

For its part, the WTO has made an effort to raise governments' awareness of the opportunities on offer and to ensure that the annual TRTA plans respond in a flexible way to the needs that have been identified. It has to be recognized, however, that some rationing is necessary. One way already mentioned is to give priority to LDCs. Another is to adjust the mix of products offered so as to ensure that all WTO Members and acceders can benefit from a range of technical assistance activities. So, while the WTO continues to offer the resource-intensive 12-week training courses at its headquarters and similar activities in different regions and sub-regions, it has put a large part of its available resources into short activities organized on a regional or sub-regional basis and held in the regions themselves. These are cost-effective because a relatively large number of participants attend, and the administrative expenses involved are less than for Geneva-based activities. However, the need for more targeted TRTA at the national level is obvious and has been recognized.

In 2006,[11] the WTO implemented a total of 486 technical assistance activities. Of these, 163 were regional events, 246 were national events, and 77 were activities organized by other agencies with WTO participation. A total of 442 of these activities were held outside the headquarters in Geneva. The average length of these activities was five days. Representatives of all 32 acceders except Andorra attended WTO TRTA activities during the course of the year 2006, an average of 17 events per applicant. Officials from many applicants benefited from the longer general trade policy training courses. Despite efforts to raise awareness on the availability of technical assistance activities provided by the WTO, only 44 national events were organized for acceders during that year.

On the whole, the WTO has been successful in giving priority to LDCs. Several products, such as the three-week introduction course, reference centres, the Netherlands trainee programme and the financing of participation in WTO Ministerial Conferences, have been developed to meet their needs.[12]

The main products relevant to acceders include:

- National activities
  - technical missions of several days to deal with issues specific to the individual applicant that cannot be dealt with at the regional or sub-regional level. LDCs are entitled to receive three national activities per year and developing countries, two.
- General trade policy courses
  - twelve-week training courses at headquarters in Geneva
  - twelve-week training courses in regions and sub-regions
  - three-week introduction courses for LDCs in Geneva
  - short (mostly one to two weeks) training courses in regions and sub-regions

The relatively long training courses, which originated in the 1950s, are still the WTO TRTA's flagship product. The training courses in the regions and sub-regions are often held in cooperation with local universities and the aim is that these local bodies should progressively take more responsibility and ownership of the courses. These are designed to ensure that participants are exposed to all activities of the WTO and develop relevant practical skills as well as an extensive network of contacts.

[11] This paragraph is based on WTO document WT/COMTD/W/157 and information provided by the WTO Secretariat.

[12] WTO document WT/COMTD/W/146, para 15.

- Specialized courses in Geneva
  One- or two-week courses on e.g. dispute settlement or trade negotiations that include briefing on WTO work in progress and emphasize interactive learning, practical exercises, case studies and debates. Infrequent because costly.
- Geneva Week:
  One-week events for delegations that do not have a representation in Geneva, held twice a year to brief them on developments in the work of the WTO and to provide them with an opportunity of making their views known. These events have proved of great value to acceders who often hold meetings in connection with their accession on the margins of Geneva Week.
- Topic-based regional and sub-regional activities
  Usually seminars and workshops (which include case studies and simulation exercises as well as simple presentations). They usually focus on narrowly defined subjects, e.g. anti-dumping, customs valuation or technical barriers to trade, but may also deal with broader aspects of the system, such as dispute settlement or the multilateral trade negotiations. They take place in the region or sub-region concerned.
- Trainee programmes and internships
  Regular interns are attached for up to 24 weeks to the WTO Secretariat or to Permanent Missions in Geneva. The aim of one programme is to provide up to 20 junior public servants per year with the possibility of spending up to ten months with the WTO or their mission in order to complete well defined tasks of specific relevance to the beneficiary government, such as an assessment of their needs for TRTA.[13]
- Reference centres
  The centres are usually located in the Ministry responsible for the WTO, to provide access to on-line and off-line WTO-related trade information and documentation. Initial training is provided and coordinators at each centre help users learn how to access technical and legal documentation.
- eTraining programme
  The objective of eTraining is to ensure that participants obtain a strengthened understanding of the multilateral trading system and its operation. The eTraining website provides interactive courses over the internet and allows government officials online access to the training material and their assigned tutors. The programme is evolving and the aim is to reorganize the courses and to increase the number and variety of subjects covered. Further information will be found on the WTO website.[14]

[13] Netherlands Trainee Programme (www.wto.org/English/tratop_e/devel_e/train_e/netherlands_prog_e.htm).

[14] http://www.wto.org/english/res_e/d_learn_e/d_learn_e.htm.

WTO MEMBERS AND OTHER ORGANIZATIONS

Some Members provide technical assistance to acceders bilaterally, sometimes on a large scale, on matters such as the preparation of the accession documentation, the implementation of domestic reforms (e.g. the transition to market economy), the establishment of the necessary legal and institutional framework and the drafting of WTO-consistent legislation.

International organizations, such as the International Bank for Reconstruction and Development (World Bank), the International Monetary Fund (IMF), the International Trade Centre (ITC), the United Nations Conference on Trade and Development (UNCTAD), the United Nations Development Programme (UNDP), the World Customs Organization (WCO) and the World Intellectual Property Organization (WIPO), also provide technical assistance relevant to WTO accession.

Formal agreements between the WTO and the IMF and the World Bank provide a framework for consultations aimed at achieving greater coherence in global economic policy-making.[15] Among the matters of operational concern are the interaction among the three organizations in their work relating to the governments that are in accession to the WTO[16] and cooperation in TRTA and capacity-building in this respect.[17] The WTO and the World Bank also cooperate in the design and delivery of Joint Regional Training Courses for acceders.[18]

Cooperation with UNCTAD has been close. UNCTAD has extensive experience in the provision of technical assistance to acceding governments. The general objectives are to: assist national officials in elaborating optimal approaches in the initial phase of the WTO accession process, particularly in the preparation of an inventory of relevant problems to be solved both internally or externally; to improve national officials' negotiating capacity by strengthening their understanding of strategies and techniques used in multilateral trade negotiations; to provide advice in trade policy formulation, particularly relating to WTO accession negotiations; and to strengthen the capacities of trade-supporting national institutional structures (including the academic community) through training and joint analysis of relevant issues.[19] UNCTAD has delivered this assistance by undertaking advisory missions and working directly with national negotiating teams; helping in the preparation of documentation required by the WTO accession negotiations; preparing analytical

15 Agreements between the WTO and the IMF and the World Bank – Decision adopted by the General Council at its meeting on 7, 8 and 13 November 1996, WTO document WT/L/194.

16 IMF/World Bank/WTO, "Report of the Managing Director, President and Director-General on Coherence" of 21 October 1998 (WTO document WT/GC/13).

17 WT/GC/W/140. 18 WTO document WT/COMTD/W/157, para 248.

19 Source: UNCTAD, Review of Technical Cooperation Activities of UNCTAD (Report by the Secretary-General of UNCTAD) to the Trade and Development Board, Working Party on the Medium-term Plan and the Programme Budget, Forty-first session (Geneva, 15–19 September 2003): WTO documents TD/B/50/2/Add.1 and TD/B/WP/163/Add.1 (11 August 2003).

papers and briefings for national policy-makers; organizing brainstorming meetings and seminars; and disseminating trade policy information.[20]

The WTO also participates in multi-agency programmes in which the agencies provide technical assistance to applicants, each within its own area of competence. A useful tool in this context is the Integrated Framework for Trade-Related Technical Assistance for Least-Developed countries (IF) initiated in October 1997 by the WTO together with the International Monetary Fund (IMF), the International Trade Centre (ITC), the United Nations Conference on Trade and Development (UNCTAD), the United Nations Development Programme (UNDP) and the World Bank.[21] Its existence is a recognition that increased international trade can generate resources needed for sustainable development and poverty alleviation but that LDCs will be able to take advantage of the trading opportunities created by WTO only if they address supply-side constraints by building their capacity to trade and by integrating trade policies into their national development strategies. The IF facilitates a coordinated response by the six agencies and development partners (each in their own area of competence) to the needs identified by each LDC participant. The IF process is in four parts: awareness-building of the importance of trade for development; preparation of a Diagnostic Trade Integration Study (DTIS), including a plan of action for integrating into the global trading system; integrating the plan of action into the national development plan; and implementing the plan of action in partnership with the development cooperation community.

The relevance of the IF for acceding LDCs is evident. Their decision to accede is also a decision to integrate into the world economy but to do this successfully they need to accord trade the necessary priority in their development strategies and to mobilize the necessary resources to deal with supply side constraints. Ten of the 43 LDCs now participating in the IF have either already acceded to the WTO (Cambodia and Nepal) or are in the process of accession (Cape Verde, Ethiopia, Lao PDR, Samoa, Sao Tomé and Principe, Sudan, Vanuatu and Yemen). Only one acceding LDC is not yet a participant (Bhutan). Lao PDR, Sao Tomé and Principe and Sudan are in the early stages of the process but Window II projects have already been approved for Cambodia, Ethiopia, Nepal and Yemen.[22] The IF Working Group has agreed to undertake technical reviews of Vanuatu, and Afghanistan.

The Joint Vienna Institute was launched in 1992 by the Austrian authorities and a number of international organizations (the WTO, the IMF, the World Bank, the Bank for International Settlements (BIS), the Organization for European Cooperation and Development (OECD), the European Bank for Reconstruction and Development (EBRD)) to respond to the demand from economies in transition, including acceders, to train officials in market economics and the free enterprise system. It provides training to governments making the transition from

[20] Ibid, para 58.

[21] See http://www.integratedframework.org and http://www.wto.org/Development – The Integrated Framework.

[22] http://www.integratedframework.org.

centrally planned to market-based economies and offers approximately 60 seminars, generally of short duration, in specialized topics that reflect the expertise of its various sponsoring organizations, and a ten-week course in applied economic policy.[23]

The Standards and Trade Development Facility (STDF) was launched in 2002 as a joint initiative of the WTO and the UN Food and Agriculture Organization (FAO), the World Organization for Animal Health (OIE), the World Bank and the WHO. Its aim is to assist developing countries enhance their expertise and capacity to analyze and to implement international sanitary and phytosanitary (SPS) standards, improving their human, animal and plant health situation, and thus their ability to gain and maintain market access. The STDF provides grant financing for developing countries seeking to comply with international SPS standards and hence gain or maintain market access. There have been 22 projects and 23 project preparation grants (PPGs) approved since the STDF's creation and in 2006 the first projects were successfully completed. PPGs have been approved for Cambodia and Nepal, which have already acceded, and for Cape Verde, another LDC in the process of accession. A new medium-term strategy agreed in December 2006 puts much greater emphasis on information sharing and co-ordination in the supply and receipt of SPS-related technical co-operation but the STDF continues also to act as a source of funding for projects. So far, 11 donors have committed funds to the STDF and, with a new operating strategy in place, it is hoped that the annual funding target of US$5 million will be met. Forty percent of facility resources are committed for LDCs and other low-income economies.[24]

23 See http://jvi.org.

24 See www.standardsfacility.org. For a database of SPS technical assistance, set up partly to improve on the OECD Doha Development Agenda Trade-Related Technical Assistance and Capacity Building Data Base (TCBDB) which did not distinguish between TBT and SPS, see http://tcbdb.wto.org. For an update on the operation of the STDF, see WTO document G/SPS/GEN/718 of 31 July 2006.

4

THE ACCESSION PROCESS: THE PROCEDURES AND HOW THEY HAVE BEEN APPLIED

1 INTRODUCTION

The format and the conduct of each individual accession negotiation are based on the procedures laid out in WTO document WT/ACC/1 entitled "Accession to the WTO – Procedures for Negotiations under Article XII," which was drawn up by the Secretariat shortly after the WTO was established on 1 January 1995.[1] These procedures were modelled after those followed by the Contracting Parties to GATT 1947, including the Complementary Procedures on Accession Negotiations agreed to by the Council of GATT 1947 in 1993 and the statement by the Chairman of the Council of GATT 1947 on the Management of Accession Negotiations in 1994.[2] The draft of the procedures was prepared by the Secretariat and revised in the light of suggestions made during extensive multilateral consultations with interested WTO Members, during which an understanding was reached that the document would not be submitted to the Ministerial Conference/General Council or individual Working Parties for formal endorsement but that it would rather serve as a practical guide for existing WTO Members and acceding governments and not as a general policy statement on accession negotiations.[3] Box 2 outlines the main steps in the process.

A glance at this schematic presentation suggests that the process of accession inevitably takes time. The length of time between application and actual accession has varied from two years and ten months[4] to 15 years and five months.[5] Six applicants that converted a request to join GATT 1947 into a request to accede to the WTO when it was created in 1995 have still not completed the process. Document references to the Reports of Working Parties on applicants that have already acceded and fuller details of the timeline for completed accessions will be found in Annex 5.

Acceders must also be prepared to submit, and to deal with, a complex range of documents. These are issued in two series: Working Party documents (the WTO document WT/ACC/- series) and documents relating to the negotiations on rules

[1] WTO document WT/ACC/1 (24 March 1995).

[2] See WTO documents L/7317 (27 October 1993) and C/COM/4 (10 November 1994).

[3] WTO document WT/ACC/1, para 2.

[4] Kyrgyz Republic.

[5] China, whose request to rejoin GATT 1947 was converted into a request to accede to WTO.

Box 2: The accession process

First Steps

Request for membership

Communication to the Director-General

Establishment of a Working Party

General Council decision

↓

Working Party

Fact-finding stage

Submission of a Memorandum on the Foreign Trade Regime; supporting documentation; responses to questions from members; Other documentation, as requested.

Negotiations stage

Multilateral negotiations on rules

Plurilateral discussions on agricultural support and export subsidies

Bilateral negotiation on market access for goods and services

Preparation of draft Working Party Report, including draft Protocol and Decision, and draft Schedules on Goods and Services

Completion of the Working Party's Mandate

Adoption by the Working Party of its Report.

↓

Final steps

Adoption of Working Party Report and terms of accession by General Council/Ministerial Conference

Acceptance of Terms by the applicant by signature or otherwise.

Notification of acceptance by the applicant

Membership thirty days after notification of ratification or acceptance

(draft Reports), market access for goods and services, including for the negotiations and discussions on agricultural support and export subsidies (WTO document WT/ACC/SPEC/-series). These can be consulted, when released, on the WTO website.[6]

[6] http://docsonline.wto.org.

2 APPLICATION FOR MEMBERSHIP AND ESTABLISHMENT OF WORKING PARTY

2.1 First contacts

Representatives of Governments interested in joining the Organization often approach the Secretariat for information before making a formal application to accede. The contact point is the Director of the Accessions Division of the Secretariat.

It is also possible for non-governmental groups, including universities or journalists, to request information on accession from the Secretariat. The contact point for media, journalists and the general public is the Director of the Information and Media Relations Division. Intergovernmental organizations, non-governmental organizations and parliamentarians should contact the Director of the External Relations Division.

2.2 Observer status for non-Member governments before application to accede

Non-member governments may become WTO observers before they make an application to accede. However, there is no obligation to do so and, increasingly, governments wanting to join the WTO have preferred to directly enter into the accession process instead of first seeking observer status.

The procedures for observer status for governments in the General Council and its subsidiary bodies make it clear that its purpose is "to allow a government to better acquaint itself with the WTO and its activities, and to prepare and initiate negotiations for accession to the WTO Agreement."[7] Under these procedures, communications from interested governments that have not yet applied to accede must "express an intent to initiate negotiations for accession to the WTO Agreement within a maximum period of five years, and to provide a description of their current economic and trade policies, as well as any intended future reforms of these policies".[8] The status is granted initially for five years and observer governments are expected to take a decision on accession within that period of time. It is however possible for an observer government that has not yet initiated a process of

[7] The Guidelines for Observer Status for Governments in the WTO are annexed to the Rules of Procedure for Sessions of the Ministerial Conference and Meetings of the General Council. WTO documents WT/GC/M/1 and WT/L/161, Annex 2 of 25 July 1996. The Guidelines also provide that Governments may seek observer status in the Ministerial Conference by addressing a communication to that body indicating their reasons for seeking such status and that such requests shall be examined on a case-by-case basis by the Ministerial Conference. These requests have normally been granted. Governments accorded observer status at sessions of the Ministerial Conference do not automatically have that status at meetings of the General Council or its subsidiary bodies, including accession Working Parties. However, governments accorded such status in the General Council and its subsidiary bodies in accordance with the relevant procedures are invited to attend sessions of the Ministerial Conference as observers. Guidelines, WTO document WT/L/161, Annex 2, para 2.

[8] Guidelines, WTO document WT/L/161, Annex 2, para 4.

negotiation with a view to acceding to the WTO Agreement, to request an extension of its status as observer. Such a request shall be made in writing and shall be accompanied by a comprehensive, updated description of the requesting government's "current economic and trade policies, as well as an indication of its future plans in relation to initiating accession negotiations."[9]

Observer status in the General Council carries with it certain rights and obligations. Observer governments have the right to observe formal meetings of the General Council and its subsidiary bodies, including accession Working Parties (with the exception of the Committee on Budget, Finance and Administration). Informal meetings, on the other hand, are held without observers in attendance. Observers have access to the main WTO document series and may also request technical assistance from the Secretariat in relation to the operation of the WTO system in general, as well as to negotiations on accession to the WTO Agreement.[10]

Representatives of governments accorded observer status "may be invited to speak at meetings of the bodies to which they are observers normally after Members of that body have spoken. The right to speak does not include the right to make proposals, unless a government is specifically invited to do so, nor to participate in decision-making."[11]

Observers have an obligation to make a financial contribution for the services provided to them of 0.015 percent of the total WTO budget, which is the same as the minimum annual contribution made by the smallest WTO Members.[12] This amounted to about SFr 26,000 for the year 2006 (about US $21,000; €16,000).

Ten governments have been granted observer status under these procedures.[13] One applied for an extension to the five-year period in the form prescribed by the Guidelines. The General Council noted that this was the first such request and agreed to its Chairman's proposal to extend the period for a further five-year period.[14]

The General Council has on two occasions deferred consideration of such requests. In one case a Member needed additional time to examine the matter.[15] In the other, the request was withdrawn shortly after its presentation when an application was made to accede to the WTO.[16]

In granting observer status in one case, the General Council took into account the applicant's unique situation and agreed to waive the requirement concerning

[9] Guidelines, WTO document WT/L/161, Annex 2, para 8.

[10] Guidelines, WTO document WT/L/161, Annex 2, para 9.

[11] Guidelines, WTO document WT/L/161, Annex 2, para 10.

[12] Guidelines, WTO document WT/L/161, Annex 2, para 11.

[13] Oman, WTO document WT/GC/M/3; Georgia, WTO document M/12; Ethiopia, WTO document M/23; Cape Verde, WTO document M/26; Bhutan, WTO document M/28; Yemen, WTO document M/40; Bahamas, WTO document M/57; Sao Tome and Principe, WTO document M/63; Equatorial Guinea, WTO document M/74; and Iraq, WTO document M/85.

[14] Ethiopia, WTO documents WT/L/ 445 and WT/GC/M/74.

[15] Request from Liberia, WTO document WT/GC/M57.

[16] The Lebanese Republic's request for observer status, WTO documents WT/L/283 and WT/GC/M/32, withdrawn and replaced by request for accession, WTO documents WT/ACC/LBN/1 and WT/GC/M/40.

the intention to initiate accession negotiations, on the understanding that this did not constitute a precedent for future decisions on requests for observer status.[17]

2.3 LETTER OF APPLICATION TO THE DIRECTOR-GENERAL

Once a government has decided that it wishes to apply for membership of the WTO, it submits a communication to the Director-General of the WTO indicating its desire to accede to the WTO under Article XII. This communication takes the form of a letter from the government of the applicant.

There is no prescribed form but the communication needs to indicate that the applicant wishes to accede under Article XII of the Marrakesh Agreement Establishing the WTO. The following text is necessary and sufficient.

Box 3: Letter of application to accede

I have the honour to inform you of the wish of [applicant A] to accede to the Agreement Establishing the World Trade Organization and to the Multilateral Trade Agreements annexed thereto, in accordance with Article XII of the said Agreement.

Of course, applicants may wish to add further language. Some communications include a request that the application be circulated to all WTO Members and included for consideration on the agenda of an early future meeting of the WTO General Council.

The application is received by the Director-General and, in accordance with standard procedure, is circulated to all Members[18] as the first in the series of formal documents relating to each accession.[19]

2.4 EXAMINATION OF APPLICATION BY THE GENERAL COUNCIL

The normal procedure is for the request for accession to then be placed on the agenda of the next or an early future meeting of the General Council.

The General Council "considers the application and the establishment of a Working Party."[20] The Chairman of the General Council typically invites the

[17] Holy See, WTO document WT/GC/M/21. [18] WTO document WT/ACC/1, para 4.

[19] These are issued in the WTO document WT/ACC series, in which each acceding country is given a three-letter identification code. The application of Afghanistan is WT/ACC/AFG/1, Andorra's is WT/ACC/AND/1, etc.

[20] WTO document WT/ACC/1, para 5. Like other items proposed for inclusion on the agenda of the General Council/Ministerial Conference, requests for accession are also approved by consensus rather than by voting, a practice to which WTO Members have consistently shown preference. This was demonstrated in the case of one accession request initially presented in July 1996 and approved by consensus on 26 May 2005 (WTO document WT/GC/M/95). Another application has still to be placed before the General Council (WTO document WT/ACC/SYR/1 of 30 October 2001, renewed in February 2004 and September 2005). One acceding country made clear that, once a Member, it would not block the decision-making process concerning the accession of another country (WTO document WT/ACC/ARM/22).

representative of the applicant government to introduce the main features of the trade and economic regime currently in place and to summarize the reasons behind the application. It is, naturally, helpful if the applicant is able to state that its existing policies are already in line with WTO requirements or that reforms are underway to ensure conformity with WTO rules. Governments often stress points of particular importance to them, such as their level of economic development or their transition to a market economy.

When requests for accession from separate customs territories have been considered, the General Council has wished to satisfy itself that the territory in question does in fact possess "full autonomy in the conduct of its external commercial relations and of the other matters provided for in [the WTO] Agreement and the Multilateral Trade Agreements" as required by Article XII of the WTO Agreement and that it intends "to undertake all the obligations associated with WTO membership and to be responsible to WTO Members for fulfilment of its obligations."[21]

2.5 Establishment of Working Party. Terms of Reference

Once the General Council considers a request for accession and finds it acceptable, it establishes a Working Party to examine the application further. All Accession Working Parties have been given the same terms of reference.[22]

Box 4: Terms of reference for accession Working Parties

"to examine the application of the Government of [name of applicant] to accede to the World Trade Organization under Article XII and to submit to the General Council/Ministerial Conference recommendations which may include a draft Protocol of Accession."

After proposing the terms of reference, the Chairman then proceeds to invite the applicant to consult with the Accessions Division of the Secretariat as to the further procedures, in particular regarding the basic documentation to be prepared for the Working Party's consideration.

2.6 Observer status for acceders

The Chairman, speaking on behalf of the General Council after establishment of a Working Party, invites the acceding government concerned, if it does not already have observer status, to attend meetings of the General Council as an observer and, as appropriate, meetings of other WTO bodies during the period when the

21 Montenegro, WTO document WT/GC/M/92, paras 27–29; Serbia, WTO document WT/GC/M/92, paras 34–36.

22 As suggested in para 5 of the Note by the Secretariat on the Procedures for Negotiations under Article XII, WTO document WT/ACC/1.

Working Party is carrying out its work. For rights and obligations of observers, see section 2.2 above.

Acceding governments are encouraged to attend meetings of Accession Working Parties other than their own, to familiarize themselves with the process and to prepare for their own negotiations. Those with enough resources often do so.

The negotiations launched at the Doha Ministerial Conference are open to observers that are in the process of accession to the WTO but decisions on the outcomes of the negotiations are taken only by Members.[23]

2.7 Chair of Working Party

In establishing an accession Working Party, the General Council authorizes its Chairperson to designate the Chairperson of the Working Party, in consultation with Members and the applicant concerned. The usual practice is for the Accessions Division to carry out these consultations on behalf of the Chairperson of the General Council and under his/her guidance. The Chairmanship is not confirmed until an announcement has been made at the General Council under "Other business".

The Chairperson is usually an ambassador resident in Geneva. The acceding government may suggest names, but the final selection also requires the agreement of all interested WTO Members. Vacancies are not necessarily filled immediately after the establishment of Working Parties but nearer the date of the first meeting of the Working Party, which takes place after the necessary basic documentation has been supplied by the applicants.

The duties of the Chairperson are not laid down in writing. It is clear that they are required to direct the discussions in their Working Parties on an impartial and objective basis. They may sometimes use the authority conferred on them by their office to make suggestions aimed at facilitating these discussions but their power of initiative is limited by the fact that the negotiations for accession are conducted between the members of the Working Parties and the acceding government.

The Chairperson and the Secretariat sometimes pay visits to acceding capitals at critical stages in the process. These visits have played an important role in activating or accelerating accession processes. Invariably, such visits have involved contacts at the highest policy levels in government and parliament, as well as meetings with representatives of the public and private sectors and the media.

2.8 Membership of Working Party

Membership of Working Parties on Accession is open to all interested WTO Members and their size has varied considerably from one accession to another. WTO Members can choose to join at any stage before the completion of the Working Party mandate.

[23] Doha Ministerial Declaration, para 48.

The largest of the Working Parties of applicants that have already acceded to the WTO had 62 members (counting the European Communities and their member States as one) and the smallest 17.[24] Five WTO Members have been members of all of these,[25] reflecting not only their particular trade interests but also their interest in the WTO system. A number of Members have joined all but one or two[26] and some other of the larger economies have been members of several Working Parties. Many other WTO Members ask for membership of individual Working Parties to demonstrate their support for the applicant concerned. Neighbouring States or close trade or diplomatic partners are therefore likely to become members of a given Working Party. The membership of Working Parties is thus not necessarily representative of the WTO membership as a whole, but tends to be commensurate with the Members' economic weight in the system and with their interest in a given accession.

Recently acceded WTO Members also have an interest in joining accession Working Parties. Two new Members joined all Working Parties which were still conducting negotiations[27] while others have been more selective.[28]

Working Party members do not always participate actively in the work. Most WTO Members do not have the resources to follow closely all accessions. In some cases, Members choose to focus on meetings relevant to their primary trade interests. This is especially true of discussions on agriculture.

The applicant takes part in Working Party discussions on an equal footing with Members as the aim of the sessions is for all concerned to reach mutual agreement on the terms of entry.

2.9 Observer status for international organizations

The rules of procedure governing observer status for international intergovernmental organizations (IGOs) in the WTO are designed "to enable these organizations to follow discussions therein on matters of direct interest to them" and requests are considered "from organizations which have competence and a direct interest in trade policy matters, or which, pursuant to paragraph V:1 of the WTO Agreement, have responsibilities related to those of the WTO".[29] The rules provide that requests for observer status from IGOs shall be considered on a case-by-case basis by each WTO body to which such a request is addressed, taking into account such factors as the nature of work of the organization concerned, the nature of its membership, the number of WTO Members in the organization, reciprocity with respect to access to proceedings, documents and other aspects of observership, and whether

[24] China, WTO document WT/ACC/CHN/2/Rev. 11, and Tonga, WTO document WT/ACC/TON/2/Rev.8.

[25] Australia, Canada, the EC, Japan, and the United States. These countries together make up 63 percent of world trade.

[26] India, and Switzerland. [27] China and Chinese Taipei. [28] E.g. Croatia and Viet Nam.

[29] Observer Status for International Intergovernmental Organizations in the WTO, WT/L/161, Annex 3. See also Minutes of the General Council of 22 October 1997 – WTO document WT/GC/M/23, page 23.

the organization has been associated in the past with the work of the GATT 1947. They specify that IGOs accorded observer status in a particular WTO body shall not automatically be accorded such status in other WTO bodies. The procedures go on to provide that "organizations with which the WTO has entered into a formal arrangement for cooperation and consultation shall be accorded observer status in such bodies as may be determined by that arrangement". Under the procedures, IGOs that do not have the formal status of observers may attend meetings of accession Working Parties on an *ad hoc* basis at the specific invitation of the Working Party concerned. Invitations may also be extended, as appropriate and on a case-by-case basis, to specific organizations to follow particular issues within a WTO body in an observer capacity.

IGOs that wish to become observers in accession Working Parties make an application to the Working Party or parties concerned. The following IGOs have obtained observer status in some accession Working Parties: EBRD, EFTA, IMF, UN, UNCTAD, WIPO and World Bank.

Non-governmental organizations (NGOs) do not qualify for observer status at the WTO and do not participate in accession Working Parties. While Article V:2 of the Marrakesh Agreement provides that "the General Council may make appropriate arrangements for consultation and cooperation with [NGOs] concerned with matters related to those of the WTO," the broadly held view is that it would not be possible for NGOs to be directly involved in the work of the WTO or its meetings given the special character of the Organization as a legally binding intergovernmental treaty of rights and obligations among its Members and a forum for negotiations. Closer consultation and cooperation with NGOs is, however, encouraged at the national level.[30]

3 THE WORKING PARTY PROCESS

The procedures followed by accession Working Parties are based on WTO document WT/ACC/1 entitled "Accession to the WTO – Procedures for Negotiations under Article XII" of 24 March 1995. This was issued by the WTO Secretariat in close consultation with Members as a practical, non-binding guide. The procedures have evolved somewhat since that date, but the document is still basically valid.

The Working Party process is divided into three distinct phases, the main features of which are:

Phase 1. This is devoted to the collection of factual information on the trade regime of the applicant. This fact-finding stage is needed in order to provide both

[30] See "Guidelines for Arrangements on Relations with Non-Governmental Organizations – Decision adopted by the General Council on 18 July 1996" (WTO document WT/L/162).

WTO Members and the applicant with a basis for their work. It has two main purposes: to clarify any changes that the applicant will need to make in order to bring laws, regulations and administrative practices into conformity with WTO requirements; and to provide a baseline for the negotiations that will take place on market access for goods and services.

The applicant first submits a Memorandum containing a detailed description of its foreign trade regime. Receipt of the Memorandum triggers the Working Party process and Members then submit written questions to the applicant asking for clarifications or additional data where necessary. Only when written answers have been received from the applicant and an adequate factual basis obtained does the Working Party hold its first meeting. The first meetings of the Working Party see a continuation of this fact-finding process and a progressively clearer identification of areas of possible inconsistency with the WTO agreements. As the information-gathering stage advances, and in order to ensure the transparency of the process, the Secretariat is often requested to circulate a Factual Summary of Points Raised – an informal document summarizing discussions in the Working Party. This document gradually develops into a draft Working Party Report.

Phase 2. At an appropriate moment, Working Parties move on to negotiate the terms of accession. All WTO Members have accepted commitments on its rules, on agricultural support and export subsidies, on customs tariffs and on services, and acceding governments are expected to do likewise. Negotiations on the general rules relating to goods, TRIPS and services take place *multilaterally* in each Working Party. Acceding governments are expected to observe these rules as well as the commitments negotiated in the Working Party. Consultations and negotiations with the applicant on the level of agricultural support and export subsidies take place *plurilaterally*, i.e. in a group consisting of the members of the Working Party interested in these issues. Other issues such as SPS, TBT, or even TRIPS have also been taken up in a plurilateral setting. Alongside with these negotiations, the applicant negotiates *bilaterally* with interested Working Party members on conditions of access to its market for goods and services. The aim of the negotiation on goods is to reach agreement on maximum permitted levels for customs duties. In the case of services, the negotiations deal not only with limitations on market access for services and service providers in different sectors but also with limitations on national treatment and any exemptions from the MFN provisions of the General Agreement on Trade and Services (GATS).

Phase 3. The text of the draft Report is examined and finalized in the Working Party. This includes the commitments on the general rules to be accepted by the acceding country and a draft Protocol of Accession. The results of the bilateral negotiations on goods and services and of the plurilateral consultations and negotiations on agricultural support are consolidated in draft multilateral Goods and Services Schedules, reviewed by the Working Party and annexed to the text of the draft Report. The Working Party then agrees the draft Report as a whole[31] and forwards it to the General Council/Ministerial Conference for adoption.

While these three stages are conceptually distinct and taken up in the above sequence, they often overlap in practice. The following sections deal with each of the steps in this process.

4 PROVISION OF FACTUAL INFORMATION ON THE APPLICANT'S TRADE REGIME

The first stage is for applicants to present factual data on their trade regime. All WTO documents must be submitted in one of the WTO official languages: English, French and Spanish. Once circulated, these are translated into the two other official languages of the Organization.

4.1 Applicant's Memorandum on its trade regime and supporting data

The basic document is the Memorandum which the applicant submits on its trade regime. This should provide a full summary of its foreign trade regime set out according to the Outline Format attached to WTO document WT/ACC/1. The Memorandum should be supplemented by information requested in the Annexes to WTO document WT/ACC/1 (see Table 1 below). The full texts of the documents referred to in this Table are reproduced in Annex 6.

Memorandum

The Memorandum is arranged under the following seven main headings:

- Introduction
- Economy, Economic Policies and Foreign Trade
- Framework for Making and Enforcing Policies Affecting Foreign Trade in Goods and Services
- Policies Affecting Trade in Goods
- TRIPS Regime
- Trade-Related Services Regime
- Institutional Base for Trade and Economic Relations with Third Countries.

A list of the subjects covered by each of these headings as set out in the Attachment to WTO document WT/ACC/1 is to be found in Annex 6.

[31] While the Goods Schedule and the Services Schedule are integral parts of the Reports of Accession Working Parties they are, for practical reasons, issued in separate addenda to the Reports.

Table 1 *Memorandum and its annexes*

Type of information	*Information required*	*WTO Document reference*
General	Memorandum	WT/ACC/1, Attachment
	Statistics and Publications	WT/ACC/1, Annex 1
	List of Laws and Legal Acts	WT/ACC/1, Paragraph 9 and Annex 2
Trade in Goods	Import Licensing Procedures Questionnaire	WT/ACC/1, Annex 3
	Customs Valuation Questionnaire	WT/ACC/1, Annex 4
	TBT Questionnaire	WT/ACC/1, Annex 5
	State Trading Questionnaire	WT/ACC/1, Annex 6
Trade in Services	Services Sectoral Classification List	WT/ACC/1, Annex 7
Foreign Trade Agreements	List of Foreign Trade Agreements	WT/ACC/1, Annex 8.

Table 2 *Supplementary factual information*[32]

Type of information	*Information required*	*WTO Document reference*
Trade in Goods	TBT and SPS Checklists	WT/ACC/8
	Domestic Support and Export Subsidies in Agriculture	WT/ACC/4
Trade in services	Trade in Services Questionnaire	WT/ACC/5
TRIPS	TRIPS Checklist	WT/ACC/9

Supporting data

Experience gained in early accessions led accession Working Parties to develop a number of documents requesting applicants to supply further factual information (see Table 2 above). The texts of these four documents are reproduced in Annex 7.

Presentation of the Memorandum

The preparation of the Memorandum dealing with all the above subjects requires a considerable investment of resources from the applicant. The timing of the submission has varied considerably from accession to accession. In one case, the applicant

[32] The full text of the documents referred to is reproduced in Annex 7.

submitted this document together with its request for accession,[33] but in another, the Memorandum was submitted over nine years after the application to accede.[34] The average for the ten most recent accessions was two years, seven months.

The Memorandum on the applicant's foreign trade regime is the foundation on which the Working Party constructs its Report. The presentation of a comprehensive and accurate document greatly facilitates the subsequent stages of the accession process.[35]

The procedures suggest that the Secretariat may check the consistency of the Memorandum with the Outline Format in WTO document WT/ACC/1. In some cases where the memoranda presented were not fully consistent with the Outline Format, Working Parties started considering information on several main sections of the Memorandum that were correct. In other cases, applicants were asked to substantiate their memoranda with additional factual information before the Working Party examination could be started.[36]

4.2 WRITTEN QUESTIONS AND ANSWERS

The procedures suggest[37] that following the circulation of the Memorandum, interested WTO Members are invited to submit questions in writing with a view to clarifying the operation of the applicant's foreign trade regime. Members may pose questions with regard to topics not listed in the outline format, and this has happened in a few instances. Answers to these questions should be provided by the applicant in writing and arranged by topic in accordance with the structure of the Memorandum. Only one round of written questions and replies was considered necessary in the great majority of cases before the first meeting of the Working Party.

5 WORKING PARTY EXAMINATION OF APPLICANT'S TRADE REGIME

The first meeting of the Working Party is scheduled once Members are satisfied that the Memorandum, and the written questions and replies, provide an adequate factual basis to begin the examination of the applicant's trade regime.

The procedures suggest that "adequate lead-time should be allowed in the preparatory stage of accession negotiations before meetings of the Working Party are convened, to enable both the applicant and members of the Working Party to better prepare themselves. As a rule, there should be a sufficient lapse of time (generally four to six weeks) between the formal circulation of documentation and meetings of the Working Party. The dates of meetings are set after the relevant documentation

[33] Estonia. [34] Nepal. [35] WTO document ACC/10, p. 9.

[36] For example, Viet Nam, WTO documents WT/ACC/VNM/3 and Corr. 1, Add. 1 and 2; Saudi Arabia, WTO documents WT/ACC/SAU/4 and Add. 1 and WT/ACC/SAU/5.

[37] WTO document WT/ACC/1, para 10.

has been circulated. The convening notice of meetings should specify the purpose of each meeting and the documentation before it".[38]

At the first meeting of each Working Party, the applicant is invited to make an introductory statement. Members then normally welcome the applicant and those intending to take an active part in the negotiations may also make some of their expectations known.

The procedures state that "at the initial meeting of the Working Party, representatives from the applicant and members of the Working Party examine the Memorandum and the questions and answers provided with a view to seeking any further clarifications that may be required in the light of the various provisions of the WTO Agreement and the Multilateral Trade Agreements."[39]

During this technical work each of the topics in the Memorandum is examined in turn using the Memorandum as a basis, together with the questions and answers and the other supporting documentation circulated. Members may ask for copies of relevant laws and regulations. Discussions are normally based on questions from interested WTO Members. The acceding delegation provides oral answers to these questions to the extent it is able to do so. It is usual for the leader of its delegation to answer but other members of the delegation may also do so if asked by the leader.

The primary aims of the question and answer process are to identify the laws, regulations and practices that are relevant to each topic and to understand if these are in conformity with WTO requirements. This discussion will already begin to reveal changes that may be necessary to ensure conformity.

At the end of each meeting of the Working Party, the Chairperson generally sums up the state of play and the next steps required for future meetings. This preparation is carried out, *inter alia*, through informal consultations with the applicant, members of the Working Party and the Secretariat.

After the meeting, members submit written questions, some of which would have already been raised at the meeting. Applicants are then required to prepare written replies to all questions and to forward them to the Secretariat. The questions and replies documents circulated after each meeting of the Working Party constitute a record of the discussions.

Further fact-finding meetings may be held as necessary before the Working Party begins to negotiate the terms on which the applicant will accede. The number of such meetings and the length of time this process takes have varied considerably, depending on a number of factors including the interest generated by a particular accession, the complexity of the policies examined, the adequacy of the information supplied, and the tabling of initial offers. The process is accelerated and time used most productively if acceding governments submit in good time the information asked for, and responses to the questionnaires and checklists listed above. Once the

[38] WTO document WT/ACC/1, para 8.

[39] WTO document WT/ACC/1, para 11.

fact-finding work has provided a sufficient factual basis for the negotiations, the Working Party moves to the negotiating phase.[40]

The Secretariat is often requested, at an appropriate stage, to prepare an informal Factual Summary of Points Raised in order to consolidate the information contained in the Memorandum, the supplementary documents, and the questions and replies documents. The subjects covered in the factual summary are broadly the same as in the Memorandum. The purpose of this Summary is to facilitate the work of the applicant and the members of the Working Party by identifying the points that are established and those that require further clarification, as well as to make the process more transparent. As work proceeds and as negotiations on multilateral commitments advance, the Factual Summary of Points Raised will gradually evolve into a draft Report of the Working Party which will contain not only factual information but also commitments to be accepted by the new Member. During this process, further revisions are prepared and circulated to Working Party members, as necessary.

In consultation with WTO Members, the Secretariat and Working Party members have worked together with applicants to streamline the accession process for LDCs. The steps taken included drafting a Factual summary at an early stage of the proceedings, and keeping the number of Working Party meetings at a minimum[41] by ensuring that maximum progress is made between meetings without the acceding governments having to visit Geneva, and by organizing bilateral market access negotiations on goods and services in the acceding government's capital or through the Secretariat to the extent possible.

6 NEGOTIATION OF TERMS ON WHICH THE APPLICANT WILL ACCEDE

WTO document WT/ACC/1 describes the procedures governing the negotiating phase in less detail than the procedures for the initial fact-finding or the concluding stages in which the results of the discussions are formalized and adopted. The main aim of these procedures is to define a framework for negotiations between WTO Members and the acceding government.[42]

Negotiations on terms of accession take place in four main parts: multilateral negotiations in the Working Party on the rules to be accepted; plurilateral negotiations among interested parties on agricultural domestic support and export subsidies (which sometimes also deal with SPS and technical barriers to trade [TBT]);

[40] WTO document WT/ACC/10/Rev.3, p. 11. In some cases initial offers on goods and services were tabled before the first meeting of the Working Party (Andorra, Tajikistan) but this is exceptional. In another exceptional case, 9 meetings were held before the offers on both goods and services were made available (Russian Federation).

[41] WTO document WT/COMTD/LDC/W/27 (WT/ACC/12).

[42] WTO document WT/ ACC/1, para 12.

bilateral negotiations between interested parties on concessions on goods; and bilateral negotiations between interested parties on specific commitments on services.

Members of the Working Party may hold bilateral meetings with the applicant at any stage of the work. These bilateral meetings may cover any matter connected with the accession of the applicant. In the initial fact-finding phase, some members may want to hold bilateral meetings on complex issues which are more efficiently discussed bilaterally than in the Working Party. Members may also want to make their expectations known on matters being discussed in the Working Party, to explore the reactions of the applicant and to reach common understandings on commitments that it is prepared to undertake. Bilateral meetings are not attended by the Secretariat and much of this process is confidential and not publicly documented.

Bilateral meetings, plurilateral meetings and the multilateral meetings of the Working Party therefore proceed in parallel. However, all agreements reached at the bilateral and plurilateral levels must be multilateralized before the negotiations are concluded and the Working Party must concur with their inclusion in the accession package consisting of the draft Report, including a draft Protocol and Decision, and draft Goods and Services Schedules. These documents are prepared by the Secretariat and presented to the Working Party for adoption.

The following four sections describe the procedures followed in the negotiations on rules, agricultural support and export subsidies, tariffs and services.

6.1 Negotiation on Rules

The suggested procedures simply state that the move from the fact-finding phase to the negotiation phase of the work takes place when the examination of the foreign trade regime is sufficiently advanced and it is understood that fact-finding work on the foreign trade regime and the negotiating phase can overlap and proceed in parallel.[43]

The decision to move to examine commitments in the rules area is taken once Working Party members are satisfied they have established an adequate factual basis. Progress in the other areas of the negotiations may also be a factor. The negotiations on rules are generally conducted multilaterally in the Working Party although concerns on particular issues may be settled bilaterally and brought to the Working Party for consideration in the shape of proposed texts.

It has become standard practice for applicants to submit legislative action plans outlining the work programme underway to amend their legislation, as well as target dates for implementation. As the accession process advances, governments are requested to revise and update these plans. Legislative action plans dealing with specific subjects may also be required, in particular when Working Parties wish to reach a clear understanding of what remains to be done to bring the applicant's legislation and practices into full conformity with each of the main provisions of

[43] WTO document WT/ACC/1, para 12.

WTO agreements. These plans now tend to be submitted earlier in the accession process than in the past.

When it is established that applicants need to introduce new legislation, some interested Members invite legislation to be presented to them in draft form. There is of course no obligation to comply with this request and governments sometimes prefer to present legislation once it has been enacted. However, it has been argued that presentation of the draft legislation would be helpful to acceding governments, as it would ensure that they did not ask their parliaments to pass texts which, when brought to the Working Party, were found unacceptable on the grounds that they did not conform to WTO requirements. While this procedure has not always been followed, it has now become common for draft legislation to be presented, sometimes informally, for comments by interested members.

It is often a member of the Working Party that initiates the negotiations on commitments by putting forward proposed texts for inclusion in the draft Report. Applicants may also propose texts if they wish to expedite the work, for instance by offering to amend specific measures which they recognize as being not in accordance with WTO requirements.

Negotiations are considered advanced when the Secretariat is asked to prepare the text of a draft Report. When taking this decision, progress in other areas of the negotiations, including the bilateral goods and services negotiations, will be taken into account, so that the work proceeds in parallel. The end result of the negotiation on rules on each topic is a text for inclusion in the Working Party Report which often includes commitments accepted by the acceding government.

6.2 Negotiation of tariff concessions

Negotiations on tariff concessions are conducted bilaterally on the basis of offers and requests. The procedures suggest that the negotiations may be initiated either by the applicant or by the Members. However, in practice, Members tend to wait for the acceding government to submit an initial offer of proposed bound rates before requesting bilateral negotiations and submitting requests. These offers are more usefully submitted in electronic form, rather than on paper. They are sent to the Secretariat which then circulates a notice to members of the Working Party, indicating that it is available. In a few cases applicants have made their offer available to interested Members on request. The usual format for the initial tariff offer, including notes on the way in which the format for scheduling has been used, will be found in Annex 8.1.

The record shows that, typically, initial tariff offers are tabled between the first and the second Working Party meetings at about the same time as initial offers on services. To the extent possible, offers on goods and services should be tabled at the same time so that the negotiations on these two subjects can move forward together. Offers are made available to all interested Working Party members through WT/ACC/SPEC/ series WTO documents.

The tabling of market access offers triggers the bilateral negotiations. Members wishing to engage in the tariff negotiations contact the applicant to arrange bilateral meetings, which are normally held in the margins of Working Party meetings. Delegations may either arrange these meetings themselves or request the Secretariat to do so. The number of Members taking part in these negotiations varies considerably from one accession to another. The largest WTO Members always take part in these negotiations and a few other Members take part in nearly all. Geographical factors will lead some Members to negotiate with some applicants. Many Members will take part in the negotiations with the largest acceders.

The number of rounds of bilateral negotiations depends on the quality of the offers and the complexity of the issues involved.

Members who negotiate on both goods and services usually conclude both at the same time. However, some Members may negotiate only on goods or only on services. Bilateral agreements recording the agreed tariff concessions are signed and transmitted to the Secretariat. The format for these is at Annex 8.2. Three signed originals are necessary, as one has to be sent to the Secretariat and the others kept by the applicant and the Member concerned. The bilateral agreements submitted to the Secretariat remain confidential.

After bilateral agreements have been completed with all interested WTO Members, the Secretariat uses these agreements, and the commitments resulting from the consultations on agricultural domestic support and export subsidies (see below), to prepare a single, consolidated draft Goods Schedule. This multilateralizes the results of the bilateral tariff negotiations. In accordance with the most-favoured-nation (MFN) principle,[44] if an applicant has agreed to bind its tariff on an item at 20 percent in its negotiations with one Member and at 10 percent in its negotiations with another, the rate in the Schedule will be 10 percent.

The format for the Tariff Schedule is contained in Annex 8.3. The cover page of each Schedule indicates the Schedule number and the authentic language of the Schedule. Each new Member is allocated the next available Schedule number, which is expressed in Latin numerals on the cover page of its Schedule.[45] The Schedules are usually authentic in only one of the three official languages of WTO (English, French or Spanish). This language is chosen by the acceder.

When completed, the draft Schedules are formally circulated to all members of the Working Party for multilateral review and verification, enabling Members to confirm that the concessions contained in the draft Schedules reflect the results of their bilateral negotiations with the acceding government. It also presents an

[44] MFN Principle (GATT 1994, Article I.1) provides that any tariff binding granted by any Member to any product originating in any other country shall be accorded immediately and unconditionally to the like product originating in the territories of all other Members.

[45] Viet Nam, the latest applicant to have completed its accession process, has Schedule CLX, the Latin equivalent of 160. There are more Schedule numbers than there are WTO Members because some Members of GATT 1947 withdrew from that Agreement.

opportunity to ensure that the contents are in accordance with the relevant WTO provisions.

Particular attention needs to be paid in this connection to the observance of obligations relating to like products in the basic MFN provision in Article I:1 of the GATT 1994. Changes have been made to draft Tariff Schedules to remove discrimination on like products when Members claimed their GATT rights in the Working Party.[46] It may be noted that a similar point has also been raised in the General Council after a Working Party had adopted its Report. At this later stage, the Member which considered certain tariff bindings on like products to be discriminatory said that if the discriminatory rates were actually applied they would be considered a violation of Article I:1 of GATT 1994.[47]

6.3 Discussions on agricultural support and export subsidies

The discussions on agricultural commitments are based on the factual data supplied by the applicant in the format of WTO document WT/ACC/4 (Annex 7.2). Since the preparation of the supporting tables involves a thorough grasp of complex WTO requirements and detailed technical work, they are invariably revised during the accession negotiations, taking into account comments formulated by Members. The supporting tables are made available to all interested Working Party members as a WT/ACC/SPEC/ WTO document.

WTO document WT/ACC/1 states that this information may be examined and further clarified on a bilateral basis. It now appears to be accepted that the tables containing information on domestic support and export subsidies are dealt with in plurilateral meetings with interested WTO Members as this information is of more general systemic interest than concessions on specific tariff lines of interest to individual Members. These meetings are called when the applicant has submitted the necessary tables and members of the Working Party have demonstrated an interest in pursuing the matter. These meetings are usually held on the fringes of Working Party meetings, when delegations come together to focus on the accession in question.

This process leads the Secretariat to circulate a set of final tables which forms the basis for the future commitment levels in relation to the Total Aggregate Measurement of Support (Total AMS) and Export Subsides in Agriculture that are recorded in Part IV of the Schedule of Concessions and Commitments on Goods. The relevant supporting tables are also incorporated by reference in Part IV of the Schedule.

[46] Mongolian bindings on alcoholic beverages.

[47] Argentina, concerning FYROM's tariff bindings on certain cheeses and alcoholic beverages. WTO document WT/GC/M/76, para 8.

6.4 Negotiation of specific commitments on services

WTO document WT/ACC/1 notes that the procedures for the negotiations on services are similar to those for the negotiations on tariffs, being based on offers and requests.[48] Negotiations on services are usually engaged after members of the Working Party have undertaken multilateral examination of the services regime, generally based on information submitted in the outline format described in the Secretariat's Technical Note WTO document WT/ACC/5 and in written replies to specific questions. As noted above, many applicants have found it difficult to supply all the factual information requested and members of accession Working Parties have often explicitly requested them to provide the Working Party with an initial offer on services as soon as possible.[49]

The negotiations start in earnest with the multilateral circulation of the applicant's initial offer. Some applicants have taken much longer to table services offers than others. On average, initial services offers have been tabled three years after submitting their Memoranda. Typically, initial services offers are tabled at about the same time as the initial tariff offers.

Initial offers on services follow the same format as all Schedules to the GATS.[50] The format is reproduced in Annex 9, which also includes notes on the drafting of a Services Schedule. If initially inconsistent, initial offers have had to be revised to conform to the standard format.

The offer is made available to all interested Working Party members as a WT/ACC/SPEC/WTO document for the applicant concerned.[51] Although the multilateral process of questions and answers in the Working Party provides an insight into the expectations of Members and the positions of applicants, the negotiations are pursued bilaterally.

The negotiations on services and tariffs normally proceed in parallel. The tabling of the offer triggers the negotiating process. Bilateral meetings are often scheduled around meetings of the accession Working Parties. In the early stages of the negotiations some Members may simply ask applicants to improve the scope and quality of their offer and not focus on particular sectors. The initial offers are inevitably revised in the course of the negotiations. The main factor affecting the number of rounds of negotiations is the willingness of the applicant to meet Members' requests. As already noted, the procedures for the signature of bilateral agreements on tariffs and services are linked. When it has received bilateral agreements from all the Members that have negotiated, the Secretariat consolidates the bilateral agreements into a draft Services Schedule and circulates the document to Members of

48 WTO document WT/ACC/1, para 13 (iii).

49 E.g. Belarus WTO document WT/ACC/BLR/7 (19 December 1997); Kyrgyz Republic WTO document WT/ACC/KGZ/7 (11 April 1997).

50 General Agreement on Trade in Services, Article XX, Schedules of Specific Commitments.

51 By way of example, Nepal's initial services offer was distributed as WTO document WT/ACC/SPEC/NPL/4 (7 July 2000).

the Working Party and the acceding government. If commitments have been made in a given sector to two or more Members, the Secretariat will take the least restrictive of these into the draft Schedule, as a commitment to one Member must be accorded to all Members under the most-favoured-nation clause. This draft is then reviewed by the accession Working Party as part of its review of the whole accession package – an opportunity of ensuring that the draft Schedule is a correct reflection of the bilateral agreements and that it conforms to the provisions of the GATS.[52]

7 COMPLETION OF WORKING PARTY MANDATE

When the negotiations in the areas of rules, domestic support and export subsidies for agricultural products, and goods and services bilaterals are completed to the satisfaction of members and the applicant, the Working Party is in a position to finish its work under its mandate. To do this it completes its Report to the General Council/Ministerial Conference.

Working Party Reports start with short introductory sections and references to the documentation provided and go on to summarize the discussions held on WTO rules. In each specific case where commitments have been negotiated and accepted by the applicant, the Reports contain texts laying down the details. Reports conclude by making the recommendations called for in the terms of reference of the Working Party. All Reports so far adopted include as an annex draft Protocols of Accession setting out the terms on which the applicant should be invited to accede. The applicant's terms of entry form a single package which must be agreed by the membership and accepted by the applicant as a whole. The Working Party Report also annexes a draft General Council/Ministerial Conference Decision inviting the applicant to accede to the Marrakesh Agreement Establishing the World Trade Organization on the terms and conditions set out in the draft Protocol. The texts of the Decisions have all been identical (see Annex 10.1). The document numbers of Working Party Reports of applicants that have acceded to WTO are listed in Annex 5.

Most Protocols of new Members are similar although the standard text was amended in January 2001 to bring it into line with other WTO Decision documents. The basic provisions have remained the same. The common core provisions state that, upon its entry into force, the applicant accedes to the WTO Agreement pursuant to Article XII and thereby becomes a Member of the WTO with the rights and obligations of membership. The new Member is bound to observe the rules contained in the Agreement establishing the WTO, as rectified, amended or otherwise modified as of the date that its Protocol enters into force. The text common to all these Protocols is reproduced in Annex 10.2.

[52] Such as GATS Article II, its most-favoured-nation clause, under which a commitment must not be so narrowly defined as to deprive like services and service suppliers of other Members of its benefits.

In addition, each of the Protocols of the new Members that have acceded so far also contains obligations which are specific to that Member. All these Members have accepted obligations to abide by rules that are either spelled out in the Protocol itself or in the Working Party's commitment paragraphs which are incorporated by reference into the Protocol. These commitment paragraphs are thus integral parts of the Protocol and have the same status and legal effect as the commitments in the Protocol itself. These two sets of provisions are referred to below as Protocol commitments. In addition, annexes to the Protocol contain the new Member's Schedule of Concessions and Commitments on Goods, which sets out maximum rates for individual customs tariffs and commitments on domestic support and export subsidies for agricultural products, and its Schedule of Specific Commitments on Services. The Protocol provides that these shall become Schedules of GATT 1994 and GATS, respectively.[53]

The Protocols make clear that the obligations of the acceder are an integral part of the WTO Agreement to which the applicant accedes. It has been accepted in the WTO that the Agreement can be modified in this way and that the rights and obligations contained in the Protocols of Accession are enforceable through the WTO's Understanding on Rules and Procedures Governing the Settlement of Disputes.

Accession Working Parties adopt their Reports, including the whole accession package, by consensus in accordance with the usual WTO practice.[54] During the last meeting of the Working Party, the Report, including the Schedules on Goods and Services, are adopted *ad referendum* – that is subject to approval by governments. Once the adoption of the Report is confirmed, it is submitted to the General Council or, if this is to meet soon, the Ministerial Conference. In only one case has an applicant requested that an adopted Working Party Report not be forwarded to the General Council for the time being.[55]

8 INVOCATION OF ARTICLE XIII OF THE WTO

Article XIII of the WTO Agreement provides that the WTO Agreement and the Multilateral Trade Agreements annexed to it "shall not apply as between any Member and any other Member if either of the Members, at the time either becomes a Member, does not consent to such application" if they notify the General Council/Ministerial Conference before its approval of the agreement on the terms of accession.

[53] For practical reasons, the Goods Schedule and the Services Schedule are contained in separate addenda to the document containing the rest of the Report.

[54] For provisions on decision-making in the WTO, including the provisions on voting, see Agreement Establishing the WTO, Article IX:1.

[55] Vanuatu.

Article XIII has been invoked eight times. Five invocations have been withdrawn[56] and only three are still maintained.[57]

9 ADOPTION OF REPORT BY GENERAL COUNCIL/ MINISTERIAL CONFERENCE

It may first be noted that when the General Council sets up an accession Working Party, it delegates examination of the request for accession to that body and there is no procedure established for the review of accessions by the General Council. Only on very few occasions have Members raised issues relating to individual ongoing accessions in the General Council.[58]

When the Report comes before the General Council, it is introduced by the Chairperson of the Working Party. The representative of the applicant is given the floor and WTO Members welcome the outcome of the negotiations.

At the invitation of its Chairperson, the General Council/Ministerial Conference then:

- approves the text of the draft Protocol of Accession and the text of the draft Decision on the Accession of [X];
- in accordance with the Decision-Making Procedures under Articles IX and XII of the WTO Agreement agreed in November 1995,[59] adopts the draft Decision on the Accession of [X]; and
- adopts the Report of the Working Party as a whole, including the Schedule on Goods in its Addendum 1 and the Schedule on Services in its Addendum 2.

Since 1995, these decisions have been taken by consensus, in accordance with WTO practice.[60]

Before a Working Party Report is brought to the General Council, the Secretariat checks that the acceding government has paid its contribution to the WTO budget as an observer (see section on First contacts, above). It may only accede to the WTO if its financial obligations have been fully discharged. The applicants' contribution to the WTO's annual operating budget is based on its share of the total international

56 United States *vis-à-vis* Mongolia WTO document WT/L/306, Kyrgyz Republic WTO document WT/L/363, Georgia WTO document WT/L/385, Armenia WTO document WT/L/601 and Corr 1 and Viet Nam WTO document WT/L/679.

57 United States *vis-à-vis* Moldova WTO document WT/L/395, El Salvador *vis-à-vis* China WTO document WT/L/429 and Turkey *vis-à-vis* Armenia WTO document WT/L/501.

58 For instance, an issue relating to the accession of Latvia was placed on the agenda by the European Communities WTO document WT/GC/M/29, item 9. The point at issue concerned specific commitments on audiovisual services, which are dealt with in the relevant Section below.

59 WTO document WT/L/93, 15 November 1995.

60 Agreement Establishing the WTO, Article IX:1.

trade of all Members (imports plus exports).[61] According to the budget for 2006, a Member accounting for 1 percent of the trade of all Members was assessed about CHF 1.7 million (about $1.4 million, €1.1 million.). A minimum contribution of 0.015 percent was paid by Members whose share of the total trade was less than 0.015 percent of the total. In 2006, 39 Members paid a minimum contribution of about CHF 26,000 (about $21,000, €16,300). New Members also pay a one-time advance to the Working Capital Fund in accordance with the scale of contributions applicable to the budget for the year of its accession. In 2006, a new Member with 1 percent of world trade advanced about CHF 93,000 (about $77,000, €58,000.) The minimum of the advance amounts to 0.5 percent of the principal of the Fund. New Members paying the minimum would therefore be assessed some CHF 47,000 (about $39,000, €29,000) in 2006.

10 ACCESSION OF APPLICANT

In adopting the Decision, WTO Members offer terms of accession to the applicant. The applicant also accepts those terms by accepting the Protocol.[62] WTO Members do not, therefore, need to sign the Protocol. The Protocol specifies the date until which it is open for acceptance by the applicant, by signature or ratification. An authorized representative of the applicant often signs the Protocol immediately after it has been approved on an *ad referendum* basis. While a period of three to six months is usual, in practice it is the applicant who proposes the length of time needed to complete its internal procedures and accept the terms.

A few acceding governments have requested an extension of the time limit for acceptance, explaining their reasons for doing so. In all of these cases, the General Council has agreed to the extension with very little discussion.[63]

The Protocol provides that applicants become Members of the WTO thirty days after accepting the Protocol of Accession. This period is allowed in order to give WTO Members time to take any action necessary to apply the WTO Agreement to the new Member.

61 The statistics used relate to trade in goods (excluding gold held as a store of value), services and intellectual property rights as reported in the Balance of Payments statistics from the IMF. See Financial Regulations of the WTO, WTO document WT/L/156/Rev.1, 21 November 2003.

62 Depending on the constitutional law of the applicant, acceptance may be effective through signature or through subsequent ratification.

63 The most recent of these requests were made by Cambodia WTO document WT/L/561 and Tonga WTO document WT/L/651.

5

SUBSTANCE OF ACCESSION NEGOTIATIONS

The aim of this Part is to review the terms on which applicants have acceded to the WTO. The WTO Agreement simply provides that a State or separate customs territory possessing full autonomy in the conduct of its external commercial relations and of the other matters provided for in this Agreement and the Multilateral Trade Agreements may accede "on terms to be agreed between it and the WTO".[1] The terms of accession are contained in the Protocols annexed to the Reports of accession Working Parties. The documents containing the text of the Reports are listed in Annex 5. Footnotes cite the new Members concerned. These are arranged in the reverse order of accession, i.e. they cite first the applicant to have acceded more recently. This method has been adopted because, on the whole, more recent accessions are a better guide to current practice than earlier accessions. The footnotes also refer to the relevant paragraphs in these Reports and the annexed accession Protocols.

WTO Members each have different obligations. Article XII does not explain the terms on which applicants may be invited to accede. One reason for its lack of specificity is that the terms of accession are different in each case also because each acceding government negotiates its own unique concessions on customs duties, commitments on agricultural support and export subsidies and specific commitments on its services regime on the basis of its national measures.[2] A second reason is that the drafters of Article XXXIII of GATT 1947, on which WTO Article XII is based, saw the need to provide flexibility to ensure that the terms provided for a balance of advantage. One point that they had very much in mind is that GATT 1947 was based on the assumption that its Members had, by and large, free market economies and that while access to their markets was governed by the measures dealt with in its agreements (for instance, tariffs, quantitative restrictions, etc. in the goods area), access to the markets of applicants which did not necessarily have free market economies might be regulated by government decision. This point is equally valid for the WTO; Article XII adopts the same approach to accession as the corresponding provision of GATT 1947. The fact that terms of accession are not defined in advance preserves the right of Members to adapt the terms to the circumstances of each case.

[1] Article XII of the Agreement Establishing the WTO.

[2] Members of the member States of the European Communities are an exception to this rule.

WTO Members active in accession Working Parties have confirmed that, because each acceder has its own unique features, its commitments should be agreed on a case-by-case basis. However, an examination of the terms shows that certain patterns do emerge. This Part examines the subjects dealt with in the Reports of Accession Working Parties, picks out patterns where they exist and identifies other commitments undertaken by the new Members.

Each of the Accession Protocols makes the applicant a Member of the WTO with all the rights and obligations this entails, including those contained in its Protocol of Accession, which is an integral part of the WTO Agreement. The new Member therefore has an obligation to abide by the rules on goods, services and the trade-related aspects of intellectual property rights of the WTO Agreement. A list of the subjects covered by the Marrakesh Agreement Establishing the WTO is reproduced in Annex 11.

Each new Member also agrees to abide by its own Protocol commitments which are either contained in the Protocol itself or set out in the body of its Report and incorporated by reference in the Protocol.[3] In addition, its concessions and commitments on goods and services are contained in the Goods and Services Schedules, both of which are annexed to the Protocol and form an integral part of it.

The following sections of this Handbook examine each of the main subjects dealt with in the Reports of Accession Working Parties and the Protocol commitments entered into. Working Party Reports have been organized under the following main headings:

1. introduction;
2. economic policies;
3. framework for making and enforcing policies;
4. policies affecting trade in goods;
5. trade-related intellectual property regime;
6. policies affecting trade in services;
7. transparency;
8. trade agreements; and
9. conclusions.

These main headings are usually divided into sub-sections. The normal pattern is that each of the Report's sub-sections deals first with the factual information collected on the acceding country's policies; second with the questions addressed to the acceding country by members of the Working Party; third with discussions that have taken place on the terms to be offered to the applicant; and finally, the Protocol commitments accepted by the applicant on the specific rules and disciplines of the WTO in question. The concluding section of each adopted Report recommends that the applicant be invited to accede to the WTO under the provisions of Article XII and forwards texts of a Draft Decision and Protocol of Accession to the Ministerial

[3] For the text of the Protocols, see Annex 10.2.

Conference/General Council for action. Annexes to the Report contain the draft Goods Schedule and Services Schedule. A tabular presentation showing the main subjects dealt with in the Working Parties and the commitments undertaken by acceders is reproduced in Annex 12.

The last sections of the Handbook analyse the commitments that acceders have undertaken in their Schedules of Concessions and Commitments on Goods and Schedules of Specific Commitments on Services.

Before examining individual subjects, mention is made of some of the more general points that have been raised in the discussions on accession that have taken place in the General Council/Ministerial Conference or in individual Working Parties.

1 GENERAL POINTS

WTO Members request applicants to observe a standstill and not to introduce new restrictive measures while the accession negotiations are in progress.

Some Members have argued in the General Council/Ministerial Conference that new entrants should not be required to undertake Protocol commitments that are more stringent than those of original WTO Members at similar levels of economic development (sometimes referred to as WTO-plus commitments). Other Members have replied that Article XII places no limits on the terms of accession and that, in their view, the process is working well.[4] They have added that the terms on which new Members have acceded are the result of negotiations taking into account the needs and requirements in each case. Moreover, they are agreed in each case by the acceding government and the WTO membership. While there has been relatively little discussion on this subject in the WTO, three main points have emerged: Article XII indeed sets no limits to the terms that may be agreed; acceders have accepted more stringent commitments than original Members in some cases; and a consensus would have to be obtained for any change to take place in the current negotiating procedures. For their part, applicants have concentrated on negotiating specific terms rather than engaging in general debate that is unlikely to lead to an agreed result.

It appears that in some cases applicants have been asked to accept WTO-plus commitments because some Members considered that the State retained a significant degree of control over their economies. All of these applicants that have acceded to the WTO were in course of transition and were reducing the role of the State in the economy. In these cases, Members have wished to obtain details of the privatization programmes under way and the standard Protocol commitment, while going beyond the normal provisions of the WTO, has been simply to provide the

[4] See, for example, General Council WTO document WT/GC/M/40/Add.3.

WTO with reports on the implementation of those programmes.[5] In addition, the Protocols of two new Members contain provisions relating to price comparisons used in anti-dumping investigations where market economy conditions cannot be shown to prevail. These commitments spell out the methodologies for identifying and measuring subsidy benefits.[6] One of these countries, China, is by far the largest applicant to have acceded to the WTO. The terms on which it acceded are unique in important respects and are summarized in Box 5 below.

It appears that some other terms of accession more stringent than those of original WTO Members were negotiated to improve conditions of access to the markets of the new Members concerned or to reduce their ability to distort conditions of competition on world markets. Two examples are commitments to join the Civil Aircraft Agreement and to reduce the level of agricultural export subsidies to zero.

The stock response to general requests from acceding governments for special and differential treatment, reserved for developing and LDCs under the WTO agreements, has been that specific requests could be examined case-by-case. In this they were treated somewhat differently from original WTO Members. The WTO has allowed original WTO Members to decide for themselves whether they are developing countries and this procedure has stood the test of time.[7]

As a general rule, Members expect applicants to submit comprehensive legislative action plans outlining the work programme underway to achieve full conformity with all WTO rules by the date of accession. Very nearly all recent applicants have provided their Working Parties with comprehensive plans indicating the legislative and administrative action to be taken and projected dates for such action. They have proved to be a useful tool for the applicants. Action plans are, by definition, specific to the individual case and there is no set format, but they are best presented in tabular form and arranged by WTO agreement. An example is given in Annex 13.1. Applicants, particularly LDCs, may add another column indicating their technical assistance needs.

Working Party members have, on occasion, requested that drafts of the legislation be presented to them for review before the accession process is completed. This has sometimes been questioned by governments sensitive of their sovereignty. There is no obligation to comply with this request and governments sometimes prefer to present legislation once it has been enacted. However, it has been argued that presentation of the draft legislation would be helpful to acceding governments as it would ensure that they did not ask their parliaments to pass texts which did not conform to WTO requirements. It has now become common for draft legislation to be presented, sometimes informally, for comments by interested members.

5 See section on State ownership and privatization below.

6 Viet Nam, para 255, China, paras 151, 152, Protocol I.15.

7 Decision of the CONTRACTING PARTIES of 28 November 1979 on Differential and More Favourable Treatment for Developing Countries ("Enabling Clause"), GATT 1947 BISD, 26 S, p. 203.

In order to obtain more information on key subjects such as subsidies, Members also occasionally ask the applicant to prepare a draft of the initial notifications that they will be required to submit once they become a Member of the Organization.

Action plans dealing with specific subjects may also be required, in particular when Working Parties wish to reach a clear understanding of what needs to be done to bring the applicant's legislation and practices into full conformity with each of the main provisions of WTO agreements. These more detailed plans frequently deal with subjects on which applicants have been asked to respond to questionnaire or checklists, such as customs valuation, technical barriers to trade, sanitary and phytosanitary regulations and trade-related intellectual property rights. An SPS plan is, for instance, typically based on the response to the checklist of obligations in the SPS Agreement and the action being taken to fill these gaps. An example is given in Annex 13.2.

During the negotiation of commitments, applicants have sometimes explained the difficulties that they will have in achieving conformity with WTO requirements in specific areas and have requested transitional periods granting them time to bring their laws, regulations and practices into line after they accede. This was more frequently the case in earlier accessions when applicants often expected to be accorded the same sort of transitional periods that WTO agreements accorded to original Members of the Organization. However, Members have pointed out that the transitional periods for original Members have now expired. Their expectation has been that new Members observe the rules from the date of their accession to WTO. Accordingly, applicants are encouraged to use the accession process to familiarize themselves with WTO rules and adjust their legal, institutional, and administrative framework as the accession process advances. Protocol commitments therefore usually provide that new Members will abide by their obligations from the date of their accession. Members may, however, show a willingness to entertain requests for transitional periods in individual cases when applicants have demonstrated that they have done as much as possible to bring their system into line with WTO requirements. When necessary, an Action Plan can be provided to support the requests. A number of transitional periods have been agreed. Details will be found in sections below dealing with individual topics.

Transitional periods for LDCs are a feature of the General Council's Guidelines, which provide that transitional periods foreseen under specific WTO agreements shall be granted to these countries, taking into account individual development, financial and trade needs and that these shall be accompanied by Action Plans for compliance with WTO rules, supported by technical assistance and capacity building measures for the acceding LDCs. Transitional periods are negotiated on the basis of Action Plans. Action Plans should demonstrate the applicant's need for the transitional period, describe the extent to which its system is in compliance with WTO rules, and lay out the steps that remain to be taken, a calendar for progressive compliance and a date by which the applicant will be in full compliance (see example in Annex 13.2). LDCs may also include technical assistance needs, though not as a condition for compliance. Members expect that the existing degree of conformity with the provisions of the agreement will not be reduced during the transitional period, that transparency provisions are implemented as soon as possible and that critical provisions central to the issue of market access and the maintenance of a stable, predictable trade regime are in place at the time of accession to the WTO of the applicant concerned.[8] If the basic legislation is not already in conformity with WTO requirements, they will normally wish to examine draft legislation before a decision is taken on the terms for granting the transitional period and normally expect this legislation to be implemented rapidly thereafter. Transitional periods have been granted to both LDCs that have already acceded.[9] One small, vulnerable isolated developing country has been treated in much the same way as the LDCs.[10]

LDCs have been provided with technical assistance and assistance with capacity building in connection with their implementation of Action Plans for transitional periods and other aspects of the accession process on a priority basis. Discussion of the technical assistance to be provided has normally taken place outside the Working Parties and Members have not agreed to suggestions that the obligation to comply with the Action Plan be made conditional on receipt of technical assistance. The Action Plan as revised and incorporated in a Protocol commitment does not contain a column indicating the technical assistance to be provided. However, one Working Party Report contains a paragraph in which the representative of the country concerned made it clear that as an LDC with limited resources, infrastructure and institutional and technical capabilities, it would face serious difficulties to implement the WTO agreements expeditiously by its own means. This country's action plans had identified the specific areas and projects where technical assistance would be welcome. The representative acknowledged assistance already received but added that additional technical assistance would be required with respect to these and other areas of WTO implementation as noted in the action plans.[11]

The implementation of the Guidelines has also streamlined the accession process for LDCs. Since the adoption of the Guidelines, substantive demands on LDCs have been moderated in some respects. The two LDCs that have already acceded were, for instance, not required to accept WTO plurilateral agreements and the obligations that they have undertaken in their Goods Schedules and Services Schedules are less onerous than those of other applicants that have acceded in recent years.[12]

[8] See, for example, Cambodia, para 83.

[9] Transitional periods were granted to Cambodia and Nepal for the implementation of the Agreements on Customs Valuation (Cambodia, para 92; Nepal, para 57), TBT (Cambodia, para 130, Nepal, para 97), SPS (Cambodia, para 141; Nepal, para 107), and TRIPS (Cambodia, para 205; Nepal, para 137).

[10] Tonga was granted transitional periods for the implementation of the Agreements on Customs Valuation (Tonga, paras 89–91) and TRIPS (Tonga, paras 167–169).

[11] Nepal, para 152.

[12] These topics are discussed in more detail in the relevant sections of this Handbook.

Box 5: Accession of China

China's accession was exceptional for a number of reasons, including: the scope of reform – the object of domestic, legal and economic reform was to establish a socialist market economy in line with China's basic national policy of opening to the outside world; the multiple trade instruments used in its different levels of government; the inclusion in its customs territory of areas where special regimes for tariffs, taxes and regulations are established (including border trade regions, minority autonomous areas, Special Economic Zones, open coastal cities, economic and technical development zones); and its very large size and rapid growth.

China's accession package therefore includes a number of commitments which, in many ways, are unique. In particular, China's accession documents include:

- a transitional time-bound (until the end of 2008) special textiles and clothing safeguard clause[13] and a transitional time-bound product-specific safeguard mechanism authorizing WTO Members to take action if imports from China cause market disruption;[14]
- a transitional review mechanism for the review of the implementation of the WTO Agreement and the related provisions of China's Protocol;[15]
- text on non-discrimination for foreign individuals and enterprises and foreign-funded enterprises;[16]
- a commitment that WTO Members phase out all prohibitions, quantitative restrictions and other measures they maintain against imports from China in a manner inconsistent with the WTO Agreement, or deal with them in accordance with mutually-agreed terms and timetables.[17]

Information on the other terms on which China acceded will be found in the relevant sections below. These provisions are often relatively detailed. They pay special attention, for instance, to: the uniform administration of its trade policies throughout its territory[18]; and price comparisons used during a transitional period in anti-dumping investigations where market economy conditions cannot be shown to prevail and methodologies for identifying and measuring subsidy benefits.[19]

China's claim to receive the special and differential treatment accorded to developing countries was not agreed in full. For instance, a compromise was reached regarding its

[13] China, para 242. [14] China, Protocol I.16.

[15] China, para 322 and Protocol Section 18. Notifications to be made to: Council for Trade in Goods, Council for Trade-Related Aspects of Intellectual Property Rights, Council for Trade in Services, Committees on Balance-of-Payments Restrictions, Market Access (covering also ITA), Agriculture, Sanitary and Phytosanitary Measures, Technical Barriers to Trade, Subsidies and Countervailing Measures, Anti-Dumping Measures, Customs Valuation, Rules of Origin, Import Licensing, Trade-Related Investment Measures, Safeguards, Trade in Financial Services.

[16] China, paras 18, 19, 22, and 23 and Protocol I.3. [17] China, Protocol I.17.

[18] China, paras 73 and 75, and Protocol I.2(A) and (B). [19] China, para 151, Protocol I.15.

de minimis level of domestic support[20] and its entitlement to special and differential treatment under the Subsidies and Countervailing Measures (SCM) Agreement.[21]

China was provided with a certain number of transitional periods to bring its laws and regulations into line with its WTO commitments.

2 RULES

The following sections examine each of the main subjects dealt with in the Working Party Reports.

2.1 INTRODUCTORY STATEMENTS

Introductory statements made at the first meeting of Working Parties provide applicants with an opportunity to introduce themselves. They may also provide an insight into the reasons behind their application to accede. Some have stated that membership will make an essential contribution to economic development by promoting an increase in foreign exchange earnings and by providing reassurance to the foreign investors that they need to attract. Members can use the resources generated by economic development to reduce poverty. However, it has also been recognized that WTO agreements create trading opportunities to maximize its benefits, and that membership must be part of an integrated approach to development and poverty reduction designed to enable traders to take advantage of the opportunities that it creates. Some applicants value the stability promised by the system, emphasizing that membership of the WTO will be a guarantee that their trade relations will be based on commercial considerations and the rule of law, rather than on political considerations and pure bargaining power. They have also been influenced by the fact that as Members, they will be able to take part in the formulation of any future changes in the rules of the WTO. The possibility of building coalitions of like-minded Members to operate within the Organization has also been attractive to applicants, especially to smaller countries.

Introductory statements also highlight issues of particular concern to their policymakers. For instance, applicants claiming developing country status under WTO rules can present data substantiating this claim. While LDCs do not need to provide data to justify their special status under the WTO, as the WTO follows the UN definition of LDCs, this section provides them with a useful opportunity to bring home their particular concerns.

Members often outline their expectations and make general points. One request usually made, already referred to above, is for a standstill – i.e. that applicants

[20] China, para 235 (see section below on agricultural policies).

[21] China, para 171. China reserved its right to benefit from the provisions of Articles 27.10, 27.11, 27.12 and 27.15 while confirming that it would not seek to invoke Articles 27.8, 27.9 and 27.13 of the SCM Agreement.

should not increase the level of their trade restrictions during the course of the negotiations for accession.

2.2 Economic policies

The main aim of this section of the Working Party Report, and the following part dealing with the framework for making and enforcing policies affecting trade in goods and services, is to provide Members with an understanding of the context within which the applicant's WTO obligations on specific trade policy measures will operate. Certain information requested is relevant to specific WTO provisions. Discussion in the Working Parties has focussed on the following subjects: monetary and fiscal policies; foreign exchange and payments, including balance of payments measures; investment regime; State ownership and privatization; pricing policies and competition policy.

Monetary and fiscal policies

Experience indicates that information submitted by applicants on monetary policy and fiscal policy should include the objectives pursued, the responsible agencies and the policy instruments used. Summaries of fiscal policies should indicate if any tax reforms have been undertaken and any changes planned. Applicants should also indicate whether they have achieved their objectives in this area and give an account of the present situation.

The aspects of taxation covered by the rules of GATT 1994 are the subject of the sections on the application of internal taxes to imports and exports. There are no provisions in GATS on taxation.

Discussion of this item in Working Parties has usually been brief and there are no Protocol commitments in this section of their Reports.

Foreign exchange and payments

Applicants need to describe how their exchange rate is determined, whether their currency is convertible, whether foreign exchange is freely available for trade and payments purposes, whether any regulations exist relating to the retention of foreign currencies, or repatriation or surrender requirements. Applicants should also describe their balance of payments situation.

While foreign exchange questions are within the jurisdiction of the IMF and trade policy questions within the competence of the WTO,[22] foreign exchange questions and trade policy questions are interrelated. Of most direct relevance to the WTO is whether foreign exchange is freely available in payment for current account transactions, as exporters need to know how they will be paid. The WTO

[22] GATT 1994, Article X:1.

therefore recognizes this interrelationship. The GATT 1994 provides that Members must not, by exchange action, frustrate the intent of its provisions and that they must either be members of the Fund or enter into a special exchange agreement with the WTO.[23] GATS provides that Members must allow international transfers and payments for current transactions relating to specific commitments entered into under that agreement.[24]

Working Parties have been careful to respect the competence of the IMF. While Members have demonstrated an interest in obtaining adequate information on all matters dealt with in this section, they have laid stress on issues of direct relevance to international trade. They have, for instance, focussed on knowing whether applicants are members of the IMF and whether they have accepted Article VIII of its Articles of Agreement, which provides that "no member shall, without the approval of the Fund, impose restrictions on the making of payments and transfers for current international transactions." They have been particularly concerned that foreign exchange controls may be used to regulate the level and composition of trade in goods and services.

All Working Party Reports but one have been able to note that the acceding government concerned is a member of the IMF and has accepted its Article VIII obligations. The great majority of WTO Members do not pursue the matter further. In the case of the one applicant that was not a member of IMF, members noted that it would have to enter into "a Special Exchange Agreement as provided for in Article XV:6 of the GATT 1994 incorporating obligations consistent with Fund Article VIII," which it duly did.[25]

In one case, an acceder responded to concerns that elements of its foreign exchange system provided scope for practices that distorted trade flows by stating that in the context of accession to the WTO, it was prepared to comply with the provisions of Article XV of the GATT 1994 regarding its foreign exchange restrictions.[26] Similar concerns were raised in two other cases. The two acceding countries accepted a Protocol commitment that, in accordance with these obligations, and unless otherwise provided for in the IMF's Articles of Agreement, they would implement its obligations with respect to foreign exchange matters in accordance with the provisions of the WTO Agreement and related declarations and decisions of the WTO that concerned the IMF. They further committed that they would not resort to any laws, regulations or other measures, including any requirements with respect to contractual terms, that would restrict the availability to any individual or enterprise of foreign exchange for current international transactions within its customs territory to an amount related to the foreign exchange inflows attributable to that individual or enterprise.[27] One of these acceders stated, in addition, that

[23] GATT 1994, Article XV:6–8. [24] GATS Article XI.

[25] Chinese Taipei, para 10. The Special Exchange Agreement between the WTO and Chinese Taipei forms an integral part of Chinese Taipei's Protocol of Accession (see Annex II of Chinese Taipei's Protocol of Accession).

[26] Chinese Taipei, para 10. [27] Viet Nam, para 31, China, paras 36 and 40.

it "would provide information on exchange measures as required under Article VIII, Section 5 of the IMF's Articles of Agreement, and such other information on its exchange measures as was deemed necessary in the context of the transitional review mechanism."[28] The other committed not only to implement its obligations with respect to foreign exchange matters in accordance with the provisions of the WTO Agreement and related declarations and decisions of the WTO that concerned the IMF but also with the relevant provisions of the IMF's Articles of Agreement itself.[29]

GATT 1994 permits the imposition of quantitative restrictions to deal with balance of payments difficulties, Article XII regulating its use by developed countries and Article XVIII:B its use by developing countries. WTO Members maintaining such measures must consult with the WTO. While not modifying these rights and obligations, the Uruguay Round Understanding on this subject confirmed Members' commitment to give preference to price-based measures. Only one acceding country actually maintained balance of payments measures at the time of its accession, these taking the form of an import surcharge. Its Protocol commitment on the subject contained a timetable for its reduction and elimination and arrangements for consultations with the WTO.[30] In a limited number of other cases Working Parties have judged it necessary to obtain a commitment from applicants on balance of payments measures they might take in the future. Four accepted the commitments along the following lines: "If balance-of-payment measures were ever necessary in the future, [X] would impose them in a manner consistent with the relevant WTO provisions, including Article XII of the GATT 1994 and the Understanding on Balance-of-Payments Provisions of the GATT 1994."[31] They were therefore treated as developed countries. One LDC accepted the same commitment, modified to refer to Article XVIII.[32] Curiously, the other LDC to have acceded accepted a commitment to impose any balance of payments measures in a manner consistent with both Article XII and Article XVIII.[33] In another case the relevant GATT 1994 provision was not cited but the new Member undertook a commitment to "give preference to those measures referred to in the Understanding on the Balance of Payments Provisions of GATT 1994 as price-based measures to address the situation and [to] maintain any measures only so long as necessary. In the circumstance that [it] must resort to measures that were not price-based, [it] would transform these measures into price-based measures within 6 months after implementing the initial measures. Moreover, any measures taken for balance-of-payment reasons would not be used to provide import protection for specific sectors, industries or products".[34]

[28] China, para 37. The transitional review mechanism is dealt with in Box 5 above.
[29] Viet Nam, para 31. [30] Bulgaria, para 29.
[31] Tonga, para 14; Albania, para 65; Georgia, para 65; Estonia, para 65. [32] Cambodia, para 82.
[33] Nepal, para 50. [34] Chinese Taipei, para 88.

Investment regime

Investment policies are closely related to trade policies, and applicants are requested to provide a summary of their investment policies. They should provide details of the objectives of: the policies; the legislative framework; the government entities responsible for implementation; incentives granted to domestic and foreign investors; bans and restrictions on such investment (e.g. sectors closed to foreign investment, limitations on percentage of ownership); conditions imposed on investment (e.g. technology transfer, domestic purchasing, and trade-balancing requirements); approval procedures; access to sources of capital, land and national resources, visas and residence permits, etc.; and right of foreign investors to initiate legal proceedings and to repatriate profits. In particular, any differences between the treatment of domestic and foreign investment should be indicated. Any international investment agreements should be listed.

A number of provisions of GATT 1994 relate specifically to investment policies. The Agreement on Trade-Related Investment Measures (TRIMs), which confirms that domestic purchasing and trade-balancing requirements are contrary to the GATT rules on national treatment and quantitative restrictions, is the subject of a separate section below under the heading Trade in Goods. The provisions of the Agreement on Subsidies and Countervailing Measures (SCM Agreement) relate, *inter alia*, to subsidies providing investment incentives. The GATS deals with investment in that its definition of trade, unlike that of the GATT, includes the supply of a service by a supplier of one Member through commercial presence in the territory of another Member, which often requires investment. While the 1996 Ministerial Conference launched work in the WTO on the interaction between trade and investment, many Members opposed the initiation of negotiations on the subject in the WTO, and it was effectively dropped from the agenda at the 2003 Ministerial Conference.[35]

Policies covered by the TRIMs Agreement, the SCM Agreement and the GATS are normally dealt with under the headings devoted to these subjects with only a few exceptions. Three acceding countries were permitted to confirm that their new legislation would conform to WTO obligations before it was completed.[36] In one case, the acceding country confirmed that the "terms and conditions of technology transfer, production processes or other proprietary knowledge, particularly in the context of an investment, would only require agreement between the parties to the investment".[37] In another case, an acceding country undertook

[35] WTO document WT/L/579, para 1.g: "no work towards negotiations on [this issue] will take place within the WTO during the Doha Round."

[36] Tonga, para 24 (no benefits would be made contingent, in law or in fact, on export performance, import substitution or local content requirements); Saudi Arabia, para 69 (hiring and employment restrictions to be in conformity with Schedule of Specific Commitments on Services); China, para 42 (revision of investment guidelines would be in conformity with the WTO Agreement).

[37] China, para 49.

commitments relating to the rights of foreign investors that had established joint ventures under its legislation on investment and enterprises and to the transparency of amendments or deletions to the list of prohibited or conditional investment sectors.[38]

State ownership and privatization

Many applicants were in the process of transformation from a centrally-planned economy to a market economy. This section has given Working Parties an opportunity of learning more about the process of transformation and drawing appropriate conclusions. It was not originally designed to deal with the more limited question of the application of the GATT rules governing the trading activities of State trading enterprises and the GATS rules on Monopolies and Exclusive Service Suppliers, which are examined in the sections "State trading Enterprises" and "Trade in Services". There has nevertheless been a certain overlap between the discussions under the present heading and the specifically rule-based discussions in these later sections. In some cases, the discussion on State trading has been merged with this section.

When examining the policies of applicants with privatization programmes, WTO Members have been particularly interested in understanding the extent to which the State is still an actor in the marketplace, the extent to which the changes made have increased competition, how much remains to be done under the programme, and the length of time that it will take to complete.

It is important therefore that applicants provide full information concerning any privatization programme that they have adopted, the legal framework for that programme, the progress already made in implementing it and expectations for the future. Each entity in which the State has an interest should be listed, together with details of State participation, and a privatization plan and schedule for each. They will be asked to improve the information supplied where necessary and to update it during the accession process in order to demonstrate that the programme is being actively pursued. They may expect to be asked whether foreigners can invest in entities being privatized.

One early Working Party is particularly significant. A number of its members noted that while the acceding country was constructing the legal framework for equality of treatment of private enterprises with State firms and the eventual separation of former State firms from government association after privatization, the current rules for the management of State-owned firms contemplated a State role in enterprise operations. It was also their view that the acceding country was facing a huge task as the number of firms involved was very large and that the setting up of an economic basis independent of the State would be a long-term project. The relationship between the State and its trade and industry had to be clear and

[38] Viet Nam, para 117.

as a minimum they expected transparency and dialogue as its economic transition progressed.

The applicant concerned stated that it could not undertake commitments exceeding the regular membership obligations but was committed to fulfil the notification requirements ensuing from the existing procedures in the WTO agreements. It also confirmed that the former State monopoly in foreign trade had been abolished and that no restrictions existed on the right of foreign and domestic individuals and enterprises to import and export goods and services, except as provided for in WTO agreements. It agreed that it was important to ensure full transparency and to keep WTO Members informed of progress in transforming its economic and trade regime. Its government would provide, every 18 months to WTO Members, information on developments in its programme of privatization along the lines of that provided to the Working Party, and on other issues related to its economic reforms as relevant to its obligations under the WTO.[39]

This case set a pattern that was followed in later accessions of countries in the course of transformation to a market economy. In these, a standard commitment provides for transparency of the process of transformation which is supplemented where appropriate with commitments specific to the case in question. The transparency commitment is along the following lines: "The representative of [X] confirmed its readiness to ensure the transparency of its ongoing privatization programme and to keep WTO Members informed of its progress in the reform of its transforming economic and trade regime. He stated that his government would provide annual reports, along the lines of that provided to the Working Party, to WTO Members on developments in its programme of privatization as long as the privatization programme would be in existence. He also stated that his government would provide annual reports on other issues related to economic reforms as relevant to its obligations under the WTO."[40] The baseline commitment provides for annual reports, except that one LDC is to make reports "periodically" rather than every year.[41] The above text states that reports on privatization programmes would be made only as long as these are in existence. It is less clear as to how long reports would continue to be made on "other issues" and a few of the Protocol commitments add an end-date for these.[42]

States that intervene to a large extent in the economy have not only been asked to accept a commitment to ensure the transparency of the privatization process but also substantive commitments. Some of these commitments deal with a complex of different measures that do not fit into the standard headings and are therefore dealt with here. For instance, one acceder committed itself to bring the operations

[39] For the full text, see Bulgaria, paras 24–26. This illustrates, *inter alia*, the relationship between economic transition and trading rights. For a discussion of trading rights, see the section below on that subject.

[40] Viet Nam, para 95; FYROM, para 37; Armenia, para 23; Chinese Taipei, para 155; Moldova, para 30; Lithuania, para 19; Croatia, para 26; Albania, para 30; Georgia, para 24; Estonia, para 21; Latvia, para 18; Kyrgyz Republic, para 14; Mongolia, para 35.

[41] Cambodia, para 25.

[42] Estonia, para 21; Latvia, para 18.

of its tobacco and wine monopoly in the area of international trade and domestic distribution into conformity with GATT 1994 and the other obligations of the WTO. It also agreed that any special privileges granted to this monopoly in the domestic distribution and international trade of alcohol and tobacco products would be eliminated from the date of accession and that both domestic and foreign firms would be eligible to participate in the distribution and trade of these products on an equal basis. Further commitments relate to the binding of its domestic subsidies on tobacco and grapes, equal access to inputs for all firms producing tobacco and alcohol products on its territory, participation of new entrants under the reform programme, fees charged, annual reports, disposal of contraband imports.[43]

A tendency is emerging of borrowing language from Article XVII of GATT 1994, which deals with trade in goods, and applying it to enterprises that supply goods and/or services. Such commitments fit better under the present heading than under corresponding headings in the sections devoted to goods and to services.

One acceder accepted a Protocol commitment to ensure that from the date of accession, 17 enterprises identified by the Working Party as State-owned or -controlled, or enterprises with special or exclusive privileges "would make purchases of goods and services, which are not for government use, and sales in international trade in accordance with commercial considerations, including price, quality, availability, marketability and transportation, and would afford enterprises of WTO Members adequate opportunity, in conformity with customary practice, to compete for such purchases or sales".[44]

In the case of two acceding countries, Members considered that the influence of the State on their economies made it necessary to obtain supplementary commitments of a more general nature. In the first of these cases, the acceding government confirmed that "[it] would ensure that all State-owned and State-invested enterprises would make purchases and sales based solely on commercial considerations, e.g., price, quality, marketability and availability, and that the enterprises of other WTO Members would have an adequate opportunity to compete for sales to and purchases from these enterprises on non-discriminatory terms and conditions. In addition, [it] would not influence, directly or indirectly, commercial decisions on the part of State-owned or State-invested enterprises, including on the quantity, value or country of origin of any goods purchased or sold, except in a manner consistent with the WTO Agreement". This acceding country also confirmed that "all laws, regulations and measures relating to the procurement by State-owned and State-invested enterprises of goods and services for commercial sale, production of goods or supply of services for commercial sale, or for non-governmental purposes would not be considered to be laws, regulations and measures relating to government procurement. Thus, such purchases or sales would be subject to the provisions of Articles II, XVI and XVII of the GATS and Article III of the GATT 1994".[45] Once again, wording was taken from GATT 1994 and applied to both

[43] Chinese Taipei, paras 158 and 160.
[44] Saudi Arabia, para 52.
[45] China, paras 46 and 47.

goods and services. The commitments of the second of these countries are very similar.[46]

Pricing policies

This section deals with laws and regulations that regulate the prices or profit margins that may be charged for goods and services. Governments may limit the price of certain goods or services, for instance to cap the price of essential foodstuffs or medicines or to restrain monopolies.

The basic GATT rule is that any laws and regulations to regulate internal prices must provide national treatment for imported goods. More precisely, imports must be accorded no less favourable treatment than that accorded to like products of national origin. However, it also recognized that domestic maximum price controls, even if applied on a national treatment basis, may adversely affect imported products. While the relevant provision does not give further explanation this might very well be the case for foreign products that command a premium because they are heavily advertised or because they are protected by patent. Concerns have also been expressed that some countries could maintain prices below market levels in order to limit imports.[47] In such cases, Members applying the measures have an obligation to take account of the interests of exporting Members "with a view to avoiding to the fullest practicable extent such prejudicial effects."[48] These provisions do not prevent the payment of subsidies exclusively to domestic producers. Some agricultural subsidies involve the payment of minimum prices for domestic produce but the subject of agricultural policies is dealt with in a separate section below.

Minimum import prices that apply only to imported goods would have to be enforced by a prohibition of imports priced below the minimum or by levying a supplementary charge in order to bring the price of imports up to the minimum. Prohibitions are contrary to GATT rules and the Agreement on Agriculture saw minimum import prices for agricultural products replaced by tariffs. The possibility of levying supplementary charges on non-agricultural products is limited by the existence of bindings in Goods Schedules.

The provisions relating to domestic regulations affecting trade in services are somewhat different. Here, Members have an obligation to accord national treatment to services and service suppliers of any other Members only in sectors where they have undertaken specific commitments and then only subject to any conditions and qualifications included in the Schedules. There are no provisions dealing specifically with price controls in the services area.[49]

It has been noted that governments may regulate the price at which monopolies buy or sell goods and services. Members have an obligation under GATT 1994

[46] Viet Nam, paras 78 and 79. [47] China, para 63.
[48] GATT 1994, Article III:4 and 9. [49] GATS, Article XVII. See also Article VI.

to ensure that State trading enterprises buy and sell goods "solely in accordance with commercial considerations."[50] The GATT rules on State trading enterprises are dealt with in a separate section below. Under GATS, Members are obliged to ensure that a monopoly supplier of services does not abuse its monopoly position in a manner inconsistent with their specific commitments.[51]

Applicants will be asked if they maintain any price controls on goods and services and, if so, to provide details. Members would like to see a list of all goods (by HS number) and services subject to price or profit controls, a citation of the legal authority for these requirements, an account of the conditions under which such controls are normally applied and a description of any plans for changing their scope of application. Members have shown an interest in all forms of price control, including more informal forms such as administrative guidance on pricing.[52]

In many cases, the list of goods subject to price controls has been rather short. Controls are perhaps more frequent in the services sector. Applicants can expect detailed discussions to take place in Working Parties if their list of price-controlled items is relatively long or if Members believe that they have a significant effect on conditions of competition.[53]

While the precise wording of Protocol commitments has varied, the following is typical: "The representative of [X] confirmed that in the application of price controls now or in the future [X] would apply such measures in a WTO-consistent fashion, taking into account the interests of other WTO Members as provided for in Article III:9 of the GATT 1994 and in Article VIII of the General Agreement on Trade in Services (GATS). [X] would publish a list of the goods and services subject to State controls and any that are introduced or re-introduced in the future in its Official Journal, including any changes in the list provided of current requirements in place."[54] In one case, the applicant accepted an additional commitment stating specifically that its pricing policy would be applied in compliance with the provisions of the WTO Agreement, including Article III:4 and XI:1 of GATT 1994 and Article 4 of the Agreement on Agriculture.[55]

Other Working Party Reports include additional Protocol commitments: to remove the exemption of local agricultural and fish products from price-control,[56] to reduce the incidence of price controls in the economy[57]; to ensure that price controls would not have the effect of limiting or otherwise impairing market access commitments on goods and services.[58]

[50] GATT 1994 Article XVII:1. [51] GATS Article VIII. [52] China, para 57; Viet Nam, para 100.

[53] See, for instance, Saudi Arabia paras 28–33, pricing of natural gas and natural gas liquids and paras 34–36, pharmaceuticals; Chinese Taipei, various products, paras 11 and 12.

[54] Tonga, para 35; Saudi Arabia, para 37; Cambodia, para 27; Nepal, para 20; FYROM, para 45; Armenia, para 29; Moldova, para 34; Lithuania, para 22; Croatia, para 33; Oman, para 25; Albania, para 34; Georgia, para 26; Jordan, para 32; Estonia, para 25; Latvia, para 21; Kyrgyz Republic, para 21; Panama, para 10; Bulgaria, para 16.

[55] Viet Nam, para 103. [56] Tonga, para 35.

[57] Moldova, para 34. [58] China, paras 18, 60, 62, 64, Protocol I.9.

Competition policies

Governments' competition policies are an integral part of the context within which the WTO operates and applicants are asked to supply information on this subject. Among the main points that they should deal with are whether they have a law on competition or not. If not, whether they have any plans to introduce such a law. If they have, they should submit the text of the law, summarize its main provisions including those permitting exceptions, the arrangements made to supervise its implementation, and the penalties foreseen for breaches of the law.

The WTO is, of course, essentially concerned with limitations on competition created by trade measures. Certain provisions of GATT 1994 have a direct bearing on competition policies. For instance, Article XX:d) contains an exception relating to the enforcement of monopolies permitted under Articles II:4 and XVII, the protection of patents, trademarks and copyrights (which grant their holders limited monopoly rights). The GATS provides that Members must ensure that monopolies or exclusive service providers do not act in a manner inconsistent with their MFN and specific commitment obligations. It also recognizes that certain business practices of services suppliers may restrain competition and therefore restrict trade in services. It provides for a measure of transparency.[59] The TRIPS Agreement strikes a balance between the interests of holders of the monopoly rights created by intellectual property rights and the public interest.

There is however no WTO agreement on competition polices as such. While the interaction between trade and competition policies was the subject of work in WTO following the 1996 Ministerial Conference, no consensus was reached at the 2003 Ministerial Conference on further action to be taken on the subject and the subject has effectively been dropped from the Organization's agenda.[60]

WTO Members have demonstrated their interest in obtaining information on this subject[61] but no applicant that has acceded has undertaken a Protocol commitment on this subject.

2.3 Policy framework

Powers of executive, legislative, and judiciary branches of government. Judicial review

An applicant needs to provide a description of the structure and powers of the government, describing the constitution and its relation to the main branches of government, the executive, legislative, and judiciary and the powers of each.

59 For details, see GATS Articles VIII and IX.

60 WTO document WT/L/579, para 1g: "no work towards negotiations on [this issue] will take place within the WTO during the Doha Round."

61 For a sample of questions asked in Working Parties, see Moldova, para 37; Croatia, para 34; Oman, para 26; Estonia, para 26; Latvia, para 22.

Among the matters Members of Working Parties have indicated to be of most importance in the context of accession are: the application of WTO law in the domestic system, including the way in which the accession Protocol will be executed; the Ministries and other government entities responsible for making and implementing the policies subject to WTO disciplines; the relationship between international treaties including the WTO Agreement and domestic legislation; and the right of review and appeal of administrative action to independent tribunals on matters subject to WTO provisions.

The WTO Agreement provides that each WTO Member shall ensure the conformity of its laws, regulations and administrative procedures with its obligations as provided in the agreements annexed to it. Various WTO agreements provide for a right to appeal administrative decisions taken in pursuance of their provisions.[62]

Most of the commitments in this area relate to the subject of the review and appeal of administrative decisions. The basic text of a Protocol commitment on this subject has been: "The representative of [X] confirmed that from the date of accession [X's] laws would provide the right to appeal administrative rulings on matters subject to WTO provisions to an independent tribunal in conformity with WTO obligations, including but not limited to Article X:3(b) of the GATT 1994."[63] One recent commitment added references to Article 23 of the Agreement on Subsidies and Countervailing Measures, Article 11 of the Agreement on Implementation of Article VII of the GATT 1994, Article 62 of the Agreement on Trade-Related Aspects of Intellectual Property Rights and Article VII of GATS.[64]

Two Protocols amplify this text by adding commitments to provide that the acceding country concerned "would revise its relevant laws and regulations so that its relevant domestic laws and regulations would be consistent with the requirements of the WTO Agreement on procedures for judicial review of administrative actions" and that "the tribunals responsible for such reviews would be impartial and independent of the agency entrusted with administrative enforcement, and would not have any substantial interest in the outcome of the matter."[65] In one of these cases, the acceding country also accepted commitments relating to tribunals, contact points and procedures for the prompt review of all administrative actions and the opportunity for appeal, without penalty, by individuals or enterprises affected by any administrative action subject to review.[66]

One detailed Protocol commitment provides that the country concerned would, from the date of its accession, "establish or designate tribunals or procedures for the prompt review of all administrative actions relating to the implementation of laws, regulations, judicial decisions and administrative rulings of general application

[62] See, *inter alia*, WTO Agreement, Article XVI:4, GATT 1994, Article X:(b) and (c) and GATS Article 2(a) and (b).

[63] Nepal, para 31; Cambodia, para 36; Armenia, para 34; Croatia, para 37; Oman, para 32; Georgia, para 35. For a broader commitment, see Kyrgyz Republic, para 26.

[64] Saudi Arabia, para 85. [65] Viet Nam, para 135; China, paras 78 and 79, Protocol 2 (D).

[66] See China, Protocol 2 (D) for the full text.

referred to in Article X:I of the GATT 1994 and Article VI of the GATS". It further provides, *inter alia*, that "the tribunals or procedures would also include actions relating to the implementation of national treatment, conformity assessment, the regulation, control, supply or promotion of a service, including the grant or denial of a licence to provide a service and other matters".[67]

The commitment of an LDC on this subject confirmed that it was in the process of establishing the necessary draft law and commercial court system and the date by which these would be operational.[68]

One acceding country confirmed that all laws and legislative instruments necessary for the application of WTO provisions would be adopted and in place prior to the legal conclusion of its WTO accession.[69]

Another Working Party Report contains detailed commitments designed to ensure that relevant treaty commitments would prevail over national legal normative documents.[70]

Under this heading, Working Parties sometimes touch on the need for the uniform application of WTO obligations throughout the territory of acceders but this issue is usually dealt with under the next heading – authority of sub-central governments.

Authority of sub-central governments. Uniform administration

Some countries are highly centralized while others, notably federal States, may be decentralized to a greater or lesser extent. Even highly centralized States normally have local governments and decentralized States have regional and local levels of government, the names given to these units varying from country to country. The issue relevant to accessions is the extent to which these sub-central governments and authorities legislate on matters subject to WTO provisions and have the responsibility of enforcing these provisions. Obviously, regional and local governments deal with regional and local affairs and most constitutions give central governments the power to regulate trade and commerce with other countries. However, the precise interpretation of these provisions is sometimes unclear and central governments have sometimes hesitated to test the outer limits of their competence. The wide scope of the WTO Agreement has perhaps been a complicating factor.

In the area of goods, the GATT 1994 provides that each WTO Member is responsible for the observance of all its provisions and "shall take such reasonable measures as may be open to it to ensure observance of the provisions of this Agreement by the regional and local governments and authorities within its territories." The approach taken in the area of services by GATS is different. It simply provides that "this Agreement applies to measures by Members affecting trade in services" as this term is defined in the Agreement. Whether the measure is taken by central, regional or local government bodies is not relevant. The Agreement on Trade-Related Aspects

[67] Tonga, para 43. [68] Cambodia, para 36. [69] Armenia, para 37.

[70] Viet Nam, paras 119 and 517. For further Protocol commitments, see China, para 68; Jordan, para 43; Estonia, para 30; Latvia, para 124.

of Intellectual Property Rights does not refer to sub-central governments and enjoins Members to "give effect to the provisions of this Agreement."[71]

Applicants need to describe their constitutional arrangements in this respect. Some Members have wanted to satisfy themselves that acceding governments have effective control over their territory and that their WTO obligations will be applied uniformly throughout that territory. Members have also asked applicants to confirm, where appropriate, that their sub-central governments do not have competence in trade matters.

Protocol commitments are often made up of different elements.

First, some acceders have "confirmed that sub-central entities had no autonomous authority over issues of subsidies, taxation, trade policy or any other measures covered by WTO provisions."[72] One went on to confirm that it would "in a timely manner" annul local regulations, government rules and other local measures that were inconsistent with its obligations.[73]

Second, some acceders have also "confirmed that the provisions of the WTO Agreement, including [its] Protocol, would be applied uniformly throughout its customs territory and other territories under its control, including in regions engaging in border trade or frontier traffic, special economic zones, and other areas where special regimes for tariffs, taxes and regulations are established."[74] One country's obligations relate to its special economic areas and all laws, regulations and other measures pertaining to or affecting trade in goods, services, TRIPS, or the control of foreign exchange.[75] Another country committed itself to "apply the WTO provisions . . . uniformly throughout the entire customs territory controlled by [its] central government".[76]

Third, some acceding governments have undertaken a commitment that "when apprised by a WTO Member of a situation where WTO provisions were not being applied or were applied in a non-uniform manner, central authorities would act to enforce WTO provisions without requiring affected parties to petition through the courts" or "would act to correct the situation and enforce the WTO provisions" or "would eliminate or nullify measures taken by sub-central authorities in [its territory] that are inconsistent with WTO provisions from the date of accession."[77]

71 The relevant provisions of GATT 1994, GATS, and TRIPS are: GATT 1994 Article XXIV:12 and the Understanding on the Interpretation of that Article; GATS Article I:1 and 2; TRIPS Article 1:1.

72 Tonga, para 48; Armenia, para 36; Moldova, para 48; Lithuania, para 29; Croatia, para 41; Albania, para 38; Georgia, para 40; Jordan, para 43; Estonia, para 30; Latvia, para 30.

73 China, para 70.

74 Tonga, para 48; Saudi Arabia, para 88; Moldova, para 48; Lithuania, para 29; Croatia, para 41; Albania, para 38; Jordan, para 43; Estonia, para 30.

75 China, Protocol 2(A). These areas include border trade regions and minority autonomous areas, Special Economic Zones, open coastal cities, economic and technical development zones and other areas where special regimes for tariffs, taxes, and regulations are established.

76 Georgia, para 40.

77 Tonga, para 48; Chinese Taipei, para 15; Armenia, para 36; China, para 73; Moldova, para 48; Lithuania, para 29; Croatia, para 41; Albania, para 38; Georgia, para 40; Jordan, para 43; Estonia, para 30; Latvia, para 30.

One Protocol establishes "a mechanism under which individuals and enterprises can bring to the attention of the national authorities cases of non-uniform application of the trade regime" and provides that "when non-uniform application is established, the authorities would act promptly to address the situation utilizing the remedies available under [its] laws, taking into account [its] international obligations and the need to provide a meaningful remedy".[78] One other Working Party Report qualifies this commitment by providing that the national authorities of the acceder would investigate claims that WTO provisions were not being applied or were being applied in a non-uniform manner and would act to enforce WTO provisions if the charges were found to be valid.[79]

2.4 Rules on trade in goods

Trading rights

While GATT provisions relate to imported products not to importers, the regulation of traders may create obstacles to trade in goods which contravene GATT provisions. Governments frequently adopt laws and regulations requiring traders to register the fact that they engage in the business of importing and exporting. Conditions attached to the right to trade in goods are inconsistent with the basic GATT principles of non-discrimination if they provide that goods imported from one country or set of countries are to be treated less favourably than those imported from other WTO Members (in terms of GATT Article I: MFN treatment), or if they treat imported goods less favourably than domestically-produced goods (GATT Article III: national treatment). Limitations on trading rights may also create restrictions on imports contrary to the provisions of GATT. These may be of two types: those that are quantity-based and those that are price-based. For example, any law which requires all traders to register and provides that no trader may import specified products amounts to a ban on imports of those products, i.e. to a quantity-based restriction (GATT Article XI). Regulations may also create import restrictions, for instance if they provide that traders may only import a specified quantity of a good during a given period of time, or that traders must obtain an authorization (which might be refused) each time they want to import goods (GATT Article XI). Price-based obstacles to trade would, for instance, be created if fees for the right to deal in imported goods are higher than the corresponding fees for the right to trade domestically-produced goods (GATT Article VIII).

Members of the WTO have been particularly interested in seeing if the basic GATT principle of non-discrimination is being observed. In recent Working Parties, some members have asked applicants if all enterprises in their country have the right to trade in all goods and have stated that any conditions attached to the right to trade, other than simple and automatic registration, would contravene GATT provisions and that the right of foreign-invested businesses to trade should not be restricted to

[78] China, para 75 and Protocol I.2(A).

[79] Viet Nam, para 134.

importation for production purposes and exportation. They have therefore wished to establish that there are no restrictions on the right of individuals and enterprises in acceding countries to import or export goods into the territory of the acceder based on their registered scope of business, except as provided in WTO agreements.[80]

Some members have also stated in recent Working Parties that limitations should not be imposed on foreign firms who wish to be importers of record, i.e. to engage in importing goods without being established in the acceding country and without selling or distributing the goods in that country. In particular applicants have been asked to confirm that importers of record are not subject to limitations on equity and are not required to invest in the acceding country.[81]

Working Party discussions also relate to specific features of applicants' measures. For instance, in one Working Party questions were asked about the scope and availability of trading rights and goods subject to designated trading – designated entities permitted to import goods and conditions attached to their right to trade in these goods.[82]

The subject of trading rights was not dealt with in the first few accession Working Parties[83] but, all subsequent Working Parties have addressed this subject and all of these Working Party Reports contain Protocol commitments on it. A pattern was set by the Protocol commitments in an early Report which "confirmed that from the date of accession, [X] would ensure that all of its laws and regulations relating to the right to trade in goods, and all fees, charges or taxes levied on such rights would be in full conformity with its WTO obligations, including Articles VIII:1(a), XI:1 and III:2 and 4 of the GATT 1994 and that it would also implement such laws and regulations in full conformity with these obligations."[84]

This text forms the base of the commitments on the subject of many of the applicants that acceded thereafter.[85] However recent Reports have tended to add further commitments and only one of these (on the accession of an LDC) maintains this basic text without additions.[86] Another adds a commitment that "[X] would, in implementing its obligations under GATT 1994, modify the relevant laws, regulations and requirements to permit foreign firms, including sole proprietorships of other WTO Members, to register strictly to engage in importation without limitation on equity or requirement to invest in [X]".[87] Some recent Reports contain an additional commitment to the effect that any registered entity could be an importer or exporter of record. One clarifies this by stating that "foreign firms and individuals

[80] E.g. Viet Nam, para 136; China, para 80; Chinese Taipei, para 19.

[81] E.g. Saudi Arabia, paras 90 and 101.

[82] China, paras 85 and 86. [83] Panama, Mongolia, Bulgaria, and Ecuador.

[84] Kyrgyz Republic, para 30.

[85] Tonga, para 52; Saudi Arabia, para 103; Nepal, para 36; Cambodia, para 50; FYROM, para 65; Armenia, para 47; Moldova, para 54; Lithuania, para 42; Croatia, para 47; Oman, para 40; Albania, para 48; Georgia, para 44; Jordan, para 53; Estonia, para 41; Latvia, para 40.

[86] Nepal.

[87] Oman, paras 37 and 40, which contain some additional material, e.g. on the relationship between relevant provisions of GATT and GATS.

with no commercial presence in [X], which were importers of record, would be able to register to engage solely in importation without limitation on equity or requirement to invest in [that country] and could obtain any necessary import licenses".[88] Another uses similar language but goes on to deal in some detail with the relationship between importers of record and individuals and firms that have the right to distribute goods in the country concerned.[89] Commitments relating to importers of record now appear to have set a new standard.

The Protocol commitment of one acceding country provides, *inter alia*, for a three-year transitional period to progressively liberalize the scope and availability of trading rights, within which all enterprises in that country whether local-invested or foreign-invested would be granted the right to trade in all goods throughout its customs territory, with the exception of goods which continue to be subject to State trading. Except as otherwise provided for in the Protocol, all foreign individuals and enterprises, including those not invested or registered in the country, would be accorded treatment no less favourable than that accorded to enterprises in the country with respect to the right to trade. All necessary legislative procedures to implement these provisions would be completed during the transition period.[90]

An LDC also negotiated a transitional period of eight months in order to bring its legislation into line with its commitments.[91]

Import regulation

Ordinary customs duties

The term "ordinary customs duties" is taken from Article II:1(b) of GATT and Article 4.2 of the Agreement on Agriculture. Accession Working Parties have taken the rates included in the customs tariff of each applicant as a basis for their work.

GATT 1994 provides that customs duties may be maintained provided that they are applied in accordance with its basic most-favoured-nation rule[92] but also recognizes that they often create serious obstacles to trade and that they should be subject to negotiation and binding against increase.[93] Each WTO Member has negotiated a Goods Schedule containing its tariff bindings – legally binding maximum rates of "ordinary customs duties" that it may apply to imports of the products listed in its Schedule. Applicants must do the same. Schedules are usually prepared in the

88 This is the language of the Cambodian Report, para 50. The text of the Saudi Arabian para 103 commitment is more specific: "The representative of Saudi Arabia confirmed that . . . from the date of accession foreign firms and individuals with no commercial presence in Saudi Arabia, which were importers of record, would be able to register to engage solely in importation without limitation on equity or requirement to invest in Saudi Arabia and could obtain any necessary import licenses".

89 Viet Nam. For the full text, see paras 139, 146, and 147.

90 China. For the full text, see paras 83, 84, 86, and Protocol I:5.

91 Cambodia, para 50.

92 Called the most-favoured-nation rule because it provides that any benefits granted to imports from the most-favoured nation must be accorded to like products from all WTO Members. For the precise text of the basic MFN provision, see GATT 1994, Article I:1. There are a number of exceptions to this rule, *inter alia* for preferences for developing countries and for customs unions and free trade areas.

93 GATT 1994, Article XXVIII *bis*.

version of the World Customs Organization Harmonized System (HS) nomenclature applied at the time of accession. The tariff negotiations are conducted bilaterally and the results recorded in the Goods Schedule of the new Member.[94] There has been little discussion on "ordinary customs duties" in accession Working Parties. Only a few acceders have made Protocol commitments. In some cases Members have wished to ensure that seasonal, specific or mixed specific and compound duties imposed in future do not exceed the bound rate.[95]

One acceding country made Protocol commitments on the level of its customs duties on specified items. One of these provided that the same rates of duty would be applied under preference programmes or regional agreements as to all imports of wood and paper products. In another, the undertaking was that any new tariff lines for completely knocked down kits for motor vehicles or semi-knocked down kits for motor vehicles would be subject to tariff rates of no more than 10 percent.[96]

Another country undertook to apply tariffs on an MFN basis to all countries and separate customs territories with which it had a WTO relationship, but a later section of the Report makes clear that this does not prevent it from joining customs unions or free trade areas.[97]

Other duties and charges

This section deals with any duties or charges levied on imported goods but not on domestically produced goods, other than charges equivalent to internal taxes, anti-dumping duties, countervailing duties and fees and charges for services rendered (for which, see below). Other duties and charges (ODCs) provide revenue for the government and protection to domestic production and therefore, like customs duties, directly affect access to markets. The WTO provides that if the customs duty on an item is bound in a Member's Schedule, then any other duties and charges on that item are also bound.[98]

WTO Members have shown that they are particularly interested in obtaining full information about any ODCs, ensuring their removal, and obtaining binding at zero in their Goods Schedules.

In some cases ODCs have been eliminated.[99] However, the removal of ODCs entails a loss of revenue for the government and some Working Party Reports indicate that they have been incorporated in the customs duty[100] or into internal taxes applicable to both imported and domestically-produced goods[101].

In addition, many acceders have accepted Protocol commitments on the subject. While the precise wording of these has differed, most commit the acceder in question to eliminate any existing ODCs and to bind them at zero in their

94 See section on tariff negotiations below.
95 Viet Nam, para 155; Armenia, para 53; Kyrgyz Republic, para 34. 96 China, paras 91 and 93.
97 Viet Nam, paras 155, 158, and 526. For membership of regional groupings, see section on Trade Agreements.
98 See Understanding on the Interpretation of Article II:1(b) of the GATT. 99 Tonga, para 58.
100 E.g. FYROM, para 68; Jordan, para 56; Bulgaria, para 31. 101 Bulgaria, para 31.

Goods Schedules.[102] Some variations have occurred however. Two Protocol commitments grant transitional periods for the elimination of certain ODCs.[103] Others provide a limited number of exceptions to the general rule that ODCs be bound at zero.[104]

Tariff rate quotas and tariff exemptions

Tariff rate quotas (TRQ)

Tariff rate quotas (TRQ) allow a specific quantity of the product concerned to be imported at a lower rate of import duty than is charged on out-of-quota imports. No restriction of the overall quantity of goods that may be imported is involved but high out-of-quota tariff rates may prevent trade from taking place and the allocation of quotas or licenses may create trade barriers and lead to discrimination between sources of supply.

While the GATT 1994 contains a general prohibition of quotas, it does not prohibit TRQs, provided *inter alia* that: tariff bindings are observed; they are non-discriminatory; any related fees are limited in amount to the approximate cost of services rendered; they are administered in a transparent way; and any import licensing procedures conform to the agreement on that subject.[105] TRQs are used to implement the minimum access commitments provided for in the Agreement on Agriculture: in this case they were regarded as a preferable alternative to other, restrictive, measures (for section on agriculture, see below).[106]

TRQs are dealt with in the tariff negotiations and bound in the Tariff Schedule.[107] They are also discussed in Working Parties on the basis of factual information provided by the applicant.

Applicants must provide full and complete factual information on any TRQs that they maintain and must be prepared for detailed discussion of these in the Working Party as well as bilaterally, in the tariff negotiations. They need to be aware that some WTO Members consider that TRQs distort trade and are difficult to administer. While the lower rates of in-quota duty may provide additional trading opportunities, there are concerns that complex or non-transparent systems for their allocation may be discriminatory and may themselves create obstacles to trade. Members also seek to ensure, as far as possible, that acceding countries do not use TRQs and have particularly resisted their use in the non-agricultural sector. Members have also wished to ensure that any TRQs interfere as little as possible with trade flows.

102 Tonga, para 59; Viet Nam, para 162; Cambodia, para 55; Nepal, para 42; FYROM, para 71; Armenia, para 54; Chinese Taipei, para 40; China, para 96; Jordan, para 58; Albania, para 51; Mongolia, para 10; Bulgaria, para 30.

103 Nepal, para 42; FYROM, para 71.

104 Saudi Arabia, para 115; Chinese Taipei, para 40.

105 Tariff bindings, Article II; non-discrimination, Articles I and XIII (subject to exceptions for regional groups, preferences); fees, Article VIII; transparency, Article X.

106 Agreement on Agriculture, Article 5.

107 For an examination of these bindings, see the relevant section below.

In the relatively few cases that TRQs have been agreed, they have been bound in the Goods Schedule of the acceder (see Annex 5). Some Working Party Reports contain Protocol commitments that complement these bindings.

Many applicants do not use TRQs and in such cases there is often either no Protocol commitment or a very brief commitment focussing on the importance of non-discrimination and transparency in any future use. In one of these cases the Protocol commitment (which also covers tariff exemptions) reads as follows: "[X] would administer any tariff rate quota or tariff exemptions in conformity with the requirements of the WTO Agreement, in particular Articles I, II, VIII and XIII of the GATT 1994 and the Agreement on Import Licensing Procedures."[108] In another case, only Article I of GATT 1994 and the TRIMs Agreement have been picked out for particular mention.[109]

One early Working Party Report on an acceding country that used TRQs also contains similar commitments, one such providing that "from the date of accession any application of general tariff rate quotas such as those described in [the Report] would be in accordance with the provisions of Articles III and XIII of GATT 1994."[110]

If TRQs are being applied in the context of preferential trade agreements, Members will ask for any tariff rate quotas negotiated in the context of WTO accession to be reserved for MFN suppliers. If an applicant is a member of a regional grouping which provides for the opening of a TRQ for the other members of the group, third country members of WTO have asked for a TRQ reserved for them. This is illustrated by one acceding country's Protocol commitment that "TRQs included in its Schedule of Concessions and Commitments on Goods would be made available only for the importation of product from MFN suppliers and would not be used to meet [its] preferential obligations under bilateral or regional free trade agreements."[111]

Later Reports on applicants that use TRQs are more detailed. Their Protocol commitments lay down principles governing the design of TRQs. For instance, one commitment contains a general obligation to ensure that TRQs were administered on a transparent, predictable, uniform, fair and non-discriminatory basis using clearly specified timeframes, administrative procedures and requirements that would provide effective import opportunities; that would reflect consumer preferences and end-user demand; and that would not inhibit the filling of each TRQ.[112] These Protocol commitments have also extended the list of relevant WTO provisions.[113] Two Protocol commitments provide for review or consultation procedures.[114] One of these provides that consultations would be held with any Member to ensure that the TRQs on non-agricultural products would be allocated in a transparent, equitable and non-discriminatory manner and the quota would be fully utilized.[115]

108 Saudi Arabia, para 113. 109 Tonga, para 62. 110 Lithuania, para 56.
111 Lithuania, para 55. 112 China, para 116. 113 Viet Nam, para 174.
114 China, paras 116–120 and Protocol Annex 1A,IV1(a), Chinese Taipei, para 61.
115 Chinese Taipei, para 61. See also analysis of Goods Schedule below.

These commitments also specify the system for administering TRQs in detail.[116] One method in particular has given rise to some debate. Some Members, while acknowledging that there was discussion taking place within the WTO on the legality of auctioning or tendering of market access entitlements, were of the view that premiums associated with this method of allocation represented charges imposed on or in connection with imports that were inconsistent with commitments undertaken by Members under Article II:1(b) of GATT 1994. The representative of the acceder concerned accepted a Protocol commitment that, "should it be demonstrated in the WTO that charges associated with allocation by competitive processes were WTO inconsistent, [it] would promptly modify its tariff quota allocation system to bring it into conformity with WTO requirements."[117]

Members may require TRQs on non-agricultural products to be phased out. One Protocol commitment provides that TRQs on passenger cars and light commercial vehicles and certain fish products would be removed over an eight year transitional period.[118] However, another acceding country persuaded Members to allow it to maintain a TRQ on one non-agricultural product, salt, on the grounds that it was the main source of income for hundreds of thousands of poor farmers living in coastal areas where the use of land for agriculture was almost impossible.[119]

Tariff exemptions

Tariff exemptions are similar to TRQs in that they allow some imports to enter either without paying the duty normally charged or at lower rates of duty. Many are for specified end-uses, for instance those which permit diplomatic missions or charities to import goods duty-free. If conditions are attached to tariff exemptions they may contravene WTO provisions. For example, tariff exemptions that are contingent on the purchase or export of domestically produced products are contrary to the Agreement on TRIMs.[120] Exporters of products may be accorded tariff exemptions in respect of imported inputs but any reductions or exemptions that exceed tariffs actually paid on these inputs constitute a prohibited export subsidy and a duty drawback system is the preferred alternative.[121] Both TRIMs and export subsidies are dealt with in separate sections below.

Information on all tariff exemptions needs to be provided but particular attention needs to be paid to product-specific tariff exemptions, as well as policy-related exemptions (e.g. those used as investment incentives). Members will be interested in seeing whether tariff exemptions are being applied equally to imports from all WTO Members on an MFN basis and will wish to ensure that conditions attached to the granting of tariff exemptions do not violate WTO obligations.

[116] See Viet Nam, paras 165–174; Chinese Taipei, paras 36–39, 61 and Goods Schedule.
[117] Chinese Taipei, paras 36–39. [118] Chinese Taipei, para 61. [119] Viet Nam, para 165.
[120] Agreement on Trade-Related Investment Measures, Article 2 and Annex.
[121] Agreement on Subsidies and Countervailing Measures, Article 3.1(a) and Annexed Indicative List of Export Subsidies, Item (i).

Tariff exemptions have been relatively uncontroversial and only a few Working Parties have found it necessary to include Protocol commitments on this subject in their Reports. The wording of these has varied. All confirm that the tariff exemptions in question would only be implemented in conformity with the relevant WTO provisions and cite examples of these provisions. The most obvious is Article I of GATT 1994, the basic MFN clause.[122] Where it was considered necessary, reference has also been made to the provisions on TRIMs and export subsidies.[123]

Fees and charges for services rendered

The fees and charges referred to here are charges imposed by governmental authorities for services rendered on or in connection with importation, typically for such services as customs clearance, exchange control, consular transactions, such as consular invoices and certificates, sanitary and veterinary inspections, etc.[124] GATT 1994 treats them differently from customs duties and "other duties and charges" which protect domestic production and raise revenue and the basic rule in this case is that they must be limited to the approximate cost of the services rendered. GATT 1994 also recognizes the need for minimizing the incidence and complexity of import formalities, including consular formalities.[125]

Accession Working Parties have wanted detailed information on the subject and to ensure that the rules will be observed. They have pointed to the jurisprudence that makes it clear that *ad valorem* fees or charges, which are by definition related to the value of imports and not to the cost of the service provided, do not conform to this requirement.[126] They also stress that fees and charges may cover only the variable cost to the government of providing the service and not the capital cost involved, e.g. the cost of processing the customs forms but not the cost of building customs posts. If the fees and charges seem high, some Members may ask to see the calculations on which they are based. Members want details of any such fees. They also stress the importance of transparency and the rules of GATT 1994 relating to publication of laws and regulations dealing with these fees and charges.

The Protocol commitments reflect these concerns. The language is not identical in all Reports but nearly all make a specific reference to Article VIII and most to the need for transparency. Typically, the acceder has "confirmed that from the date of accession [it] would impose fees and charges for services rendered related to importation or exportation only in conformity with the relevant provisions of the WTO agreements, in particular Articles VIII and X of the GATT 1994. Information

122 Viet Nam, para 177; Saudi Arabia, para 113; Cambodia, para 59; China, para 111; Kyrgyz Republic, para 37. See also Jordan, para 63.

123 TRIMs: Viet Nam, para 177; Cambodia, para 59. Export subsidies: Viet Nam, para 177.

124 See GATT 1994 Article VIII:4.

125 GATT 1994 Article VIII:1(c). GATT BISD II/210, BISD 1S/25 and 100, BISD 6S/25.

126 GATT 1994 BISD 35S245.

regarding the application and level of any such fees, revenue collected and their use would be provided to WTO Members on request."[127]

Where relevant, the commitments also provide that acceders bring fees into conformity with WTO rules, for instance by eliminating *ad valorem* fees.[128] Commitments may also provide that the acceders shall ensure that customs fees or charges applied or administered by national or sub-national authorities are in conformity with the GATT 1994 and based on unified criteria ensuring that they are limited to the approximate cost of services rendered.[129]

Questions relating to consular formalities and charges have been raised under this heading. These have long been an irritant for many WTO Members. A few Protocol commitments provide that the requirement for notarization, authentification or consularization of trade documents would be terminated by a certain date.[130] One acceder confirmed that consular charges were not required for the authentification of documents necessary to import goods and another confirmed that regarding import/export documentation there was no requirement for authentification of the documentation by its consulates overseas, and there was no fee charged in this respect.[131]

Application of internal taxes to imports

WTO rules provide for both national treatment and MFN treatment in this area. The basic provision is the relevant national treatment rule of GATT 1994 Article III: "imported products must not be subject, directly or indirectly, to internal taxes or other internal charges of any kind in excess of those applied, directly or indirectly, to like domestic products." So Members may levy indirect taxes such as excise taxes, stamp duties, general sales taxes or value added taxes on imported goods provided that they do not afford protection to domestically-produced goods.

The general MFN rule of GATT 1994 Article I provides that, when levying these taxes, governments must not discriminate between imports from different Members. Products imported from a Member must be treated no less favourably than like products imported from any other Member, including those not members of the WTO.

It is important that applicants provide full information about their indirect taxes, such as excise taxes, general sales taxes or value-added taxes, including a list of the products subject to each tax, the rate of tax (where appropriate, the general rate of tax and a list of any products that pay lower rates or are exempt from tax) and the

127 Tonga, para 68; Viet Nam, para 184; Saudi Arabia, para 123; Nepal, para 44; Cambodia, para 62; FYROM, para 84; Armenia, para 60; Chinese Taipei, para 45; China, para 103; Lithuania, para 59; Croatia, para 58; Oman, para 49; Albania, para 53; Georgia, para 53; Jordan, para 72; Estonia, para 50; Latvia, para 48; Kyrgyz Republic, para 44; Panama, para 23; Mongolia, para 10.

128 Viet Nam, para 184; Cambodia, para 62.

129 China, para 103 and Protocol I: 11.

130 Saudi Arabia, para 122 (31 December 2007, two years after accession); Jordan para, 72 (providing for the termination of its consular formalities by 31 December 2002).

131 Moldova, para 61; Armenia, para 54.

base for the calculation of the tax. Tax rates applied to imported and to domestic products should be clearly stated.

Working Parties scrutinize internal taxes in detail. During the fact-finding stage, if the methodology for the calculation of taxes makes it difficult to compare the taxes applied to imported and domestically produced goods, Members are likely to request the acceder to simplify its system.[132] Members of accession Working Parties are particularly interested in any differences between the treatment of imported products and domestically-produced products or of imports from different origins and any differences in the treatment of like products. There is no general definition of the term "like products" in the WTO and the practice is to determine whether imported and domestic products are "like" on a case-by-case basis. An extensive jurisprudence on the subject does, however, provide guidance on this issue.[133]

Some Members consider that the exemption of the domestic output of very small producers from application of the sales tax, while all imports were subject to that tax without exception, constituted a breach of national treatment with regard to the application of that tax.[134] VAT thresholds have been discussed and accepted in some instances.

It is difficult to speak of a standard Protocol commitment on this matter. However, the following text is a succinct expression of the basic point: "The representative of [X] confirmed that, from the date of accession, [X] would apply its domestic taxes, including value-added and excise taxes, in a non-discriminatory manner consistent with Articles I and III of the GATT 1994".[135] Some other texts call for the non-discriminatory application of domestic taxes to imports but refer specifically only to Article III of GATT 1994.[136]

Many acceders have needed to modify internal taxes to bring them into line with WTO requirements. In these cases, it is standard practice either to note the changes already made to bring them into line or to agree a Protocol commitment.

Some applicants have based their border tax adjustments on the origin principle, rather than the destination principle. This means that goods are subject to the tax in the exporting country, rather than the importing country. It has been pointed out in Working Parties that the application of the destination principle to imports from some countries and the origin principle to imports from others might lead to breaches of the MFN rule in Article 1 of GATT 1994. Some acceders therefore agreed to apply the destination principle to all imports.[137]

[132] Chinese Taipei, para 53; Mongolia, para 11.

[133] See GATT and WTO Analytical Indexes for relevant cases.

[134] Mongolia, para 12. See also Tonga, para 72; Viet Nam, para 190; Cambodia, paras 68 and 71; Nepal, para 61.

[135] For this and similar texts, see Tonga, para 75; Saudi Arabia, para 171; Cambodia, para 71; Nepal, para 64; Armenia, para 72; Croatia, para 64; Oman, para 51; Jordan, para 76; Estonia, para 62.

[136] Viet Nam, para 198 (basic commitment); FYROM, para 97; Chinese Taipei, para 50; Moldova, para 74; Lithuania, para 66; Albania, para 58; Bulgaria, para 45.

[137] See: Armenia, para 71; Moldova, para 66; Georgia, para 61; Kyrgyz Republic, paras 47 and 48.

The Protocol commitments of several acceders provide for changes in the tax base in order to ensure that imported products are treated no less favourably than domestically-produced products. For example, changes were made to the base for the levying of a commodity tax, to the timing of payments of an excise tax on domestically produced goods and imports, to eliminate the use of minimum values, including domestic wholesale prices or any other domestic prices, for the application of its domestic taxes to imports.[138]

In a significant number of cases, acceders charged higher rates of tax on certain imported products than on the "same" products when domestically produced and committed themselves to eliminate this discrimination. Products concerned included agricultural products, alcohol and tobacco products, and new and used automobiles.[139]

WTO Members have also taken issue with applicants for charging higher rates of tax on certain products that were imported than on "like" products that were produced domestically. These cases all concerned alcoholic beverages or tobacco products. In all of these cases, the acceders concerned accepted obligations to remove the differentiation involved.[140]

In some cases short transitional periods have been granted to provide time for new Members to implement their commitments in this area. An acceding country was allowed a transitional period of three and a half years to equalize its taxes on spirits and beer.[141] In another case that involved a change in an integral part of the country's agricultural support system, a period of about six years was agreed. In this instance the acceding country was required to notify the General Council annually of the status of the tax exemption and its scope and level and, upon request, to consult with WTO Members concerning the status of the VAT exemption and its effect on their trade.[142] A few other of the Protocol commitments also contain provisions to ensure transparency during the transitional period.[143]

Quantitative import restrictions, including prohibitions, quotas, and licensing systems

The WTO provisions demonstrate a strong preference for the use of price-based measures to protect domestic production over quantity-based restrictions on imports. The basic WTO principles are simple. While Members may use customs duties, but should be prepared to negotiate for their reduction or elimination,[144] they

138 Respectively, Chinese Taipei, paras 49 and 50; Moldova, para 69; and Georgia, para 62 .

139 Cambodia, para 64; Armenia, para 65; Chinese Taipei, para 55; Moldova, para 68; Jordan, para 75; Estonia, para 57; Latvia, para 52; and Ecuador, para 19.

140 Alcoholic beverages: Viet Nam, paras 190, 198, 199; Nepal, para 64; FYROM, para 91; Armenia, para 70; Moldova, para 72; Lithuania, para 66; Albania, para 57; Georgia, para 57; Bulgaria, paras 43 and 45. Tobacco products: FYROM, para 97; Albania, para 57; Georgia, para 57; and Bulgaria, para 45.

141 Lithuania, para 66.

142 Armenia, para 65.

143 Viet Nam, paras 198 and 199; FYROM, para 97; Armenia, para 64; Lithuania, para 66; Kyrgyz Republic, para 48; Bulgaria, para 45; and Ecuador, para 19.

144 WTO Article III:2, Agreement on Agriculture Article 4:1 and 2, GATT Article XXVIII *bis*.

may only use quantitative restrictions, including prohibitions, quotas and restrictive licenses in specific, carefully defined cases. However, these exceptions are quite numerous and further provisions are required to govern the application of the permitted restrictions.[145] A number of these exceptions are dealt with in other sections of this Handbook, for instance those dealing with balance of payments; safeguards; technical regulations; and sanitary and phytosanitary measures.

A separate WTO Agreement on Import Licensing Procedures deals specifically with import licensing, defined as the administrative procedures used for the operation of import licensing regimes requiring the submission of an application to a government body as a prior condition for importation. They may themselves create obstacles to trade. The Agreement distinguishes between automatic and non-automatic procedures. Automatic procedures are deemed not to have trade-restrictive effects if specified conditions are met and must, for instance, be granted in all cases within ten working days. Non-automatic licenses should not have trade-restrictive or distortive effects on imports additional to those caused by the imposition of the restriction itself.[146]

Quantitative restrictions directly affect access to markets and members of Working Parties have scrutinized any restrictions carefully in order to reach a judgment on their compatibility with the WTO rules.

The language of Protocol commitments varies and the nearest that can be found to a core commitment on quantitative restrictions and import licensing requirements reads as follows: "The representative of [X] confirmed that [it] would, from the date of accession, eliminate and shall not introduce, re-introduce or apply quantitative restrictions on imports, or other non-tariff measures such as licensing, quotas, bans, permits, prior authorization requirements, licensing requirements and other restrictions having equivalent effect that cannot be justified under the provisions of the WTO Agreement. [X] further confirmed that the legal authority of the government of [X] to suspend imports and exports or to apply licensing requirements that could be used to suspend, ban, or otherwise restrict the quantity of trade will be applied from the date of accession in conformity with the requirements of the WTO, in particular Articles XI, XII, XIII, XVIII, XIX, XX and XXI of the GATT 1994, and the multilateral trade agreements on Agriculture, Application of Sanitary and Phytosanitary Measures, Import Licensing Procedures, Safeguards and Technical Barriers to Trade."[147]

145 The following are among the relevant provisions. GATT 1994. Basic prohibition: Article XI:1. Exceptions: Articles XII, XVIII, XIX, XX, XXI. Administration of Restrictions: Articles VIII, X, XIII, XIV, XV. Multilateral Agreements. Agreement on Agriculture Agreement on Safeguards, Agreement on Technical Barriers to Trade, Agreement on Sanitary and Phytosanitary Measures, Agreement on Import Licensing Procedures.

146 Agreement on Import Licensing Procedures.

147 Croatia, para 73. See also Tonga, para 84; Viet Nam, para 227; Saudi Arabia, paras 155 and 158; Nepal, para 50; Cambodia, para 82; FYROM, para 107; Armenia, para 87; Chinese Taipei (same subject, different commitment), para 73; Moldova, para 83; Lithuania, para 71; Jordan, para 88; Latvia, para 59; Kyrgyz Republic, para 60.

Many Reports also contain commitments to bring specific restrictions into conformity with WTO rules. One Working Party Report contains a list of specific import licenses, quotas and import tendering requirements imposed at the national and sub-national levels to be phased out over periods of up to three years and detailed commitments on the procedures and criteria to be used in order to ensure non-discriminatory allocation and utilization of the measures.[148] A number of Reports provide for transitional periods.[149] One Report provides that the acceding country "would not introduce any other import quotas in future".[150]

One set of Protocol commitments provides that the duration of validity of import licenses shall be increased to one year and that the country concerned shall provide an initial notification.[151]

Customs valuation

The aim of the WTO rules in this area is to lay down a fair, uniform and neutral system for the valuation of goods for customs purposes that precludes the use of arbitrary or fictitious customs values.[152] The relevant rules are contained in Article VII of the GATT 1994 and the WTO Agreement on the Implementation of Article VII of the GATT 1994, including its Interpretative Notes. The Customs Valuation Agreement provides that the basis for the valuation of the goods being imported should, to the greatest extent possible, be "the transaction value, i.e. the price actually paid or payable for the goods when sold for export to the country of importation", suitably adjusted. When the transaction value cannot be determined, the Agreement establishes a hierarchy of alternative valuation methods and the conditions under which these may be used. Certain valuation practices, including the use of minimum customs values, are specifically prohibited under the Agreement.[153]

These are key GATT provisions, as the valuation of goods has a direct impact on access to markets. The rules are there not only to ensure that the benefits derived from tariff bindings are protected but also to provide predictability so that traders know, with a reasonable degree of certainty, how much duty they will pay.

The main aim of the active members of accession Working Parties has been to ensure as far as possible that the WTO rules on valuation are implemented in full from the date on which new Members accede. The baseline Protocol commitment is therefore: "The representative of [X] confirmed that [it] would implement the provisions of the WTO, including the Agreement on the Implementation of Article VII, concerning customs valuation in full from the date of accession to the WTO."[154]

148 China, paras 122–136, 421, Protocol I, 7 and 8. See also Viet Nam, paras 206–227.

149 Bulgaria, para 45; Chinese Taipei, para 71; FYROM, para 107; Cambodia, para 77.

150 Oman, para 57.

151 Armenia, paras 80 and 86.

152 Agreement on the Implementation of Article VII of the GATT, Preamble.

153 Agreement on the Implementation of Article VII of the GATT, Articles 1:1 and 8.

154 In some cases, reference is also made to Article VII of GATT 1994. See Viet Nam, para 238; Saudi Arabia, para 164; FYROM, para 111; Armenia, para 97; Moldova, para 90; Lithuania, para 80; Croatia, para 83; Oman, para 64; Albania, para 74; Georgia, para 69; Jordan, para 94; Estonia, para 71; Latvia, para 62; Kyrgyz Republic, para 63.

This commitment has frequently been augmented by reference to the WTO Customs Valuation Committee Decisions which interpret the basic provisions. Decision 3.1 on the Treatment of Interest Charges in Customs Value of Imported Goods deals with the way in which interest charges should be treated in customs value. Paragraph 2 of Decision 4.1 on the Valuation of Carrier Media Bearing Software for Data Processing Equipment provides that, exceptionally, the customs value of imported carrier media bearing data or instructions may be either the transaction value or only the cost or value of the carrier medium itself and not the value of the data or instructions.[155] Some Members have asked that acceders implement these Decisions and that only the cost of the carrier medium itself would be accounted for in the customs value. Recent practice has varied however. In some cases the Protocol commitment has required acceders to implement not only Article VII of GATT 1994 and the Customs Valuation Agreement but also Decision 3.1 and paragraph 2 of Decision 4.1.[156] On the other hand, certain Protocol commitments do not specify which option the acceder concerned will choose for the valuation of carrier media when implementing the Decisions[157] and three other recent commitment paragraphs, two of which relate to LDCs, make no mention of these Decisions.[158] Two Reports conclude that the new Member concerned would apply the provisions of the Decision on the Valuation of Carrier Media as soon as practicable but in any event no later than two years from the date of accession.[159]

In some cases acceders have accepted a commitment making clear that, as an international agreement, the provisions of the WTO Customs Valuation Agreement would supersede domestic law after accession.[160] WTO Members have wanted to identify any deficiencies in existing legislation and to verify that all relevant legislation would conform to WTO requirements by the date of accession of the new Member concerned, as is clear from a number of commitment paragraphs.[161]

Members have wanted to see that all the provisions of the Customs Valuation Agreement will be observed but they have been particularly vigilant in ensuring that new Members conform to certain of these provisions, focussing, for instance, on the necessity of eliminating and not reintroducing any prohibited valuation methods, such as the use of minimum customs values and any system of reference prices or fixed valuation schedule applied in lieu of the transaction value.[162] The

[155] VAL/8, 10 October 1984.

[156] Saudi Arabia, para 164; FYROM, para 111; Armenia, para 97; Moldova, para 90; Oman, para 64; Albania, para 74; Georgia, para 69; Estonia, para 71.

[157] China, para 143; Croatia, para 83; Jordan, para 94; Latvia, para 62; Bulgaria, para 73.

[158] Nepal, paras 53 and 57; Cambodia, para 93; Chinese Taipei, paras 78 and 80.

[159] Viet Nam, para 238; China, para 143.

[160] Moldova, para 90; Albania, para 74; Estonia, para 71; Kyrgyz Republic, para 63; Bulgaria, para 73.

[161] See, for example: Saudi Arabia, para 164; Armenia, para 97; Chinese Taipei, paras 78 and 80; Moldova, para 90; Lithuania, para 80; Croatia, para 83; Albania, paras 73–75; Georgia, para 69; Panama, para 35.

[162] For prohibited valuation methods, see Agreement on the Implementation of Article VII of the GATT, Article 7:2. Viet Nam, para 238; China, para 140; Moldova, para 90; Lithuania, para 79; Oman, para 64; Estonia, para 71; Kyrgyz Republic, para 63; Panama, para 34.

implementation of some other provisions, for instance those relating to the valuation of cinematographic films, the posting of bonds for prompt clearance of goods, the right of appeal to an independent administrative tribunal, have also received particular attention.

Some of the Protocol commitments specifically state that the provisions of the Customs Valuation Agreement would be implemented in full from the date of accession to the WTO "without recourse to any transitions."[163]

Working parties have granted transitional periods for the implementation of the Agreement on Customs Valuation to the two LDCs that have so far acceded, in pursuance of the Guidelines for the Accession of LDCs after providing a detailed Action Plan with a timetable for full implementation of the Custom Valuation Agreement. In the discussion of such requests, some members expected that legislation on the valuation of imports for customs and taxation purposes conforming to the requirements of the Agreement would be examined by the Working Party before a decision was taken on the terms of accession of the applicant requesting a transitional period and would be enacted promptly thereafter. In one case it was made clear the use of any prohibited methods of valuation beyond the products currently listed in its legislation should not be expanded, and the prohibited methods of valuation should not otherwise be used.[164] Tonga was also granted a transitional period on similar conditions.[165]

Rules of origin

Rules of origin are required for the implementation of any measures which distinguish between imports from different countries, such as MFN treatment, anti-dumping and countervailing duties, safeguard measures, free trade areas and preferential schemes. GATT 1947 had no provisions on the subject despite the effect that such rules had on international trade. The negotiation of the WTO Agreement on Rules of Origin was a recognition of their importance. However, its main provisions govern only non-preferential rules of origin and its programme for the harmonization of rules of origin has not yet produced agreed results. The Agreement lays down certain disciplines and procedural requirements for publication and notification. It provides, for instance, the right to request an advance assessment of origin, even before trade in the good concerned has begun.[166] An annex to the Agreement sets out a "common declaration" with respect to preferential rules of origin.

Standard Protocol commitments establish that the new Member will observe the provisions of the Agreement on Rules of Origin, paying particular attention to the clauses regarding the issuance of assessments of the origin of imports and to

163 Saudi Arabia, para 164; Chinese Taipei, para 80; Croatia, para 83; Georgia, para 69; Jordan, para 94; Latvia, para 62.

164 This paragraph is based mainly on the experience of Cambodia and Nepal. For the relevant commitments, see Cambodia, paras 89–93 and Nepal, paras 53–57.

165 Tonga, paras 89–91.

166 Agreement on Rules of Origin, Article 2(h) and Paragraph 3(d) of Annex II.

the need for these to be incorporated in domestic law by the date of accession. A baseline commitment reads: "The representative of [X] confirmed that from the date of accession [X's] preferential and non-preferential rules of origin would comply fully with the WTO Agreement on Rules of Origin, and that the requirements of Article 2(h) and Annex II, paragraph 3(d) of the Agreement, which require provision upon request of an assessment of the origin of the import and outline the terms under which it will be provided, would be established in [X's] legal framework prior to accession".[167] Commitments sometimes specify that these assessments would be issued by the relevant government authorities "or preshipment inspection agencies acting on their behalf."[168]

The Protocol commitment of one LDC recorded that it would be able to comply fully with the provisions of the WTO Agreement on Rules of Origin in the application of preferential and non-preferential rules of origin after enactment of its new Customs Law and its implementing regulations, no later than 1 January 2005.[169]

Other customs formalities

This section deals with Customs formalities not dealt with under other headings. The range of these formalities can best be seen from the coverage of the WCO's International Convention on the Simplification and Harmonisation of Customs Procedures (Kyoto Convention), especially from its annexes on individual procedures. These formalities are the subject of negotiation in the WTO under the heading of Trade Facilitation.

The main provision of the WTO is GATT 1994, Article VIII:1(c), which contains rules on formalities imposed on or in connection with importation (and exportation) as well as the fees and charges dealt with above.

Applicants are invited to provide information on these customs formalities. Under this heading they should, for instance, indicate whether they are a party to the WCO Kyoto Convention, which of the annexes to this Convention they have accepted and whether they have signed the Draft Protocol on the Amendment of this Convention. They should also provide information on any steps taken to simplify customs procedures, to make these more transparent, and to improve the enforcement capability of customs services.

The customs procedures of most general interest to WTO Members are dealt with in other sections dedicated to them. However, some of the formalities in this residual section may attract their attention. Members have, in at least one case, wished to assure themselves that applicants have control of their customs territory and would be able to enforce the WTO provisions and terms of their accession package.[170] If difficulties have been reported Members may also ask questions concerning efforts to combat smuggling and to limit incentives to smuggling and

[167] Moldova, para 94. See also Tonga, paras 95 and 96; Viet Nam, para 244; Saudi Arabia, para 167; Nepal, para 68; FYROM, para 115; Armenia, para 102; Chinese Taipei, para 82; China, paras 100, 101, and 102; Lithuania, para 86; Croatia, para 88; Oman, para 67; Albania, para 79; Georgia, para 73; Jordan, para 100.

[168] Armenia, para 102; Croatia, para 88

[169] Cambodia, para 96.

[170] Croatia, paras 90 and 91.

the discretion allowed customs officials. One acceding country, urged to establish prompt, simplified and more transparent customs procedures including the enforcement capability of border measures, confirmed that customs procedures had already been reformed to facilitate trade and investment and to ensure compliance with its international obligations, without, however, entering into a Protocol commitment on the subject.[171] An LDC confirmed that its government was in the process of establishing a dispute settlement mechanism within its customs service to accept and act upon complaints about customs practices from traders and governments and undertook a Protocol commitment to pass a law to establish this by a specified date: this mechanism was authorized in a new Customs Law and would be established prior to a specific date.[172] Finally, several Working Party Reports record that the countries concerned do not maintain any requirements for notarization, authentication or consularization of trade documents.[173]

Preshipment inspection

Some governments, mainly of developing countries and countries in transition, have used preshipment inspection companies for the mandatory inspection and verification of the quality, quantity, price of goods to be exported to their countries. Exports are sometimes also subject to this sort of preshipment inspection (PSI). The purpose of this type of PSI is to compensate for inadequacies in administrative infrastructures and to safeguard national interests (e.g. prevention of capital flight, commercial fraud, or customs duty evasion). However, the activities of the PSI companies concerned may themselves hinder or distort international trade. The WTO Agreement on PSI recognizes both that developing countries may need to use PSI and that the activities of PSI companies contracted or mandated by governments should be brought under multilateral disciplines.

The obligations placed on PSI user governments by the Agreement include non-discrimination, transparency, protection of confidential business information, the avoidance of conflicts of interest by the PSI agencies, avoidance of unreasonable delay and the use of specific guidelines for conducting price verification. The obligations of exporting contracting parties include non-discrimination in the application of domestic laws and regulations, prompt publication of such laws and regulations, and the provision of technical assistance where requested on mutually agreed terms.

This subject is primarily important for applicants that operate a mandatory system of PSI. Normally, Members have been interested in finding out whether acceding governments have concluded contracts with PSI firms. They have also wanted to find out if acceding governments have considered using the services of PSI

[171] Viet Nam, paras 245 to 247. [172] Cambodia, para 99.

[173] Cambodia, para 97; Nepal, para 69; FYROM, para 117; Estonia, para 72; Panama, para 22. This issue is sometimes dealt with under the heading "Fees and Charges for Services Rendered" (see that section above).

enterprises and whether a legislative framework for the use of PSI exists. Requests have been made for a description of any PSI services provided. Members have wanted to establish that any mandatory PSI will only be used until such time as the customs authorities were able to carry out the activities performed by PSI companies. Particular attention has been paid in some Working Parties on the fees charged by PSI entities.[174] Questions have also been asked about provisions ensuring the transparency of PSI activities and the possibility of appealing decisions of PSI entities to the courts. Some members have been interested in establishing that an acceding government was prepared to take responsibility for the activities of the PSI enterprises that operated in its name and to ensure that they observed WTO provisions.[175]

The Protocol commitments of acceders that did not use PSI have been relatively brief. Some early Reports committed them to ensure that the operation of PSI firms would be consistent with the provisions of the Agreements on PSI and Customs Valuation.[176] Some others added a commitment to observe GATT 1994 Articles VIII (fees related to the approximate cost of the services rendered) and X (transparency).[177]

The Protocol commitment of the first user government to accede was much broader in scope.[178] User governments can expect to be asked to undertake a commitment along the following lines: "The representative of [X] stated that, from the date of accession to the WTO, [it] would ensure that the requirements of the Agreement on Preshipment Inspection were met in full. He further confirmed that [X] would ensure that the operations of any preshipment inspection companies retained by [X] met the requirements of the WTO agreements, including the Agreements on Technical Barriers to Trade, Sanitary and Phytosanitary Measures, Import Licensing Procedures, Customs Valuation, Rules of Origin, Implementation of Article VI (anti-dumping), Subsidies and Countervailing Measures, Safeguards and Agriculture. The establishment of charges and fees would be consistent with Article VIII of the GATT 1994, and [X] would ensure that the due process and transparency requirements of the WTO agreements, in particular Article X of the GATT 1994, would be satisfied."[179] One recently acceded country that did not use PSI and was not considering its use accepted a similar commitment.[180]

Two user governments received somewhat different treatment.[181]

[174] Cambodia, para 103 and Georgia, para 75, respectively.

[175] On this last point, see for example, Moldova, para 96.

[176] Panama, para 36; Mongolia, para 45; Ecuador, para 29. The PSI Agreement refers to the Agreement on Customs Valuation in its footnote 4.

[177] Nepal, para 71; Chinese Taipei, para 84; Moldova, para 96; Jordan, para 103. Tonga, para 98, and Albania, para 81 provide exceptions, each undertaking, for instance, to "take full responsibility to ensure that such enterprises operating on its behalf complied with the provisions of WTO Agreements".

[178] Georgia, paras 74–76.

[179] See Saudi Arabia (no longer a user at the date its Report was adopted), para 174; Armenia, para 104; Georgia, para 76.

[180] Viet Nam, para 250.

[181] For details, see Cambodia, para 105; China, paras 145 and 146.

Anti-dumping, countervailing, safeguard measures

Anti-dumping duties and countervailing measures are used to counteract the effects of dumping and subsidization respectively. Safeguard measures are imposed on imported products that cause or threaten to cause injury to domestic producers.

The WTO lays down rules disciplining the imposition of these measures. Anti-dumping duties may, for instance, not exceed the margin of dumping and countervailing duties may only offset the subsidies granted in exporting countries. Both may only be imposed on imports that cause or threaten material injury to domestic producers. These measures are unusual in the WTO in that they are levied only to the dumped or subsidized imports and not on an MFN basis. The WTO also disciplines the use of safeguard measures, which must be imposed on a MFN basis.[182]

While more countries have adopted anti-dumping, countervailing duty and safeguard legislation than used to be the case, WTO agreements do not oblige Members of the Organization to adopt a legislative framework for the imposition of these measures, nor to impose them, and members of accession Working Parties do not press applicants to do so. Working Parties rapidly evolved a fairly similar approach to Protocol commitments in these cases. Applicants may expect to be asked to accept a commitment along the following lines: "The representative of [X] confirmed that [X] would not apply any anti-dumping, countervailing or safeguard measures to imports from WTO Members until it had notified and implemented appropriate laws in conformity with the provisions of the WTO Agreements on the Implementation of Article VI, on Subsidies and Countervailing Measures and on Safeguards. He confirmed that [X] would ensure that such legislation would be in full conformity with the relevant WTO provisions, including Articles VI and XIX of the GATT 1994 and the Agreement on the Implementation of Article VI, the Agreement on Subsidies and Countervailing Measures and the Agreement on Safeguards. After such legislation was implemented, [X] would only apply any anti-dumping duties, countervailing duties and safeguard measures in full conformity with the relevant WTO provisions."[183]

Working Parties have usually not insisted that pre-existing laws and regulations which do not comply with the WTO obligations be amended before accession, but

[182] Main relevant WTO provisions. Anti-Dumping: GATT Article VI and the Agreement on Implementation of Article VI of GATT, Ministerial Decisions and Declaration Relating to the Agreement on Implementation of that Agreement adopted by the Trade Negotiations Committee on 15 December 1993. Countervailing measures: GATT 1994 Article XVI and the Agreement on Subsidies and Countervailing Measures. Safeguards: GATT 1994 Article XIX and Agreement on Safeguards.

[183] Saudi Arabia, para 178. See also Tonga, para 100; Viet Nam, para 253; Cambodia, para 108; Nepal, para 75; FYROM, para 122; Armenia, para 106; Moldova, para 98; Lithuania, para 91; Croatia, para 99; Oman, para 73; Albania, paras 84 and 86; Georgia, para 78; Jordan, para 107; Estonia, para 78; Latvia, para 66; Kyrgyz Republic, para 70.

have maintained that such laws and regulations not be used until they were brought into conformity.

In two cases some Members noted that the applicants concerned were continuing the process of transition towards a full market economy and that under those circumstances, in the case of imports from those countries into a WTO Member, special difficulties could exist in determining cost and price comparability in the context of anti-dumping investigations and countervailing duty investigations. The acceding countries concerned agreed that importing WTO Members might, under some circumstances, use alternative methodologies in determining price comparability under Article VI of the GATT 1994 and the Anti-Dumping Agreement and in identifying and measuring the subsidy benefit under the Agreement on Subsidies and Countervailing Measures. The use of alternative methodologies in determining price comparability will expire once the acceding country concerned establishes, under the national law of the importing WTO Member, that it is a market economy and, in any event, at the end of a transition period of 15 years in one case and 12 years in the other.[184]

Export regulation

Customs tariffs, fees and charges for services rendered, application of internal taxes to exports

Customs tariffs are imposed less frequently on exports than on imports and for different reasons, e.g. for revenue purposes, to relieve shortages of foodstuffs or to provide an incentive to process raw materials domestically. Under GATT 1994, WTO Members are obliged to apply these on an MFN basis, to provide transparency and to be prepared to negotiate for their reduction.[185] Very few tariff bindings on export duties have been negotiated in the history of the Organization.

Members will seek full information on any export duties levied by acceding governments and these are described in the Working Party Report. They have demonstrated an interest in the elimination of any tariffs that may distort trade and reduce their access to supplies of basic materials. They expect to receive information on fees and charges and the application of internal taxes on exports but, as they have frequently dealt with them in connection with imports, rarely ask for separate Protocol commitments on these subjects.

One Working Party Report contains a Protocol commitment in which the acceding country agreed "to apply export duties, export fees and charges, as well as internal regulations and taxes applied on or in connection with exportation in conformity with GATT 1994".[186] Relatively few Protocol commitments deal specifically with export tariffs. One such is: "The representative of [X] confirmed that [X] would apply export duties only in accordance with the provisions of the WTO and any

184 Viet Nam, paras 254 and 255; China, Protocol I.15.

185 GATT 1994, Articles I:1, X:1, XXVIII *bis*:1.15

186 Viet Nam, para 260.

such duties would be published in [its] Official Journal. Changes in the application of such measures would also be published in the Official Journal."[187] Another commitment provides that "[X] would apply all fees and charges for services rendered to exports in accordance with WTO agreements, in particular Articles VIII:1(a), XI:1 and III:2 and 4 of the GATT 1994."[188]

Some commitments relate to individual measures. One acceding country accepted a Protocol commitment not to impose export duties on iron and steel scrap[189] and another to reduce its export duties on ferrous and non-ferrous scrap metals.[190] A third agreed to charge export duties only on products specified in its Protocol and not to increase the currently applied rates on these products except under exceptional circumstances following consultations with affected Members.[191] One LDC undertook to transform an *ad valorem* export service fee into a specific fee.[192]

Export restrictions

Quantitative restrictions on exports, including bans, quotas and restrictive licenses, are generally prohibited by GATT 1994 as are import restrictions. There are, however, a number of exceptions to this rule, that permit, *inter alia*, restrictions applied: temporarily to prevent or relieve critical shortages of foodstuffs or other essential products; to protect national treasures; to conserve exhaustible natural resources if domestic production or consumption is also restricted, etc. Restrictions which Members consider necessary for the protection of their essential security interests are also permitted.[193]

Applicants are expected to list all export restrictions that they maintain and any reasons for their continued application. They must expect to remove any that cannot be justified. They will also be asked to provide information on the entities responsible for the authorization of exports, the way in which they are implemented, including methods for allocating any licenses, and on measures taken to ensure transparency.[194]

The baseline Protocol commitment is: "The representative of [X] confirmed that, from the date of its accession, [X] would apply any export licensing requirements or other export restrictions in conformity with WTO provisions, including those contained in Articles XI, XVII, XX and XXI of the GATT 1994."[195] A simpler version has recently been used in one case: "The representative of [X] confirmed that, on accession, any remaining export restrictions and management measures would be applied in a manner fully consistent with WTO provisions".[196]

187 Croatia, para 101. 188 Tonga, para 102. 189 Saudi Arabia, para 184.
190 Viet Nam, para 260. 191 China, Protocol I.11. 192 Nepal, para 79.
193 General prohibition: GATT 1994, Article XI:1. For the exceptions quoted, see: GATT 1994, Articles XI: 2(a), XX and XXI.
194 See, for instance, Saudi Arabia, paras 179 to 183 and China, paras 157 to 165.
195 Tonga, para 106; Saudi Arabia, para 183; Nepal, para 84; Armenia, para 112; Oman, para 77; Georgia, para 86; Jordan, para 116; Estonia, para 83.
196 Viet Nam, para 269.

In some cases, Protocol commitments also contain publication and notification requirements.[197]

Export subsidies

The Agreement on Subsidies and Countervailing Measures prohibits the granting of subsidies on exports of non-agricultural products and defines these as subsidies contingent, in law or in fact, upon export performance. The Agreement contains an Illustrative List of such subsidies which, while not exhaustive, provides a guide to this matter.[198] This prohibition does not apply to LDCs and low-income developing countries. The latter will be struck off the list when their GNP per capita reaches $1,000 per annum.[199]

Members will seek full information on existing export subsidy programmes and their compatibility with the disciplines of the Agreement on Subsidies and Countervailing Measures. Some applicants have granted export subsidies. Members' main objective is to ensure that any such subsidies are eliminated by the date of accession.[200]

Many applicants have not had the resources to grant export subsidies but sometimes provide tax exemptions which could meet the definition of export subsidies. For instance, questions have been raised in more than one accession Working Party concerning the conformity of schemes to exempt certain investors in export-oriented industries from import duties on their inputs even if some of their production is not exported. WTO Members have insisted that these schemes be replaced by duty drawback schemes, even in the case of LDCs which have argued that they were entitled to maintain export subsidies and that they lacked the administrative resources to implement such a scheme properly at present.[201]

Subsidies contingent upon the use of domestic over imported goods are also prohibited and Working Parties usually deal with these together with export subsidies.[202] The baseline Protocol commitment is therefore: "The representative of [X] confirmed that [X] did not/would not maintain subsidies, including export subsidies, that met the definition of a prohibited subsidy, within the meaning of Article 3

[197] Saudi Arabia, para 179; China, para 165 and Protocol I: 8.

[198] For the full text of the definition of subsidies and export subsidies, see Agreement on Subsidies and Countervailing Measures, Articles 1 and 3. For the Illustrative list of export subsidies, see Annex of that Agreement. For a discussion of agricultural export subsidies see section on agricultural support commitments below.

[199] Agreement on Subsidies and Countervailing Measures, Annex VII.

[200] Transitional periods provided for the other original Members of WTO to bring their existing export subsidy programmes into conformity with the relevant provisions of the Agreement have now expired. Agreement on Subsidies and Countervailing Measures, Articles 27, 28, and 29.

[201] See Cambodia, paras 116 to 120.

[202] Agreement on Subsidies and Countervailing Measures, Article 3:1(b).

of the Agreement on Subsidies and Countervailing Measures and that it would not introduce such prohibited subsidies in the future".[203]

This wording encompasses import substitution subsidies as these are also prohibited. Occasionally, Working Parties have found it necessary to be more specific on this subject and in one case a transition period of three years was granted to phase out subsidies provided to manufacturers of automobiles and motorcycles using domestically developed and designed parts.[204]

While a few countries have been granted transitional periods to phase out prohibited subsidies,[205] the usual practice now is not to grant transitional periods and the words " . . . would therefore not seek a transitional period for the elimination of such measures" are sometimes added at the end of the baseline commitment.[206]

In response to the suggestion by some Members that one acceding country should be added to the list of low-income developing countries permitted to maintain export subsidies because its per capita GNP was under $1,000 per annum, a Member noted that this list was of specific countries and was not a self-nominated or expanding list of countries. While ready to consider some flexibility as to how this developing country would phase out its prohibited export subsidies, this Member maintained that, as it would be acceding to the WTO after the lapse of the phase-out period for export subsidies by developing countries, it should phase out its export subsidy schemes upon accession. The acceding country in question agreed to eliminate all prohibited subsidies (i.e. subsidies contingent upon export performance or the use of domestic over imported goods) to the textile and garment industries, as of the date of accession and was granted a five-year grace period to phase out benefits to current beneficiaries of investment incentives contingent on export performance.[207]

The Protocol commitments of the two LDCs to have acceded include two elements: one to eliminate certain programmes considered to constitute export subsidies and a second to administer its subsidy programmes in full conformity with the WTO Agreement on Subsidies and Countervailing Measures, including Article 27, which exempts least-developed Members from the Article 3 prohibition of export subsidies.[208] One of these LDCs agreed to replace a system of remission of import fees and waiver of certain duties by a duty drawback system within a period of nine years.[209]

[203] Tonga, para 115; Saudi Arabia, para 186; FYROM, para 132; Moldova, para 105; Lithuania, para 102; Oman, para 81; Albania, para 92; Georgia, para 89; Estonia, para 85; Bulgaria, para 57. Occasionally, more specificity may be added (China, para 167).

[204] See Chinese Taipei, paras 101, 113, and 116.

[205] Jordan, para 126; Kyrgyz Republic, para 84; Panama, para 63.

[206] Tonga, para 115; FYROM, para 132; Lithuania, para 102; Croatia, para 108; Bulgaria, para 57.

[207] Viet Nam, paras 272, 286, and 288. It may be noted that in the case of this acceding country, information on export subsidies has been included in the section on Industrial Policies. Viet Nam's Working Party Report does not include any separate section on export subsidies.

[208] Cambodia, para 120; Nepal, paras 88 and 89.

[209] Cambodia, para 120.

Internal policies

Industrial policy, subsidies

GATT 1994 does not contain obligations on industrial policies as such and while this heading provides an opportunity to discuss industrial policies in general, discussions under it have tended to concentrate on the specific subject of subsidies. Aspects of industrial policies are taken up under a number of other headings, such as TRIMs, trade in civil aircraft and textiles and clothing.

While WTO provisions do not prohibit Members from granting domestic subsidies, they permit countervailing measures to be taken, under defined circumstances, against exports if these benefit from specific subsidies granted to certain enterprises.[210] Definitions of subsidies are typically tailored to specific purposes and vary considerably in scope. As defined in the Agreement on Subsidies and Countervailing Measures (SCM), subsidies exist: if they involve a financial contribution of one sort or another from the government; or if the government forgoes revenue; or if there is any form of income or price support; and a benefit is thereby conferred.[211] Article 27 of the SCM Agreement contains a number of paragraphs providing developing countries and LDCs with special and differential treatment.

The Agreement applies to all products but the provisions of the Agreement on Agriculture and the negotiation of binding commitments in the areas of domestic support and export subsidies for agricultural products are discussed below.

The way in which Working Parties have approached questions relating to subsidies on non-agricultural products has varied. One or two early Working Parties dealt with domestic subsidies under the heading of export subsidies.[212] Others have taken up questions relating to export subsidies for non-agricultural products and subsidies contingent upon the use of domestic over imported goods under the present heading.[213] The points made on these two subjects are discussed above, in the section on export subsidies.

Most Working Party discussions on this subject therefore first concentrate on obtaining full information on any subsidies granted by applicants. This could be done by completing a draft notification pursuant to Article 25 of the SCM Agreement. As domestic subsidies are not prohibited but may have adverse effects on international trade, the multilateral trading system has always stressed the importance of transparency in this area and WTO Members are required to provide notifications on existing subsidy programmes on a regular basis.

The baseline Protocol commitment is well established: "The representative of [X] confirmed that [X] any subsidy programmes would be administered in conformity with the Agreement on Subsidies and Countervailing Measures and that all

210 GATT 1994 Article XVI, Agreement on Subsidies and Countervailing Measures.

211 For the complete text of the definition see Agreement on Subsides and Countervailing Measures, Article 1.1.

212 Panama, para 63; Bulgaria, para 57.

213 Nepal, para 88; Chinese Taipei, paras 106, 113, and 116; China, para 174; Lithuania, para 104; Croatia, para 111; Jordan, para 131; Mongolia, para 23; Viet Nam, para 276 et seq.

necessary information on programmes would be notified to the Committee on Subsidies and Countervailing Measures in accordance with Article 25 of the Agreement upon entry into force of [X's] Protocol of Accession."[214]

Additional commitments were agreed by two acceding countries. Both agreed to progressively work towards a full notification of subsidies, as contemplated by Article 25 of the SCM Agreement.[215] One agreed to a compromise relating to its claim to developing country status in this area.[216]

Technical barriers to trade

While technical regulations making the observation of product specifications mandatory and the procedures used to enforce these are adopted for legitimate purposes, such as the protection of human, animal or plant life or health and protection of the environment, such measures inevitably create barriers to trade since products that do not conform cannot be put on the market. Product standards may also sometimes create obstacles to trade, even though they are not mandatory.

The aim of the WTO in this area is to minimise the obstacles to trade created by technical regulations, standards and procedures for the assessment of conformity with these. The WTO's main instrument in this area is its Agreement on Technical Barriers to Trade (TBT). In order to reduce impediments to trade caused by a multitude of different national measures, this Agreement promotes the use of international standards and the acceptance of the results of other Members' conformity assessment procedures. It relies on appropriate international standardizing bodies to draw up these standards and encourages Members to participate fully in these bodies. Another considerable innovation was the inclusion in the TBT Agreement of the Code of Good Practice for the preparation, adoption and application of standards, which are not mandatory and are often drawn up by non-governmental bodies.

Acceding governments are asked to supply full information on their TBT measures. They are also asked to complete a Checklist to enable applicants (and Members) to verify that their measures conform to WTO rules.[217] The existence of this Checklist is evidence that Members show an interest in ensuring that all the provisions of the TBT Agreement are observed. Particular emphasis has been placed on the implementation of its provisions on the establishment of enquiry points and transparency.

While practice has varied somewhat, Working Parties soon evolved a basic Protocol commitment in this area, providing that: "The representative of [X] confirmed that [X] would apply all obligations under the WTO Agreement on

[214] Tonga, para 115; Saudi Arabia, para 189; Nepal, para 89; Cambodia, para 122; Armenia, para 119; Moldova, para 109; Lithuania, para 104; Croatia, para 111; Oman, para 88; Albania, para 94; Georgia, para 92; Jordan, para 131; Estonia, para 88; Latvia, para 77.

[215] China, para 173; Protocol I.10. For a similar commitment, see Viet Nam, para 288.

[216] China, para 171. [217] WTO document WT/ACC/8.

Technical Barriers to Trade from the date of accession without recourse to any transition period."[218]

One Protocol commitment provides that the acceding country concerned will incorporate key provisions of the TBT Agreement in its domestic measures.[219] Some Members have been interested in securing Protocol commitments to ensure the modification of particular measures.[220] Some Members have also wished to ensure that certain applicants will review their technical regulations, standards and/or conformity assessment procedures in order to bring them into line with the Agreement on TBT and in securing Protocol commitments designed to ensure this. One acceding country agreed to review all mandatory standards to ensure their replacement voluntary standards or technical regulations.[221]

Countries in the course of transition to a market economy have also made major changes in this area. Mandatory standards, such as Soviet-era GOST standards, were used in the past to ensure that products conformed to the directives issued by central authorities. Some acceders have therefore had to agree to ensure that the application of these standards would be made voluntary and that they would only be mandatory if they became technical regulations adopted by a public authority in accordance with legitimate objectives such as health and safety.[222]

In another case an acceding country accepted a range of commitments *inter alia*, to ensure that: conformity assessment procedures are applied to imported products only to determine compliance with technical regulations and standards that are consistent with the provisions of this Protocol and the WTO Agreement; that technical regulations, standards and conformity assessment procedures applied to imported and domestic products on a national treatment basis and that it will play a full part in the development of relevant international standards and of international guides and recommendations relating to conformity assessment procedures.[223]

In one unusual case, the acceding country had not adopted any technical regulations, standards or conformity assessment procedures to date, and had no plans to do so. It accepted a detailed commitment, *inter alia*, to introduce regulations to ensure that its National TBT Notification Authority and Enquiry Point would be operational as from the date of its accession.[224]

A few acceders have agreed to accept the Code of Good Practice for the Preparation, Adoption and Application of Standards annexed to the TBT Agreement.[225]

218 Viet Nam, para 303; Saudi Arabia, para 205; FYROM, para 145; Armenia, para 136; Chinese Taipei, para 127; China, para 197; Lithuania, para 113; Croatia, para 122; Oman, para 97; Albania, para 104; Georgia, para 100; Jordan, para 140; Estonia, para 98.

219 Viet Nam, para 303.

220 Shelf-life standards: Saudi Arabia, para 201; Oman, para 103; Jordan, para 145. See also Section on SPS below. Registration and initial imports of chemical products, procedures to obtain and apply safety marks, unified non-discriminatory legislation applied to automobiles and parts, safety and quality licence system for boilers and pressure vessels: China, para 196. Definition of whisky: Chinese Taipei, para 126 *bis*.

221 Jordan, para 137. 222 Moldova, para 124. 223 China, para 187; Protocol I.13.

224 Tonga, paras 117 and 119. 225 Armenia para, 136; China, para 180.

Pursuant to the Guidelines on the Accession of LDCs, both of the LDCs that have acceded were accorded transitional periods allowing them to implement the TBT Agreement progressively, after providing a detailed Action Plan including a specific timetable for attaining full compliance with its provisions.[226] Transitional periods have also been accorded to some of the acceding countries that have agreed to review, and where necessary revise, whole categories of their existing measures.[227]

Sanitary and phytosanitary measures

The aim of sanitary and phytosanitary (SPS) measures is to protect human, animal and plant life and health. These measures ensure that food is safe for consumers and prevent pest or diseases from spreading among animals and plants. They apply to both domestically-produced and imported products and may require products to come from disease-free areas, the inspection of products, the use of specified treatment or processing of products, maximum levels of pesticide residues or the use of only certain food additives. By their very nature, they restrict trade in products that do not conform to their requirements.

The WTO Agreement on Sanitary and Phytosanitary Measures supplements the relevant provisions of GATT 1994, including its basic national treatment provision. It recognizes the right of governments to apply measures necessary to protect human, animal or plant life and health and to set the level of protection they each consider appropriate but it is designed to ensure that these measures do not create unnecessary barriers to international trade. It does not apply only to agricultural products as it is, for instance, relevant to other products such as fish and forestry products.[228] A distinguishing feature of the SPS Agreement is that SPS measures must be based on scientific principles. The SPS Agreement contains specific provisions with respect to the performance of assessments of the risk involved to human, animal or plant life or health. It encourages its Members to participate fully in the relevant international organizations, in particular the Codex Alimentarius Commission, the International Office of Epizootics, and international and regional organizations operating within the framework of the International Plant Protection Convention.

Acceding governments are asked to supply full information on the measures maintained in their country, whether by the central government or by any sub-central governments. They are also asked to complete a Questionnaire,[229] designed to help applicants to provide the necessary data which emphasizes the need to supply information on steps taken to ensure transparency, and a Checklist,[230] to enable applicants (and Members) to verify that their measures conform to WTO rules.

226 Cambodia (two years), para 131; Nepal (two years, nine months), para 98.

227 China, paras 180, 184, Protocol I.13.4(b); Moldova, para 124; Georgia, para 99; Jordan, para 137.

228 Agreement on Agriculture, Annex 1, para 2.

229 WTO document WT/ACC/1, Annex 5.

230 WTO document WT/ACC/8.

The baseline Protocol commitment for sanitary and phytosanitary measures is similar to that relating to technical barriers: "[The representative of [X] confirmed that [X] would apply all obligations under the WTO Agreement on Sanitary and Phytosanitary Measures from the date of accession without recourse to any transition period".[231]

Here again, the two LDCs that have acceded were accorded a transitional period allowing them to implement the SPS Agreement progressively, after providing a detailed plan of action and specific timetable for attaining full compliance with its provisions (see Annex 10).[232] One developing country was granted a short transitional period to bring specific measures in line with the Agreement.[233]

The Protocol commitment of one small developing country contains precise obligations on transparency, opportunity for review of and comment on draft measures, non-discriminatory application of measures and training of relevant government officials.[234]

One acceding country accepted a commitment to notify all its SPS measures within 30 days of accession.[235] In only one case has an acceding government committed itself to reviewing its SPS measures, harmonizing them with international standards and reporting annually on progress until their standards were in conformity with WTO requirements.[236]

A number of Working Party Reports contain commitments on specific issues discussed in their Working Party. For example, three acceding countries have accepted an additional commitment not to require additional certification or sanitary registration for products which have been certified as safe for human use and consumption by recognized foreign or international bodies.[237] The other particular issues addressed in Protocol commitments include: elimination of unnecessary inspections of, and national treatment for imported meat, abolition of a prohibition on the use of powdered milk by industrial users of dairy products[238] and removal of a ban on imports of live swine.[239] Some Members have obtained commitments relating to particular shelf-life measures that they consider to be restrictive, arbitrary, non-transparent and not consistent with relevant international standards.[240]

Only one Working Party Report contains very detailed Protocol commitments relating to SPS measures. These commitments followed a request of some Members that an Action Plan be provided by the acceding country concerned containing a timetable for bringing the SPS regime into conformity with the provisions of the SPS Agreement. This case also demonstrates, *inter alia*, that some Members are

[231] Tonga, para 126; Chinese Taipei, para 137; Lithuania, para 122; Oman, para 105; Albania, para 108; Georgia, para 107; Estonia, para 98; Latvia, para 88; Bulgaria, para 64. Some Working Parties have elaborated on the theme without changing the basic thrust of the commitment: Viet Nam, para 328; Saudi Arabia, para 224; FYROM, para 153; Armenia, para 143; China, para 200; Moldova, para 125; Croatia, para 135; Jordan, para 151; Kyrgyz Republic, para 103.

[232] Cambodia (three years), para 142; Nepal (two years nine months), para 107.

[233] Jordan, paras 145, 148, and 149. [234] Tonga, para 126. [235] China Protocol I.14.

[236] Kyrgyz Republic, para 100. [237] FYROM, para 153; Kyrgyz Republic, para 103; Bulgaria, para 64.

[238] Jordan, para 149. [239] Chinese Taipei, para 135. [240] For example, Viet Nam, paras 315 and 316.

interested in checking applicant's legislation to ensure that it reproduces the exact wording of WTO agreements; ensuring transparency (including the establishment of an enquiry point and, in this case, a commitment to disseminate information about its SPS regime and measures through a website); and verifying the observance of the substantive rules of the SPS Agreement.[241]

Trade-related investment measures

The scope of this subject in this context is defined by the WTO Agreement on Trade-Related Investment Measures (TRIMs) that reaffirms and clarifies two sets of existing GATT obligations – those relating to domestic purchasing requirements contrary to the national treatment provisions of its Article III:4 and trade balancing requirements contrary to the obligation of general elimination of quantitative restrictions in Article XI:1.[242] Developing country Members may deviate temporarily from these obligations to the extent that balance of payments provisions permit.[243]

Members have therefore sought to verify that the acceding government applies no requirements that could be construed as a prohibited TRIM under this Agreement and to ensure that new TRIMs are not introduced.

The usual Protocol commitment in this area is: "The representative of [X] confirmed that [X] would not maintain any measures contrary to the TRIMs Agreement and would apply the TRIMs Agreement from the date of accession without recourse to any transitional period."[244]

Few applicants have, in fact, been found to apply TRIMs. One recent acceder undertook an obligation to remove, upon accession, local content and sourcing requirements applied to the production of automobiles and motorcycles and a mixing regulation relating to the use of coal.[245] An acceding government eliminated TRIMs during the accession process.[246] Another acceding country undertook commitments to remove requirements relating to foreign exchange balancing (as well as trade-balancing), as well as to amend its industrial policy for the automobile sector and relax restrictions affecting motor vehicle producers and restrictions on investments in this sector.[247]

One LDC that has acceded undertook the usual Protocol commitment. The other had reviewed the relevant legislation but had not found any measures contrary to the Agreement. It agreed to notify any TRIMs subsequently uncovered as part of its initial WTO notification. It also undertook, from the date of accession, not to introduce any TRIMs unless they were in conformity with the Agreement.[248]

241 Saudi Arabia, paras 207, 208, 210, 212, 215, 216, 218, 222, 223, and 224.

242 For details, see the illustrative list of TRIMs which is annexed to the Agreement.

243 Agreement on TRIMs, Article 4.

244 Tonga, para 130 (also states tha Tonga's laws would implement this commitment); Saudi Arabia, para 226; FYROM, para 155; Armenia, para 144; Croatia, para 137; Oman, para 107; Albania, para 110; Georgia, para 109; Jordan, para 98; Latvia, para 90. For a variation, see Viet Nam, para 332; Chinese Taipei, para 141.

245 Chinese Taipei, para 140.

246 Viet Nam.

247 China, paras 203–207, P I7:3.

248 Cambodia, para 144; Nepal, para 109.

Another acceding country undertook commitments to remove requirements relating to foreign exchange balancing (as well as trade balancing), as well as to amend its industrial policy for the automobile sector and relax restrictions affecting motor vehicle producers and restrictions on investments in this sector.[249]

State trading entities

This section comes under the heading Trade in Goods and was designed to deal with the State trading provisions of GATT 1994, which regulate State-owned enterprises and other enterprises that have been granted exclusive or special rights or privileges that enable them to influence imports or exports of goods. The provisions of the GATS on monopolies and exclusive service providers are dealt with in the section on Trade in Services below. See also the related section on State Ownership and Privatization above in which it is noted that a tendency is emerging of negotiating Protocol commitments which borrow language from Article XVII of GATT 1994 and applying it to enterprises that supply goods and/or services.

WTO provisions do not prevent Members from maintaining State-owned enterprises. However, GATT 1994 rules recognize that the operation of these enterprises may create serious obstacles to trade in goods which may be price-based (e.g. created when State trading enterprises increase the resale prices of products they import more than the resale prices of like domestic products) or quantity-based (e.g. when they restrict the quantity of products imported). The basic principles behind the GATT rules are that such enterprises are to operate solely in accordance with commercial considerations and that notifications are required to ensure that their operations are transparent.[250] Applicants are therefore asked to complete the standard notification on State trading enterprises covered by Article XVII. This requests governments to list any State trading enterprises, to state the reason and purpose for introducing and maintaining each of these, to describe their functioning, and to provide relevant statistical information.[251]

Corresponding obligations in the area of services[252] are similar in some respects and the basic principles are the same but the terminology used and the specific obligations differ. For instance, the corresponding services provision is entitled 'Monopolies and Exclusive Service Providers' and its provisions on non-discrimination reflect the different approaches to this subject taken in the area of goods on the one hand and the area of services on the other.[253] However, Working Parties have often dealt with goods and services under this heading and applied wording drawn from the WTO provisions on goods to both goods and services.

[249] China, paras 203–207, Protocol I.7.3.

[250] These may be governmental or non-governmental, including marketing boards. For the full text of these provisions, see GATT 1994 Article XVII and the Uruguay Round Understanding on the Interpretation of that Article.

[251] The questionnaire is reproduced in Annex 6.7.

[252] The main provision in the General Agreement on Trade in Services is Article VIII.

[253] GATT Article III contains a general obligation to grant national treatment while GATS Article XVII makes national treatment the subject of negotiations on specific commitments.

The wording of Protocol obligations varies but the following text is representative of recent common practice: "The representative of [X] confirmed that his government would apply its laws and regulations governing the trading activities of State-owned enterprises and other enterprises with special or exclusive privileges in full conformity with the WTO Agreement, in particular Article XVII of GATT 1994 and the Understanding on that Article and Article VIII of the GATS and would notify any enterprise falling within the scope of Article XVII".[254] A number of Working Party Reports use the term "State trading enterprises" rather than 'State-owned enterprises'.[255]

Some Protocol commitments also state that the acceder would ensure conformity with the obligations relating to non-discrimination and the application of commercial considerations in the sale and purchase of State traded commodities.[256]

One of the LDCs to have acceded accepted a standard Protocol commitment. The other confirmed that the operations of the enterprises to be retained as State-owned were consistent with the provisions of GATT Article XVII, "and that no new privileges in terms of Article XVII would be granted to these or other entities".[257]

Most Protocol commitments in this area are phrased in general terms but some others deal with specific issues that have been raised in Working Parties. Two acceders undertook a number of specific obligations in this area. Both agreed to ensure that no price increase by State trading enterprises would result in protection beyond that allowed in their Schedule of Concessions and Commitments on Goods, and not otherwise justified under WTO rules.[258]

Free zones, special economic areas

The GATT 1994 does not deal with free zones as a separate topic and so has not adopted a standard terminology. Documentation submitted by applicants refers to free zones and free economic zones but also uses other terms such as special economic areas, free ports, industrial zones, high-tech parks, export zones and export processing zones. Assistance provided to minority autonomous regions and other areas of economic poverty has also been dealt with in one Report under this heading.[259]

The main point that these entities have in common is that they are "parts of the territory of the country concerned where any goods introduced are generally regarded, insofar as import duties and taxes are concerned, as being outside the

254 See for example, Tonga, para 133; FYROM, para 160; Armenia, para 148; Lithuania, para 135; Croatia, para 146; Albania, para 115; Georgia, para 111; Latvia, para 93.

255 Cambodia, para 149; Chinese Taipei, para 152; Moldova, para 141; Oman, para 114; Jordan, para 161; Latvia, para 93.

256 Moldova, para 141; Oman, para 114; Jordan, para 161; Estonia, para 103; Kyrgyz Republic, para 113; Panama, para 83; Mongolia, para 29; Bulgaria, para 69.

257 Cambodia, para 149; Nepal, para 111.

258 For details, see China, paras 210, 212, 213, 215, 217, Protocol I:6; Chinese Taipei, paras 147–152.

259 China, para 223.

customs territory".[260] Governments may also provide incentives for producers that locate in these zones.

Acceding governments are expected to provide information on regulations and incentives pertaining to existing zones and/or concrete plans to establish such zones in the future. Members will want to ascertain that goods manufactured and subsequently sold within the ordinary customs territory of the acceding government, will be subject to the duties and taxes normally levied on imported products. They are also concerned that new Members should not use prohibited subsidies as incentives to locate in its export processing zones and about the enforcement of WTO rules on TRIPS.

The main elements of Protocol commitments are as follows: "The representative of [X] stated that [X] would administer free zones or special economic areas established in its territory in compliance with WTO provisions, including those addressing subsidies, TRIMs and TRIPS, and that goods produced within the zones under tax and tariff provisions that exempt imports and imported inputs from tariffs and certain taxes would be subject to normal customs formalities when entering the rest of [X], including the application of tariffs and any taxes and charges."[261]

A few acceders have also agreed to ensure that existing or draft laws and regulations are brought into line with this commitment.[262] One accepted commitments relating to the uniform implementation of its policy throughout its customs territory, the provision of detailed notifications and the application of WTO provisions on non-discrimination and national treatment in special economic areas.[263]

Barter

This is trade by exchange of goods for goods (or goods for services) and is also called counter trade.

Accession Working Parties have not concerned themselves with private-sector barter transactions. WTO Members want to find out if governments of acceding countries have concluded any trade agreements which provide for barter transactions and, if so, whether these contain binding commitments to import or export specified products or merely indicative targets. They may question the consistency of such binding commitments with the MFN clause, since it can be argued that these reduce access to the market for other countries.

[260] See International Convention on the Simplification and Harmonization of Customs Procedures (Revised Kyoto convention), June 1999, WCO, Specific Annex D, Chapter 2, Free Zones.

[261] Tonga, para 135; Saudi Arabia, para 228; Nepal, para 112; Cambodia, para 151; FYROM, para 165; Armenia, para 150; China, para 222; Moldova, para 145; Lithuania, para 138; Croatia, para 148; Oman, para 116; Albania, para 118; Georgia, para 113; Jordan, para 164; Latvia, para 95; Kyrgyz Republic, para 115; Panama, para 77; Mongolia, para 51; Ecuador, para 61. See Viet Nam, para 339 for similar commitments.

[262] Viet Nam, para 339; Cambodia, para 151; FYROM, para 165; Kyrgyz Republic, para 115.

[263] China, paras 222, 223, 225, and 227, Protocol I.2(A).

Only six Working Party Reports have a section dealing with this subject[264] and only one contains a Protocol commitment, in which the acceder concerned undertook "upon accession, [to] eliminate or bring into conformity with the WTO Agreement all special trade arrangements, including barter trade arrangements, with third countries and separate customs territories, which are not in conformity with the WTO Agreement".[265]

Government procurement

In the context of trade in goods, GATT 1994 defines government procurement as procurement by government agencies of products purchased for government purposes and not with a view to commercial resale or with a view to use in the production of goods for commercial sale. The GATS definition substitutes the word "goods" with the word "services."

It is generally agreed that laws, regulations and requirements regulating government procurement are excluded from the rules of the multilateral trading system.[266] While the subject of transparency in government procurement was the subject of work in the WTO following the Singapore Ministerial Conference, no consensus was reached at the Doha Ministerial Conference on further action to be taken on the subject and the subject has effectively been dropped from the Organization's agenda.[267]

A plurilateral Agreement on Government Procurement is, however, annexed to the Agreement Establishing the WTO. Parties to the Agreement on Government Procurement agree to grant national treatment to products imported from other members of the Agreement but only if they are purchased by entities on a list that they have negotiated with other members. Acceders must negotiate their own entity list. Accession to plurilateral agreements is governed by the provisions of each of these agreements.[268]

Government procurement contracts characteristically represent a significant percentage of GNP and applicants are expected to provide information about their government procurement practices, including their general legal regime and procedures for tendering, dealing with tenders and award of contracts. Some Working Party members are interested in access to the market that the procurement contracts open up. Applicants can therefore expect questions about their practices in the Working Party designed to obtain full information on the subject.

264 FYROM, paras 166 to 169; Chinese Taipei, paras 168 and 169; China, para 323; Moldova, para 151; Croatia, paras 149 and 150; Albania, para 120.

265 China, Protocol I.4.

266 See the provisions of GATT Articles III:8(a) and XVIII:2 and GATS Article XIII.

267 WTO document WT/L/579, para 1g, p. 3: "no work towards negotiations on [this issue] will take place within the WTO during the Doha Round".

268 Agreement Establishing the WTO, Article XII:1 and 3.

Some Members have also asked applicants to accept commitments regarding accession to the Agreement on Government Procurement. An early acceder undertook a Protocol commitment to "seek observer status in the Committee for the Agreement on Government Procurement at the time of its accession with a view to initiating negotiations for membership thereafter"[269] and a standard Protocol commitment emerged soon thereafter: "The representative of [X] stated that [X] would initiate negotiations for membership in the Government Procurement Agreement upon accession by tabling an entity offer at that time. He also confirmed that, if the results of the negotiations were satisfactory to [X] and the signatories of the Agreement, [X] would complete negotiations for membership in the Agreement by [date]." Seventeen acceders have accepted such a commitment, or commitments that are variations on the same theme.[270] The main variations concern the date by which they expect to complete their negotiations for membership of the GPA. Most of the commitments insert a certain date, which is normally about one year after the date of their accession to the WTO, but which in one case was as little as three months.[271] Several commitments insert a period of time of one or, in one case, two years rather than a specific date.[272] One commitment provides for early accession, the exact timing of which would depend on the date by which the necessary government laws were enacted.[273]

In only one case does the commitment simply provide that the [acceder] would "initiate negotiations for membership of the GPA by tabling an Appendix 1 offer as soon as possible". In this case, the [acceder] also entered into a commitment that, until it became a member of the GPA, it would provide transparency and would provide MFN treatment, i.e. if a procurement was open to foreign suppliers, all foreign suppliers would be provided with equal opportunity to participate in that procurement.[274]

As provided in the Guidelines for their accession, the two LDCs that have acceded have opted not to have a Protocol commitment on this subject.[275] No commitment was asked of another acceder, whose representative had "noted that this plurilateral agreement had not been drawn up with the situation of very small developing countries, such as [his own], in mind. Few, if any, [of its] government contracts would be covered due to the value thresholds applied under the Government Procurement Agreement. Moreover, large contracts were often implemented in the context of economic aid programmes, which would be covered by the procurement rules of the organizations concerned."[276]

[269] Mongolia, para 59.

[270] Saudi Arabia, para 231; FYROM, para 177; Armenia, para 153; Chinese Taipei, para 166; China, para 341; Moldova, para 150; Lithuania, para 140; Croatia, para 156; Oman, para 121; Albania, para 123; Georgia, para 117; Jordan, para 179; Estonia, para 107; Latvia, para 100; Kyrgyz Republic, para 120; Panama, para 68; Bulgaria, para 80.

[271] Albania. [272] Saudi Arabia, FYROM (two years); Moldova, Jordan.

[273] Chinese Taipei. [274] China, paras 339 and 341.

[275] See the section on WTO Rules in the Guidelines on the Accession of LDCs in Annex 4.

[276] Tonga, para 135.

Transit

Transit can be of vital importance to some countries, for instance those that are land-locked. The WTO recognizes this: the relevant provision contains a careful definition of traffic in transit and provisions to ensure freedom of transit.[277]

Information should be provided on procedures and requirements relating to the transit of goods through the customs territory in the light of the provisions of Article V of the GATT 1994 (freedom of transit).

One applicant described in some detail the steps that it had taken to modify its provisions on transit with a view to ensuring freedom of transit as required by GATT 1994.[278]

The geographical configuration of some countries is such that an extensive discussion of transit rules is unnecessary.

Only nine Working Party Reports contain Protocol commitments on this subject. The baseline wording is: "The representative of [X] confirmed that his government would apply its laws and regulations governing transit operations and would act in full conformity with the provisions of the WTO Agreement, in particular Article V of GATT 1994."[279] One Report adds: "In this regard, he stated that [X] would not deny right of transit to exports from any country."[280]

Agricultural policies

In many respects the rules of the multilateral trading system apply equally to agricultural and non-agricultural products. MFN treatment and national treatment are to be accorded to agricultural products in the same way as other products. The rules on customs valuation or technical barriers to trade apply to all products. The commitments accepted by acceders analysed above also normally relate to all products, including agricultural products. However, agriculture is special, and the Agreement on Agriculture lays down rules that apply only to agricultural products, which it defines (in its Annex 1) as all products in Chapters 1 to 24 of the Harmonized System, less fish and fish products, plus a short list of other products. It should be noted that forestry products are not considered to be agricultural products for the purposes of the Agreement on Agriculture.[281] Under the Agreement, WTO Members converted their non-tariff measures into tariffs[282] and reduced their tariffs, domestic support measures and export subsidies. If there is a conflict between the Multilateral Trade Agreements and the Agreement on Agriculture, the provisions of the latter prevail.[283]

277 GATT 1994 Article V, Freedom of Transit. 278 Viet Nam, paras 351–354.

279 Viet Nam, para 355; Saudi Arabia, para 235; Cambodia, para 158; Armenia, para 156; Lithuania, para 143; Croatia, para 160; Georgia, para 119; Estonia, para 109; Latvia, para 102.

280 Croatia, para 160.

281 Work is ongoing to refine the definition of agricultural products in the Doha negotiations.

282 For a list of "measures of the kind which have been required to be converted into ordinary customs duties", see Agreement on Agriculture, footnote to Article 4:2.

283 Agreement on Agriculture, Article 21:1.

Applicants are asked to provide information of their policies affecting imports and exports of agricultural products. These are: customs duties; non-tariff measures such as quantitative restrictions; domestic support measures; and export subsidies.[284] The agricultural sector is important to many WTO Members and applicants must expect their policies in this sector to be the subject of a thorough verification and review in their Working Parties.

Factual information on agricultural measures will have been obtained under other headings dealt with above, such as: customs duties; tariff-rate quotas; tariff exemptions; prohibitions, quotas, import licensing procedures; technical barriers to trade; sanitary and phytosanitary measures; State trading enterprises, etc. The Protocol commitments on these subjects normally relate to both agricultural and non-agricultural products. The negotiations for tariff bindings, which are conducted bilaterally, also relate to both agricultural and non agricultural products. These are the subject of section 3.1. The examination of agricultural support programmes and the elaboration of commitments on domestic support and export subsidies for the most part take place plurilaterally in informal groups of representatives with an interest in the subject, rather than in the Working Parties. They are dealt with in section 3.2.

Discussions of agricultural policies in Working Parties therefore address any issues not dealt with under other headings and provide an opportunity for a multilateral review of developments in the negotiations on agriculture. In addition, each Working Party must approve the resulting commitments for inclusion in the Goods Schedule.

In one Report, a Protocol commitment records the fact that the acceder will bind all tariffs applied on imports of agricultural products.[285] A few Working Party Reports contain Protocol commitments to eliminate all WTO-inconsistent non-tariff measures on agricultural products, to conform to WTO obligations[286] or to eliminate specific measures.[287] A few Working Party Reports also contain Protocol commitments on agricultural domestic support and export subsidies. Some of these simply note the fact that the acceder has undertaken such obligations in its Goods Schedule.[288] One Working Party agreed that the applicant should be treated as a developing country for the purposes of a provision relating to domestic support[289] and a compromise commitment on the *de minimis* level was recorded in the Working Party Report of another country.[290] The Protocol commitment of one country accorded a transitional period for the implementation of its domestic support commitments.[291]

[284] WTO documents WT/ACC/1 and WT/ACC/4 provide guidance on the information to be provided on these subjects.

[285] Chinese Taipei, para 180.

[286] Chinese Taipei, para 180; Panama, para 86; Ecuador, para 31.

[287] Jordan, para 177; Ecuador, paras 41 and 48.

[288] Cambodia, para 164; Chinese Taipei, para 181; China Protocol I.12.1; Moldova, para 159; Jordan, para 18. Two Reports also contain a commitment not to maintain or apply export subsidies: Viet Nam, para 366 (without prejudice to its rights and obligations arising from existing WTO rules); China, para 234 and Protocol I.12.1.

[289] Jordan, para 189.

[290] China, para 235.

[291] Latvia, para 109.

Finally, one country entered into commitments relating to: the linkage of import policies for agriculture with domestic production policy; administrative guidance which could have the effect of influencing the quantity and composition of agricultural imports; export subsidies; and notification of fiscal and other transfers by State-owned enterprises in the agricultural sector (whether national or subnational).[292]

Trade in civil aircraft

Members of the Agreement on Trade in Civil Aircraft bind their customs duties on civil aircraft and parts at zero in their Goods Schedules and accept the Agreement's provisions limiting trade-distorting subsidies. Its dispute settlement provisions are inoperative as they foresee recourse to the dispute settlement provisions of GATT 1947 which are no longer in force. The Agreement is a plurilateral agreement, accession to which is governed by its own provisions and not by the provisions governing accession to the Agreement Establishing the WTO and its Multilateral Trade Agreements.[293]

Applicants are asked to provide information on import duties and taxes applicable to the importation of aircraft and parts and major producers of these products are interested in access to markets for their products.

Eight of the acceders accepted a Protocol commitment to join the Agreement on Civil Aircraft upon accession.[294] The wording in this case is usually very straightforward: "The representative of [X] confirmed that [X] would become a signatory of the Agreement on Civil Aircraft upon accession to the WTO." Four of these confirmed in addition that they would implement the Agreement without exceptions or transitional period.

Two undertook to "initiate negotiations for membership in the Agreement on Trade in Civil Aircraft immediately after accession to the WTO" without specifying a time-frame and confirmed that its Schedule of Concessions on Goods establishes duty free treatment for products used in civil aircraft.[295] One country agreed to "become signatory to the Agreement on terms and conditions acceptable to it and the other parties to that Agreement within a reasonable period of time, but in no case later than the date on which it accords duty-free treatment on the products covered by the Agreement to another country which has become a signatory to the Agreement."[296] Another acceding country said that it "will become an observer in the Agreement upon accession and will join within three years of accession."[297]

One acceding country's Protocol commitment is of a different type, confirming that it "would not impose any provisions of offsets or other forms of industrial

[292] China, paras 231 to 233. See also Protocol I.12.

[293] WTO Agreement, Article XII: 1 and 3.

[294] FYROM, para 180; Armenia, para 213; Chinese Taipei, para 223; Protocol I.5; Lithuania, para 157; Croatia, para 168; Albania, para 154; Georgia, para 125; Estonia, para 116; Latvia, para 110.

[295] Armenia, para 213; Moldova, para 153.

[296] Kyrgyz Republic, para 122.

[297] Oman, para 128.

compensation when purchasing civil aircraft, including specified types or volumes of business opportunities."[298]

In accordance with the Guidelines, the two LDCs that have acceded opted not to join the Agreement.

Textiles and clothing

For many years, a series of Agreements negotiated within the framework of GATT 1947 permitted importing Members to conclude bilateral agreements with exporting countries imposing discriminatory quantitative restrictions on imports of textiles and clothing that were disrupting their markets. The Agreement on Textiles and Clothing annexed to the WTO Agreement reintegrated this sector into the multilateral system by providing that all quantitative restrictions maintained under these bilateral agreements would be phased out by 1 January 2005.[299] The normal GATT remedies of anti-dumping, countervailing or safeguard measures have been available if problems arise in this sector.

Applicants whose exports of textiles and clothing were under restriction had an interest in becoming a Member of WTO during the lifetime of the Agreement so that its provisions could be made applicable to their restricted exports. Six acceders concluded Protocol commitments in their accession Working Party Reports providing that the quantitative restrictions on imports maintained by WTO Members on textiles and clothing originating in their territories will be phased out over a ten-year period from the date of their accession to WTO.[300]

2.5 Trade-related intellectual property rights

By the term "intellectual property," the TRIPS Agreement means copyright and related rights, trademarks, geographical indications, industrial designs, patents, layout designs of integrated circuits, and undisclosed information. This Agreement applies the basic MFN and national treatment principles to TRIPS and extends the WTO rules and procedures on dispute settlement to disputes on TRIPS, albeit with some qualifications.[301] The Agreement recognizes the underlying public policy objectives of systems to protect intellectual property (IP), lays down detailed minimum standards Members must adopt to protect the private rights of IP holders and provides means that Members must make available under their law to enforce those rights. Its minimum standards incorporate by reference the substantive obligations of the main conventions previously negotiated in other bodies,

[298] China, para 240.

[299] Agreement on Textiles and Clothing, Article 9. The Annex to this Agreement sets out its product coverage.

[300] Nepal, para 119; Cambodia, para 166; FYROM, para 192; Chinese Taipei, para 167; China, para 241; Oman, para 130.

[301] Understanding on Rules and Procedures Governing the Settlement of Disputes. Agreement on Intellectual Property Rights, Article 64.

notably the World Intellectual Property Organization,[302] but also adds significantly to these obligations. Its enforcement provisions provide for civil judicial procedures and remedies, provisional measures, administrative procedures and remedies, special border measures, and, exceptionally in the WTO context, criminal procedures.

Transitional arrangements for the application of the TRIPS Agreement by WTO Members provided for in the Agreement have by now come to an end, the grace period for least-developed Members having terminated on 1 January 2006. However, under the terms of a separate decision, LDC Members are not obliged, with respect to pharmaceutical products, to implement or apply certain provisions related to patents until 1 January 2016.[303]

Concern about the gravity of the public health problems afflicting many developing and LDC countries, especially those resulting from HIV/AIDS, tuberculosis, malaria and other epidemics led to an amendment of the TRIPS Agreement, making it easier for Members to obtain generic versions of patented medicines.[304]

The Secretariat has circulated a checklist of the main obligations of the TRIPS Agreement asking applicants to check whether their legislation faithfully reflects each of these.[305] Members of the Working Party will wish to satisfy themselves that this legislation is in full conformity with the requirements of the TRIPS Agreement and that the applicant concerned is in a position to implement its legislation from the date of accession. Where necessary, applicants will be asked to present an action plan setting out a timetable for the completion of each step in this process. Some applicants have presented draft legislation to Members with a request for comments. It is the clear expectation of Working Party members that acceders have this legislation in place by the time of the adoption of their Working Party Report and that it will be implemented as from the date of their accession.

The baseline Protocol commitment on this subject is very brief and to the point: "The representative of [X] stated that [X] would apply fully all the provisions of the Agreement on Trade-Related Aspects of Intellectual Property Rights from the date of accession to the WTO, without recourse to any transition period." Eighteen of the new Members accepted this type of Protocol commitment.[306] Five of these

302 The Paris Convention for the Protection of Industrial Property, Berne Convention for the Protection for the Protection of Literary and Artistic Works, International Convention for the Protection of Performers, Producers of Phonograms and Broadcasting Organizations (Rome Convention), Treaty on Intellectual Property in Respect of Integrated Circuits. See TRIPS Agreement, Article 1:3, footnote.

303 Decision of the Council for TRIPS of 27 June 2002, IP/C/25.

304 Doha Ministerial Conference, Declaration on the TRIPS Agreement and Public Health, WTO document WT/MIN(01)/DEC/2, 14 November 2001. Decision of 6 December 2005, WT/L/641.

305 WTO document WT/ACC/9 and Corr.1.

306 Viet Nam, para 471; Saudi Arabia, para 272; FYROM, para 238; Armenia, para 197; China, para 305; Moldova, para 216; Lithuania, para 166; Croatia, para 202; Oman, para 140; Albania, para 153; Georgia, para 161; Jordan, para 230; Estonia, para 126; Latvia, para 116; Kyrgyz Republic, para 164; Panama, para 111; Mongolia, para 54; Bulgaria, para 85.

also recognized that specific changes still needed to be made in their legislation to bring it fully into line with the provisions of the Agreement and to provide effective enforcement of its provisions and committed themselves to make these changes by the time of their accession.[307]

Two recent acceders, one of them an LDC, have accepted Protocol commitments specifying the way in which they will implement the obligation in Article 39.3 of the TRIPS Agreement to provide effective protection against unfair commercial use of undisclosed test or other data submitted to their authorities as required in support of applications for marketing approval of pharmaceutical or of agricultural chemical products which utilized new chemical entities.[308]

Some doubts were raised as to whether new Members would be entitled to the flexibilities provided by the Doha Declaration on the TRIPS Agreement and Public Health. Any such doubts were resolved by an uncontested statement by one LDC which is recorded in the Working Party Report on its accession[309] and by a statement made when the Report on the accession of another LDC was presented for adoption that "the terms of this accession did not preclude access of [this country] and LDCs to the benefits under the Doha Declaration on the TRIPS Agreement and Public Health".[310]

The first applicant to accede to the WTO undertook to apply the TRIPS Agreement with a limited transition period.[311] Apart from this very early case, Working Parties have only granted transitional periods to the two LDCs that have so far acceded and to one small and vulnerable economy. An acceding government seeking transitional arrangements needs to confirm that, should a transition be granted, it would ensure that existing rates of infringement would not significantly increase and that any infringement of intellectual property rights would be addressed immediately in cooperation with affected right holders and that it would seek out all available technical assistance to ensure that its capacity to fully enforce its TRIPS-consistent legal regime upon expiration of the transition periods is assured and that [it] would make available all legislation in draft and promulgated form to WTO Members so that advice on TRIPS-consistency can be obtained. It also needs to submit a detailed action plan setting out the steps that still remained to be taken in order to achieve full compliance with the requirements of the TRIPS Agreement and a timetable for each step. This should state which of their existing laws and regulations are already in conformity with the Agreement, which need to be amended, which new laws and regulations will need to be adopted and what needs to be done to implement the legislation (See Annex 13).[312]

[307] Viet Nam, paras 403 and 465; FYROM, para 211; Armenia, para 193; Chinese Taipei, paras 187, 198, 207–209; China, paras 252, 256, 259, 263, 265, 270, 275, 284, 286, 288, 291, 292, 296, 299, 302, 304, Protocol VI.

[308] Cambodia, para 205; China, para 284.

[309] Nepal, para 138.

[310] Cambodia, Ministerial Conference, Cancun, 11 September 2003, WTO document WT/MIN(03)/SR/4, p. 4.

[311] Ecuador, para 78.

[312] See in particular Cambodia, paras 205 and 206; Nepal, paras 137 and 138; and Tonga, paras 167–169.

Trade in services

The share of services in the economy increased considerably in recent decades. Many governments have recognized the benefits of services liberalization for their economic growth. Ranging from architecture to telecommunications and to transport, services are the largest and most dynamic component of both developed and developing country economies. Important in their own right, they also serve as crucial inputs into the production of most goods. Their inclusion in the Uruguay Round of trade negotiations led to the GATS. The GATS is innovative in a number of ways. Trade in services is understood to take place in four different ways, often referred to as the four modes of supply.[313] The GATS is similar to the GATT in that it contains general rules that apply to all Members and specific commitments in a series of annexed Schedules which have been negotiated by each Member. However, its approach to the basic GATT principles is different: Members may take exemptions to the obligation of MFN treatment and grant national treatment only in sectors listed in their Schedules, subject to conditions and qualifications set out there.[314]

Applicants are requested to supply information on their trade-related services regime.[315] Members of the Working Party will then use the question and answer procedure and the examination of the applicant's regime in the Working Party to obtain fuller factual information. Members of the Working Party are interested in obtaining information on: legislation regulating services; the role of different government agencies; licensing procedures, judicial and arbitral appeal procedures; governance issues (e.g. separation of regulators and service suppliers); and transparency (e.g. publication, prior publication). More detail has naturally been demanded of the larger acceders with well-developed regulatory systems than of smaller countries in which many sectors are unregulated. Questions have been asked on most service sectors, but many relate to sectors such as financial services and telecommunications.

Members have concentrated more on bilateral negotiations for specific commitments on services than on general Protocol commitments related to the rules in the GATS. It should be recalled, however, that under the terms of their Protocols acceders accept the general rules contained in the Agreement Establishing the WTO and the Multilateral Trade Agreements attached to it, including the GATS, when they become Members of WTO.

Only five acceders entered into Protocol commitments related to GATS in their Working Party Reports. These relate to issues specific to the acceder concerned and

[313] General Agreement on Trade in Services, Article I:2. "For the purposes of this Agreement, trade in services is defined as the supply of a service: (a) from the territory of one member into the territory of any other member; (b) in the territory of one Member to the service consumer of any other Member; (c) by a service supplier of one Member, through commercial presence in the territory of any other Member; (d) by a service supplier of one Member, through presence of natural persons of a Member in the territory of any other Member".

[314] General Agreement on Trade in Services, Articles II:1 and XVII:1.

[315] WTO documents WT/ACC/1 and WT/ACC/5.

there is therefore no standard text of commitments. It may be noted that two acceders undertook a relatively large number of Protocol commitments: both of these were dynamic economies that were continuing the process of transition to a full market economy.[316] The others accepted a more limited number of commitments.[317]

2.6 Transparency

Transparency is a basic principle of the rule of law in general and for the WTO in particular. It is achieved in the WTO through provisions which require publication, notification and the provision of information on relevant matters, for instance by enquiry points. These provisions are specific to each of the WTO agreements.[318]

Publication

The main principles behind the various WTO provisions on publication are that all relevant measures of general application should be published in such a way as to enable governments and traders to become acquainted with them; that measures should be officially published before being enforced; and that confidential information need not be provided if contrary to the public interest or prejudicial to legitimate commercial interests of particular enterprises. However, each WTO agreement has its own provisions. Some do not contain all of the above elements: the GATS does not, for instance, require that relevant measures must be published before they are enforced. Some agreements contain additional elements: for instance, the Agreement on Technical Barriers to Trade requires that Members publish a notice at an early appropriate stage if they propose to introduce certain technical regulations or conformity assessment procedures and provide an opportunity for consultation on these.

Applicants are expected to provide information about arrangements made for the publication of their laws, regulations, etc.

The practice of Working Parties regarding Protocol commitments has varied and only half the Reports contain commitments on this subject. Nevertheless, the more recent Reports do address this issue and commitments have tended to become more detailed.

[316] Viet Nam, paras 479 (telecom and express delivery), 480 (telecom), 483, 484, and 485 (banking), 488, 489, 491 and 494 (insurance), 496 (express delivery), 498 (joint ventures), 499 retailing, 502 and 503 (joint ventures), 506 (publication of legislation), 507 (licensing procedures and conditions) and 508 (governance and transparency); China, paras 307 (publication), 308 (licensing procedures), paras 309 (independence of regulators from regulated), 310 (regulations away from fixed locations), 312 (definition of terms in Schedule), 315 (partnerships with foreign services suppliers), 317 (commodity inspection agencies), 318 (market research services), 320 (rights of minority shareholders), 475 (national treatment) and 494 and 496 (publication).

[317] Saudi Arabia, paras 276 (banking), 296, 298, and 299 (insurance); Chinese Taipei, para 211 (telecom); Croatia, para 204 (national treatment).

[318] Compare, for example: GATT Article X:1 and 2; GATS Article III:1 and 2; and TRIPS Article 63:1.

Protocol commitments sometimes deal with the WTO provisions relating to both publication and notification. One version reads as follows: "The representative of [X] confirmed that [X] would implement fully Article X of GATT 1994, and Article III of GATS and the other transparency requirements in WTO agreements requiring notification and publication".[319] Some commitments specifically provide that measures will not enter into force before they are published.[320]

One acceding country entered into a commitment making it clear that "official letters" were not recognized as legal normative documents and would be invalid if they provided for legal normative rules.[321]

Some acceders have agreed to Protocol commitments requiring them not only to publish the text of measures but also some or all of the following: the names of the authorities responsible for implementing a particular measure, the effective date of the measure and a list of the products and services affected, identified by appropriate tariff line and classification.[322]

Some acceders committed themselves to publish measures prior to implementation and to provide a minimum period of time for comment before such measures are implemented – in some but not all of these commitments an exception is made for cases of emergency or security or for which publication would impede law enforcement.[323]

The method of publication is usually specified in the commitment. Some are to be published in an official publication,[324] some in an official publication or website,[325] and some in both an official publication and a website.[326] In two cases in which the creation of a website is not foreseen, Protocol commitments provide for the establishment of one or more enquiry points where information relating to measures affecting trade in goods, services and TRIPS (in one case, also foreign exchange measures) could be obtained. These two acceders have also accepted commitments to make available translations of these measures into one or more of the official languages of WTO (English, French, Spanish) not later than 90 days after they are implemented or enforced (in one case) or enacted or issued (in the other).[327]

319 Viet Nam, para 518; Saudi Arabia, para 305; Nepal, para 147; Cambodia, para 217; Armenia, para 215; Moldova, para 235; Oman, para 150. For two early cases, see Kyrgyz Republic, para 113, and Ecuador, para 65.

320 Tonga, para 180; Viet Nam, para 518; Nepal, para 147; Cambodia, para 217; Panama, para 115; Mongolia, para 44.

321 Viet Nam, para 517.

322 Tonga, para 180; Viet Nam, para 518; Saudi Arabia, para 305; Nepal, para 147; Cambodia, para 217; China, para 332.

323 Viet Nam, para 518 (no less than 60 days); Armenia, para 215 (two weeks); Chinese Taipei, para 219 (60 calendar days), China Protocol I.2(C) 1 and 3 (a reasonable period); Bulgaria, para 40 (two weeks).

324 Tonga, para 180; Nepal, para 147; Armenia, para 215; China, para 332; Protocol I.2(C), Oman, para 150; Panama, para 115; Mongolia, para 44.

325 Cambodia, para 217. 326 Viet Nam, para 518; Saudi Arabia, para 305.

327 Chinese Taipei, para 217; China, paras 334 and 336, Protocol I.2(C). See the texts of these for the exact language of each.

Notification

The WTO agreements contain a large number of provisions requiring Members to make notifications of relevant measures that they have taken (or not taken) – and in some cases of proposed measures.[328] The notifications must be made in one of the official languages of the WTO[329] and are then translated into the other official languages. These requirements, and the existence of WTO bodies to examine them, are important to the functioning of the WTO rule-based system.

Under this heading, the main aim of members of Working Parties has been to ensure that acceders make the initial notifications required as soon as they become Members of the Organization and the standard Protocol commitment is, subject to minor variations: "The representative of [X] confirmed that at the latest upon entry into force of the Protocol of Accession [X] would submit all initial notifications required by any agreement constituting part of the WTO agreements. Any regulations subsequently enacted by [X] which gave effect to the laws enacted to implement any agreement constituting part of the WTO agreements would also conform to the requirements of that agreement".[330]

This formula was modified in a Report: "The representative of [X] said that at the latest upon accession, [it]would submit all initial notifications required by the WTO Agreement. Any laws, regulations, or other measures subsequently enacted by [X], and which were required to be notified pursuant to the WTO Agreement, would also be notified in a time and manner consistent with WTO requirements".[331]

Some applicants have been requested to present draft initial notifications during the accession process and commit themselves to make these notifications immediately after accession.[332]

One country has committed itself to provide specified information during a transitional period to subsidiary bodies of the WTO which have a mandate covering [its] commitments under the WTO Agreement or [its] Protocol.[333]

2.7 Trade agreements

These agreements are of three main types: agreements establishing international organizations, plurilateral agreements and bilateral agreements. They are either

[328] See WTO document G/L/223 and its subsequent revisions. [329] English, French, and Spanish.

[330] Tonga, para 181; Viet Nam, para 508; Saudi Arabia, para 306; FYROM, para 247; Armenia, para 217; Chinese Taipei, para 220; Lithuania, para 179; Croatia, para 216; Oman, para 151; Albania, para 160; Georgia, para 172; Estonia, para 136; Latvia, para 124; Kyrgyz Republic, para 168.

[331] Viet Nam, para 519. [332] Examples include: China, Annex 5A; Moldova, para 236; Jordan, para 240.

[333] China, para 322, and Protocol I.18. Notifications to be made to: Council for Trade in Goods, Council for Trade-Related Aspects of Intellectual Property Rights, Council for Trade in Services, Committees on Balance-of-Payments Restrictions, Market Access (covering also ITA), Agriculture, Sanitary and Phytosanitary Measures, Technical Barriers to Trade, Subsidies and Countervailing Measures, Anti-Dumping Measures, Customs Valuation, Rules of Origin, Import Licensing, Trade-Related Investment Measures, Safeguards, Trade in Financial Services.

based on the MFN principle or preferential in nature. The WTO permits agreements in the second category only if they are free trade areas or customs unions as defined in GATT 1994, if they are preferential agreements between or among developing and LDC countries within the scope of the GATT 1994 Enabling Clause, or if they are agreements liberalizing trade in services that meet the requirements of GATS.[334]

Applicants provide a full list of international agreements to which they are party, but members of Working Parties are mainly interested in obtaining information on non-MFN agreements. They have, however, not explored the conformity of these with the relevant WTO provisions in any depth during the accession process.

This is a subject on which there is a clear baseline Protocol commitment: "The representative of [X] confirmed that [X] would observe the provisions of the WTO, including Article XXIV of the GATT 1994 and Article V of the GATS, in its trade agreements, and would ensure that the provisions of these WTO Agreements for notification, consultation and other requirements concerning free trade areas and customs unions of which [it] was a member were met from the date of accession."[335] Some Reports add a reference to the GATT 1994 Enabling Clause.[336]

If the applicant is a member of a preferential agreement that has not yet been notified to the WTO, the Working Party will request it to accept a Protocol obligation to supply notifications and copies of its preferential agreements for review by the Committee on Regional Trade Agreements (and the Committee on Trade and Development for Enabling Clause notifications).[337]

3 NEGOTIATION OF MARKET ACCESS CONCESSIONS AND COMMITMENTS

The negotiation of tariff concessions, commitments on agricultural support and export subsidies, and specific commitments on services take place either bilaterally or, in the case of commitments on agricultural support, in relatively small informal groups. This section focuses on the documentation on which these negotiations are based and the results of these negotiations.

Some active members of accession Working Parties have indicated that acceders should be prepared to undertake market access commitments that are "commercially

334 GATT Article XXIV, which also permits interim agreements necessary for the formation of a customs union or of a free trade area; Decision on Differential and More Favourable Treatment, Reciprocity and Fuller Participation of Developing Countries (Enabling Clause) of 28 November 1979, GATT BISD 16 S/17; GATS Article V.

335 Viet Nam, paras 523 and 526; Saudi Arabia, para 314; Cambodia, para 223; FYROM, para 254; Armenia, para 212; Moldova, para 232; Lithuania, para 188; Croatia, para 224; Oman, para 156; Albania, para 166; Georgia, para 179; Jordan, para 247; Estonia, para 140; Latvia, para 130; Kyrgyz Republic, para 172; Bulgaria, para 78.

336 Tonga, para 187; Nepal, para 151; Panama, para 80; Mongolia, para 48; Ecuador, para 70.

337 Viet Nam, para 523; Saudi Arabia, para 314; Cambodia, para 223; FYROM, para 254; Armenia, para 212; Moldova, para 232; Georgia, para 179.

viable," or "meaningful in trade terms." Some emphasize that these should be "appropriate to the level of economic development of the applicant". It will be recalled that the Guidelines on the Accession of LDCs provide that in the area of market access, WTO Members are to "exercise restraint in seeking concessions and commitments on trade in goods and services from acceding LDCs, taking into account the levels of concessions and commitments undertaken by existing WTO LDCs' Members." For their part, acceding LDCs are expected to offer "reasonable market access concessions and commitments on goods and services commensurate with their individual development, financial and trade needs," in line with relevant WTO provisions on goods and services.[338]

3.1 GOODS SCHEDULE – TARIFF CONCESSIONS

This section examines the format for initial offers, the way in which the results of the negotiations have been scheduled and the level of the tariff commitments undertaken by new Members.

Formats for initial offers and scheduling of tariff concessions

The formats for initial offers and scheduling of tariff concessions, including notes on the way in which the format for scheduling has been used to reflect the results of negotiations, are at Annex 8.

Results of the negotiations – all products

With very few exceptions all applicants that have acceded to the WTO have bound all of their tariffs in their Schedules. The great majority are *ad valorem* bindings. The average of the final bound *ad valorem* rates varies from 5.8 percent in the case of Chinese Taipei to 26.0 percent in the case of Nepal. The first four applicants to accede bound their tariffs at relatively high levels which may be regarded as unrepresentative of current practice. In the case of the applicants to have acceded since then, there appears to be no correlation between the average level of bindings and the date of their accession, their per capita income or the level of their applied duties at the time the negotiations took place.[339] However, some points do emerge. The two LDCs, Cambodia and Nepal, are in a category of their own with average bindings of 19 percent and 26 percent respectively, in keeping with the Guidelines on LDC accession. Three developing countries, Tonga, Jordan and Oman, bound their tariffs at between 13.8 percent and 17.6 percent. All the other new Members bound the average of their *ad valorem* tariffs at between 5.8 percent and 12.7 percent.

[338] WTO document WT/L/508.

[339] Data on the duties applied during the base period for the negotiations are not available. Table 3 shows the nearest approximation to this that is available.

Table 3 *New Members: average final bound tariffs – all products*

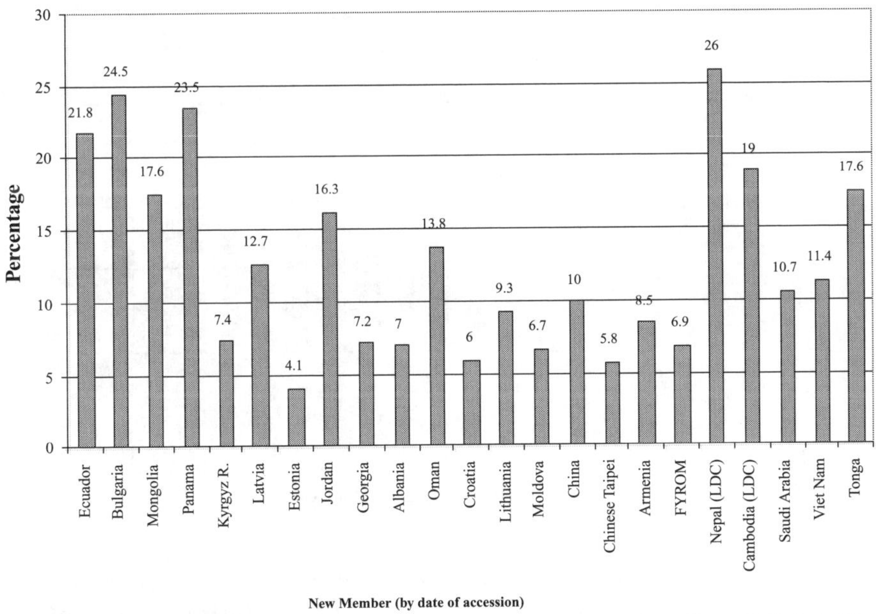

Source: WTO Trade Profiles.

Results of the negotiations – agricultural products

As a general rule WTO Members, including the recently acceded Members, have bound their tariffs on all agricultural products.[340]

Table 4 presents the simple average of final *ad valorem* tariff bindings of agricultural products accepted by the new Members. This demonstrates that the results of the accession negotiations vary considerably, the average in this sector going from a low of 9.4[341] to a high of 41.4 percent.[342] While no strikingly clear pattern emerges, this chart does show at least two things. First, that the Guidelines on the Accession of LDCs have had an effect and that less is asked of LDCs than of other acceders. Second, that, these apart, recent acceders have bound the average level of their tariffs at lower rates than countries that acceded in the earlier days of the WTO.

Table 5 analyses the results of the tariff negotiations on agricultural products for the new Members that have acceded to date in more detail. It shows that averages do

340 With some exceptions, for example, Saudi Arabia prohibits importation and domestic production of some items for religious reasons.

341 Albania and Croatia. 342 Nepal.

Table 4 *New members: average final bound tariffs – agricultural products*

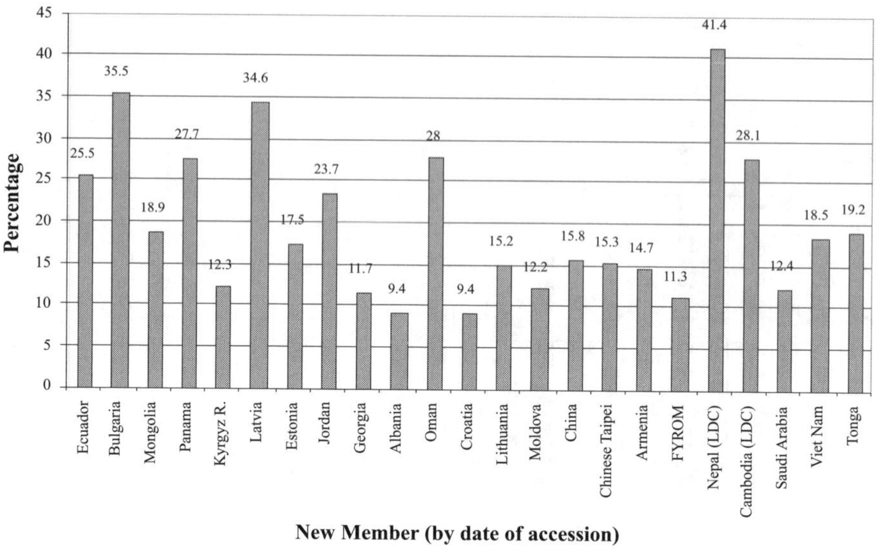

not tell the whole story and that some have a much flatter tariff structure than others, as can be seen from the fact that among more recent acceders the highest final bound rate is 15 percent in one case and 500 percent in another. This exceptionally high binding was made by the acceder with the lowest average final binding of rates on all products.

Table 5 does not analyse specific and mixed duties, but does indicate the relatively small share of these duties in the Schedules of the new Members that have acceded to date. WTO Members tend to encourage acceders to use *ad valorem* duties as these are more transparent but they may agree to the binding of specific duties, especially if they export relatively high-priced goods on which the incidence of the duty is lower than on cheaper products covered by the same tariff heading.

Table 5 also shows that the simple averages of agricultural rates bound at accession are systematically higher than the averages of final bound rates, even though in some cases this difference is minimal. This indicates that acceders have negotiated transitional periods during which they phase in their final bound rates. The length of these periods varies up to ten years.

Results of the negotiations – non-agricultural products

Acceding governments have generally bound 100 percent of their non-agricultural tariffs.

The key results of the negotiations are the final bound rates accepted by new Members. In the non-agricultural sector, the simple average of final bound rates

Table 5 *Agricultural products – bound tariffs*

	Reduction commitments	Simple average of ad valorem tariff bindings (percent)	Distribution of ad valorem tariff bindings (percent)									Share of non-ad valorem tariff bindings (percent)	Min. ad valorem duty	Max. ad valorem duty
			0 (duty-free)	0.1–5.0	5.1–10.0	10.1–15.0	15.1–20.0	20.1–30.0	30.1–40.0	40.1–50.0	50.1+			
Ecuador	*Bound rate at accession 1995*	26.2	0.0	2.0	1.4	9.0	28.5	44.5	6.9	5.1	2.4	0.0	5.0	95.0
	Final bound rate 2001	25.5	0.0	2.0	1.4	9.0	28.2	45.1	7.4	4.5	2.3	0.0	5.0	85.5
Bulgaria	*Bound rate at accession 1997*	52.3	0.1	2.5	5.5	3.8	7.2	10.6	17.1	1.3	38.1	15.8	0.0	135.0
	Final bound rate 2005	35.5	5.0	6.6	9.3	10.3	2.4	13.1	9.9	0.9	28.6	15.8	0.0	98.0
Mongolia	*Bound rate at accession 1996*	19.0	0.7	0.7	0.7	23.2	72.4	0.6	1.0	0.3	0.3	0.0	0.0	75.0
	Final bound rate 2005	18.9	0.7	0.7	0.7	23.5	72.4	0.6	1.0	0.0	0.3	0.0	0.0	75.0
Panama	*Bound rate at accession 1997*	36.9	0.3	7.2	4.7	4.5	2.0	4.2	69.4	1.2	6.3	0.0	0.0	320.0
	Final bound rate 2007	27.7	0.3	7.2	4.8	5.1	6.0	70.0	1.1	0.8	4.5	0.0	0.0	260.0
Kyrgyz	*Bound rate at accession 1998*	12.4	1.2	6.0	56.3	12.4	21.8	0.1	0.0	0.0	0.0	2.4	0.0	30.0
Republic	*Final bound rate 2003*	12.3	1.2	7.1	56.0	11.7	21.8	0.1	0.0	0.0	0.0	2.4	0.0	30.0
Latvia	*Bound rate at accession 1999*	35.8	1.5	1.6	16.7	9.6	2.4	5.9	2.9	57.5	1.5	0.4	0.0	100.0
	Final bound rate 2008	34.6	2.1	1.6	19.0	9.1	3.2	3.5	5.3	54.3	1.3	0.4	0.0	55.0
Estonia	*Bound rate at accession 1999*	19.2	8.1	7.8	23.6	11.5	15.5	18.3	7.2	7.4	0.6	0.0	0.0	59.0
	Final bound rate 2004	17.5	17.0	6.2	21.5	11.1	12.5	17.7	6.2	7.1	0.6	0.0	0.0	59.0
Jordan	*Bound rate at accession 2000*	25.8	0.9	13.1	11.9	12.2	10.5	46.2	1.0	0.0	3.5	1.0	0.0	200.0
	Final bound rate 2010	23.7	0.9	13.1	12.7	15.5	23.6	29.2	0.9	0.0	3.5	1.0	0.0	200.0
Georgia	*Bound rate at accession 2000*	13.3	0.0	0.9	0.1	85.4	6.6	4.4	0.0	0.0	0.0	2.5	4.0	30.0
	Final bound rate 2006	11.7	8.3	1.5	7.4	69.5	6.9	4.0	0.0	0.0	0.0	2.5	0.0	30.0
Albania	*Bound rate at accession 2000*	10.8	0.4	17.8	59.4	3.4	18.9	0.0	0.0	0.0	0.0	0.0	0.0	20.0
	Final bound rate 2007	9.4	10.9	17.3	54.9	1.8	15.2	0.0	0.0	0.0	0.0	0.0	0.0	20.0
Oman	*Bound rate at accession 2000*	28.1	0.0	6.9	5.2	76.3	0.1	0.0	0.0	1.2	10.3	0.0	5.0	200.0
	Final bound rate 2006	28.0	0.0	8.0	6.6	73.7	0.1	0.0	0.0	1.2	10.3	0.0	5.0	200.0
Croatia	*Bound rate at accession 2000*	13.0	13.0	24.6	13.1	15.9	9.7	3.7	3.8	3.1	3.2	18.3	0.0	90.0
	Final bound rate 2007	9.4	15.1	27.4	15.5	16.4	8.7	2.4	4.4	0.1	0.0	18.3	0.0	55.0

(cont.)

Table 5 *(cont.)*

	Reduction commitments	*Simple average of ad valorem tariff bindings (percent)*	*Distribution of ad valorem tariff bindings (percent)* 0 (duty-free)	0.1–5.0	5.1–10.0	10.1–15.0	15.1–20.0	20.1–30.0	30.1–40.0	40.1–50.0	50.1+	*Share of non-ad valorem tariff bindings (percent)*	*Min. ad valorem duty*	*Max. ad valorem duty*
Lithuania	*Bound rate at accession 2001*	16.3	9.1	13.6	31.7	14.7	4.0	11.5	6.0	4.6	1.5	3.4	0.0	100.0
	Final bound rate 2009	15.2	9.7	13.7	31.9	16.1	5.2	12.2	4.0	3.4	1.0	3.0	0.0	100.0
Moldova	*Bound rate at accession 2001*	18.1	0.4	6.9	28.5	11.2	11.4	25.2	8.0	0.0	0.0	8.3	0.0	40.0
	Final bound rate 2005	12.2	3.0	8.3	32.7	35.7	11.8	0.1	0.0	0.0	0.0	8.3	0.0	25.0
China	*Bound rate at accession 2000*	20.6	2.7	9.4	14.3	16.5	14.7	26.1	8.6	3.1	4.6	0.0	0.0	74.0
	Final bound rate 2010	15.8	2.8	11.1	25.2	24.9	18.6	12.1	2.2	0.6	2.5	0.0	0.0	65.0
Chinese Taipei	*Bound rate at accession 2002*	17.2	22.9	16.5	10.9	8.3	18.4	12.1	1.6	0.7	3.8	8.6	0.0	800.0
	Final bound rate 2011	15.3	24.6	15.9	11.5	10.3	17.6	9.9	1.5	0.1	3.8	8.6	0.0	500.0
Armenia	*Bound rate at accession 2003*	14.7	1.3	0.4	1.0	97.2	0.0	0.0	0.0	0.0	0.0	0.0	0.0	15.0
	Final bound rate 2003	14.7	1.3	0.4	1.0	97.2	0.0	0.0	0.0	0.0	0.0	0.0	0.0	15.0
FYROM	*Bound rate at accession 2003*	13.7	31.0	16.1	7.7	7.2	6.1	6.8	6.1	7.7	2.6	10.1	0.0	60.0
	Final bound rate 2007	11.3	34.0	15.9	8.2	8.7	6.7	7.7	5.1	4.3	0.6	10.0	0.0	60.0
Nepal	*Bound rate at accession 2003*	50.1	0.0	0.0	2.3	0.3	0.7	3.6	3.6	77.4	12.0	0.0	10.0	200.0
	Final bound rate 2006	41.4	0.0	0.7	2.3	0.4	4.2	28.7	33.7	21.4	8.5	0.0	5.0	200.0
Cambodia	*Bound rate at accession 2003*	28.2	0.0	2.8	6.9	17.1	11.4	16.4	43.5	0.9	0.9	0.0	5.0	60.0
	Final bound rate 2011	28.1	0.0	2.8	7.1	17.6	11.2	16.4	43.1	0.9	0.9	0.0	5.0	60.0
Saudi Arabia	*Bound rate at accession 2005*	12.5	0.0	3.6	32.3	51.6	2.3	1.7	0.1	0.0	0.1	10.7	0.0	200.0
	Final bound rate 2010	12.4	0.0	3.6	32.4	52.4	3.0	0.6	0.1	0.0	0.1	10.1	0.0	200.0
Viet Nam	*Bound rate at accession 2007*	22.4	6.9	16.0	16.9	7.8	13.7	10.8	20.5	3.2	4.0	0.0	0.0	150.0
	Final bound rate 2014	18.5	6.9	17.2	20.7	9.8	14.6	14.9	11.8	1.6	2.5	0.0	0.0	135.0
Tonga	*Bound rate at accession 2007*	19.7	0.0	0.0	0.0	15.6	68.0	11.4	0.0	0.0	0.0	5.0	15.0	25.0
	Final bound rate 2007	19.2	0.0	0.0	0.0	16.4	83.6	0.0	0.0	0.0	0.0	0.0	15.0	20.0

Table 6 *New Members: average final bound tariffs – non-agricultural products*

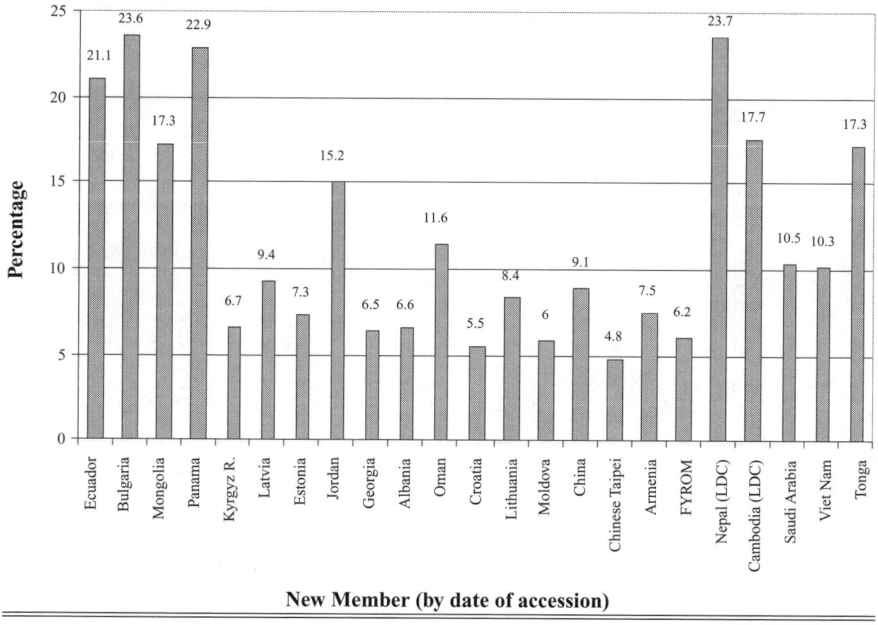

for the newly acceded Members has ranged from 4.8 percent[343] to 23.7 percent,[344] significantly lower than in the agricultural sector (see Table 6 above). At first sight, no very clear pattern emerges. However, the results fall into four groups: (i) the four countries that first acceded (because the WTO accession process was still being established and most of the concessions were negotiated during the Uruguay Round of trade negotiations); (ii) the two LDCs, Cambodia and Nepal, with 17.7 percent and 23.7 percent; (iii) three developing countries, Tonga, Jordan and Oman, at between 11.6 percent and 17.3 percent and (iv) 14 other new Members that all bound the average of their tariffs between 4.8 percent and 10.7 percent.

Table 7 provides more detail and shows that, as in the agricultural sector, some of the distribution of individual rates around the average is much greater in the tariffs of some countries than in others. The highest final bound rate in the non-agricultural tariff of six of the new Members is 20 percent. The highest individual final bound rate is 90 percent but final bound rates of more than 50 percent are quite exceptional.

343 Chinese Taipei. 344 Nepal.

Table 7 *Non-agricultural products – bound tariffs*[345]

	Reduction commitments	*Simple average of ad valorem tariff bindings (percent)*	*Distribution of ad valorem tariff bindings (percent)*									*Share of non-ad valorem tariff bindings (percent)*	*Min. ad valorem duty*	*Max. ad valorem duty*
			0 (duty-free)	0.1–5.0	5.1–10.0	10.1–15.0	15.1–20.0	20.1–30.0	30.1–40.0	40.1–50.0	50.1+			
Ecuador	*Bound rate at accession 1995*	21.1	0.0	1.9	15.8	12.4	21.3	48.2	0.2	0.0	0.0	0.0	5.0	40.0
	Final bound rate 2001	21.1	0.0	1.9	15.8	12.4	21.3	48.2	0.2	0.0	0.0	0.0	5.0	40.0
Bulgaria	*Bound rate at accession 1997*	25.7	0.3	4.0	15.2	9.2	4.8	16.6	49.9	0.0	0.0	0.0	0.0	40.0
	Final bound rate 2005	23.6	1.8	5.9	18.2	15.3	3.4	5.7	49.6	0.0	0.0	0.0	0.0	40.0
Mongolia	*Bound rate at accession 1996*	19.2	0.6	0.0	1.1	19.7	74.5	3.9	0.0	0.0	0.0	0.0	0.0	30.0
	Final bound rate 2010	17.3	1.6	0.0	19.8	0.0	74.5	3.9	0.0	0.0	0.0	0.0	0.0	30.0
Panama	*Bound rate at accession 1997*	31.6	1.2	3.7	4.6	6.1	12.8	5.0	66.5	0.0	0.0	0.0	0.0	90.0
	Final bound rate 2011	22.9	2.2	3.6	18.7	4.6	2.6	68.0	0.1	0.0	0.0	0.0	0.0	81.0
Kyrgyz Republic	*Bound rate at accession 1998*	11.8	2.4	4.8	64.1	11.6	15.3	1.2	0.0	0.5	0.0	0.0	0.0	50.0
	Final bound rate 2005	6.7	22.5	10.5	58.9	7.8	0.0	0.0	0.0	0.0	0.0	0.2	0.0	20.0
Latvia	*Bound rate at accession 1999*	10.8	3.4	9.1	59.3	18.0	6.8	2.1	0.1	0.9	0.3	0.0	0.0	55.0
	Final bound rate 2008	9.4	16.1	6.6	51.5	17.5	6.7	0.3	0.0	0.9	0.3	0.0	0.0	55.0
Estonia	*Bound rate at accession 1999*	7.6	12.6	15.1	61.3	9.9	0.3	0.8	0.0	0.0	0.0	0.0	0.0	30.0
	Final bound rate 2005	7.3	18.5	11.2	59.3	9.9	0.3	0.8	0.0	0.0	0.0	0.0	0.0	30.0
Jordan	*Bound rate at accession 2000*	19.2	3.0	20.1	11.2	6.8	12.8	43.2	2.8	0.0	0.0	0.1	0.0	35.0
	Final bound rate 2010	15.2	6.3	19.5	16.3	11.1	24.1	22.7	0.0	0.0	0.0	0.1	0.0	30.0
Georgia	*Bound rate at accession 2000*	10.2	1.3	22.6	1.6	73.8	0.6	0.0	0.0	0.0	0.0	0.0	0.0	20.0
	Final bound rate 2005	6.5	23.6	20.6	23.4	32.0	0.3	0.0	0.0	0.0	0.0	0.0	0.0	20.0
Albania	*Bound rate at accession 2000*	10.1	3.9	44.4	23.1	0.3	28.2	0.0	0.0	0.0	0.0	0.0	0.0	20.0
	Final bound rate 2009	6.6	28.4	34.5	19.1	2.4	15.5	0.0	0.0	0.0	0.0	0.0	0.0	20.0
Oman	*Bound rate at accession 2000*	14.7	1.5	0.9	2.7	92.7	2.2	0.0	0.0	0.0	0.0	0.0	0.0	20.0
	Final bound rate 2009	11.6	4.1	8.5	24.4	60.7	2.2	0.0	0.0	0.0	0.0	0.0	0.0	20.0
Croatia	*Bound rate at accession 2000*	6.7	22.9	34.4	23.0	12.7	6.7	0.2	0.0	0.0	0.0	0.0	0.0	38.0
	Final bound rate 2005	5.5	26.5	36.9	22.9	13.3	0.3	0.0	0.0	0.0	0.0	0.0	0.0	25.0

(*cont.*)

	Reduction commitments	Simple average of ad valorem tariff bindings (percent)	Distribution of ad valorem tariff bindings (percent) 0 (duty-free)	0.1–5.0	5.1–10.0	10.1–15.0	15.1–20.0	20.1–30.0	30.1–40.0	40.1–50.0	50.1+	Share of non-ad valorem tariff bindings (percent)	Min. ad valorem duty	Max. ad valorem duty
Lithuania	*Bound rate at accession 2001*	8.7	24.5	7.0	31.9	28.4	6.7	1.4	0.2	0.0	0.0	0.0	0.0	35.0
	Final bound rate 2009	8.4	24.5	7.1	36.0	24.7	6.7	1.0	0.0	0.0	0.0	0.0	0.0	30.0
Moldova	*Bound rate at accession 2001*	11.1	22.7	11.7	31.4	7.5	11.9	6.9	7.9	0.0	0.0	0.0	0.0	40.0
	Final bound rate 2005	6.0	25.6	16.9	46.4	11.0	0.1	0.0	0.0	0.0	0.0	0.0	0.0	20.0
China	*Bound rate at accession 2000*	12.7	1.8	10.4	35.2	21.0	12.1	17.7	1.3	0.2	0.3	0.0	0.0	61.7
	Final bound rate 2010	9.1	6.2	18.1	47.0	15.3	8.7	3.9	0.5	0.2	0.0	0.0	0.0	50.0
Chinese Taipei	*Bound rate at accession 2002*	6.4	13.2	44.7	25.3	12.0	2.5	0.9	0.3	0.1	0.5	0.9	0.0	106.0
	Final bound rate 2011	4.8	29.0	39.9	21.0	7.8	0.7	0.5	0.1	0.0	0.3	0.9	0.0	90.0
Armenia	*Bound rate at accession 2003*	7.7	38.6	7.6	10.4	43.4	0.0	0.0	0.0	0.0	0.0	0.0	0.0	15.0
	Final bound rate 2007	7.5	39.2	7.8	11.1	41.8	0.0	0.0	0.0	0.0	0.0	0.0	0.0	15.0
FYROM	*Bound rate at accession 2003*	9.5	23.4	23.8	18.7	11.4	7.4	8.9	6.5	0.0	0.0	0.2	0.0	32.2
	Final bound rate 2012	6.2	36.2	20.3	21.2	13.9	7.5	1.0	0.0	0.0	0.0	0.2	0.0	25.0
Nepal	*Bound rate at accession 2003*	39.4	0.1	1.2	0.7	1.4	2.4	20.6	39.4	28.0	5.4	0.0	0.0	130.0
	Final bound rate 2013	23.7	3.1	1.1	2.9	5.3	34.5	48.6	3.5	0.2	0.1	0.0	0.0	60.0
Cambodia	*Bound rate at accession 2003*	17.7	0.7	0.0	28.9	29.9	17.0	8.8	14.6	0.0	0.0	0.0	0.0	42.5
	Final bound rate 2013	17.7	1.0	0.0	28.8	29.7	17.1	8.8	14.6	0.0	0.0	0.0	0.0	42.5
Saudi Arabia	*Bound rate at accession 2005*	10.9	1.7	9.8	32.2	55.2	1.1	0.0	0.0	0.0	0.0	0.0	0.0	20.0
	Final bound rate 2015	10.5	5.6	6.6	34.4	53.0	0.4	0.0	0.0	0.0	0.0	0.0	0.0	20.0
Viet Nam	*Bound rate at accession 2007*	13.1	12.7	25.8	19.4	12.4	11.2	11.0	6.1	1.0	0.5	0.1	0.0	100.0
	Final bound rate 2019	10.3	14.3	32.8	14.1	13.8	14.4	8.5	1.3	0.4	0.4	0.1	0.0	100.0
Tonga	*Bound rate at accession 2007*	19.4	0.0	0.0	0.0	27.6	62.4	7.0	1.8	1.3	0.0	0.0	15.0	15.0
	Final bound rate 2007	17.3	0.0	0.0	0.0	53.0	47.0	0.0	0.0	0.0	0.0	0.0	15.0	20.0

[345] Source: WT/ACC/10/Rev.3, pp. 22 and 23.

To improve cross-country comparability, tariff profiles are compiled at the HS 6-digit level product classification, which offers a common structure that is not biased by the different levels of disaggregation in Members' tariffs. As a result of the HS 6-digit aggregation, double-counting may occur, which could affect the percentage distribution of tariff bindings (which may not necessarily add up to 100 percent). Minimum/maximum *ad valorem* duties, however, are compiled at the level of the national nomenclature.

For several applicants, the final bound rates were significantly lower than the bound rates at the date of accession. As in the agricultural sector, the length of these periods varies up to 12 years.

Only four new Members apply non *ad valorem* duties and in each of these cases these account for less than one percent of their final bound tariffs.

The number of zero bindings made by new Members reflect in part that most acceders have agreed to join "zero for zero" initiatives, or to become a participant in the Information Technology Agreement (ITA).

The informal "zero for zero" initiatives were negotiated plurilaterally among interested countries during the Uruguay Round and led to an agreement among the countries concerned to bind their tariffs on products in a number of sectors at zero and extend the benefits on an MFN basis. The sectors concerned are: pharmaceuticals, agricultural equipment, construction equipment, medical equipment, paper, steel, toys, furniture, beer and distilled spirits. An agreement to harmonize tariffs on chemical products was also concluded on a similar basis. An indicative list of the products included in these sectors is at Annex 15.

The Information Technology Agreement is a later development.[346] This is a formal agreement providing that tariffs and other duties and charges on the covered products must be bound at zero in the Schedules. There are no exceptions to product coverage but an extended implementation period for sensitive items is foreseen. The number of participants is now 70,[347] representing about 97 percent of world trade in information technology products.

As noted above, some new Members have joined the Civil Aircraft Agreement which requires them, *inter alia*, to bind their tariffs on covered items at zero. Some other acceders have not joined the Agreement but have nevertheless bound civil aircraft tariffs at zero.

During the bilateral tariff negotiations, some WTO Members ask applicants to join these sectoral initiatives. Table 8 shows that neither Tonga, nor the two LDCs have fully participated in any of the sectoral initiatives. It also demonstrates that most acceders have joined the ITA. One acceder participated in all 13 initiatives.[348] In many cases, acceders made commitments in a significant number of tariff lines corresponding to particular tariff initiatives, but did not fully participate in these initiatives.

Goods Schedule – agricultural commitments

This section examines the format of the initial set of support tables, the way in which the results of the negotiations have been scheduled and the level of the tariff commitments undertaken by new Members.

[346] Ministerial Declaration on Trade in IT Products, 13 December 1996 WTO document WT/MIN(96)/16. This contains a list of the products covered.

[347] August, 2007. [348] Estonia.

Table 8 *Sectoral initiatives*

country (in order of accession)	Sectors												
	ITA	Civil Aircraft Agreement	Chemical Harmonization	Pharmaceuticals	Agricultural Equipment	Construction Equipment	Medical Equipment	Paper	Steel	Toys	Furniture	Beer	Distilled Spirits
Ecuador													
Bulgaria	Full												
Mongolia			Significant										
Panama	Full		Significant	Significant									
Kyrgyz Rep.	Full	Significant	Full	Full	Full	Full	Full	Full	Full	Full	Significant		
Latvia	Full	Full	Full	Significant	Full	Full	Significant	Full	Significant	Full	Full	Full	Full
Estonia	Full	Full	Full	Full	Full	Full	Full	Full	Full	Full	Full	Full	Full
Jordan	Full		Significant	Full	Full		Significant						
Georgia	Full	Full	Significant		Significant	Significant	Full	Full	Significant	Full	Full		
Albania	Full	Full	Full	Full	Full	Full	Full	Full	Significant	Full	Full	Full	Full
Oman	Full	Full	Significant	Full									
Croatia	Full	Full	Full	Significant	Significant	Significant	Significant	Significant	Significant	Full		Full	Significant
Lithuania	Full	Full	Significant	Full	Full	Full	Full	Significant	Full	Full		Full	Full
Moldova	Full	Significant	Full	Full			Full		Full	Full			
China	Full									Full	Full	Full	
Chinese Taipei	Full	Full	Significant	Full	Full	Full	Significant	Full	Significant	Full	Full	Full	Full
Armenia		Full	Significant	Full	Full	Full	Full	Significant	Full				
FYROM		Full	Significant	Significant	Full	Full	Full	Significant		Full		Full	Full
Cambodia													
Nepal													
Saudi Arabia	Full	Significant	Full	Full									
Viet Nam	Full		Significant				Full						
Tonga													

Full participation — Significant participation (approx. >75 percent of tariff lines) — No participation

Format for data on agricultural domestic support and export subsidies and scheduling of commitments

The factual information on domestic support and export subsidy submitted by each applicant is examined plurilaterally in an informal group composed of the applicant and interested Working Party members, in accordance with the procedures outlined above. When this information is agreed, the set of final tables forms the basis for the domestic support commitments and the export competition commitments of the acceder. For the format used and notes on these see Annex 7.2.

Results of the negotiations

A summary of the commitments undertaken by the new Members is contained in Table 9.

The table shows the *de minimis* levels for these Members. In a number of cases, acceders claiming developing country status had recourse to a *de minimis* level of 10 percent.[349] In other cases Working Party Reports spell out specific provisions. An acceder accepted a 5% *de minimis* level but negotiated a transition period until 1 January 2003 during which SDR 24 million constituted its *de minimis* exemption. Another acceder agreed to a *de minimis* level of 10 percent until 31 December 2008 and 5 percent thereafter.[350] Another acceder claimed developing country status but after negotiation agreed to include Article 6.2 measures (development programmes) in its base total aggregate measure of support (AMS) and to a *de minimis* level of 8.5 percent.[351]

Fourteen governments identified no base total AMS at all, meaning either that they granted no domestic support or that all domestic support applied during the base period either satisfied the "green box" criteria, was provided in accordance with Article 6.2 (development programmes), or fell below the applicable *de minimis* threshold for "amber box" support. "Blue box" support programs have not been reported for any of the 23 newly acceded Members.

The Schedules of the other nine new Members specify their base total AMS and their final total AMS levels of "amber box" support.[352] The reductions appear to have generally been in line with the cuts made by original WTO Members under the Agreement on Agriculture – 13 percent for developing Members and 20 percent for developed Members. However, in two cases no reductions were made.[353]

One acceder implemented its final total AMS two years before it joined the WTO.[354] The developing countries called on to make reductions over negotiated implementation periods of six and ten years respectively. Implementation periods for the other new Members concerned varied from two to four years.

Two of the earliest acceders[355] undertook commitments to reduce agricultural export subsidies in Part IV of their Goods Schedules but since then all the other new Members have bound export subsidies at zero. The majority of these governments had not been providing any subsidies during the relevant base period but the four that had maintained agricultural export subsidies agreed to eliminate them fully

349 Agreement on Agriculture, Article 6.4 (b). LDCs are by definition developing countries subject to a *de minimis* of 10 percent.

350 Latvia, WTO document WT/ACC/LVA/32; and Armenia WTO document WT/ACC/ARM/23 and Corr.1 and Add.1.

351 China, para 235.

352 See Bulgaria, Jordan, Croatia, Lithuania, Moldova, Chinese Taipei, FYROM, Saudi Arabia and Viet Nam.

353 FYROM and Viet Nam.

354 Chinese Taipei.

355 Panama and Bulgaria.

Table 9 *Commitments on agricultural domestic support and export subsidies*

Member	*Year of accession*	*Base period*	*Currency*	*De minimis level*	*Base total AMS (million)*	*Final total AMS (million)*	*Percent reduction*	*Implementation period*	*Length of implementation period*
Ecuador	01/1996	n.a.	n.a.	10%	0	0		–	
Bulgaria	12/1996	1986–1988	Euro	5%	2,513	520	79%	1998	2 years
Mongolia	01/1997	n.a.	n.a.	10%	0	0		–	
Panama	09/1997	1991–1993	USD	10%	0	0		–	
Kyrgyz Republic	12/1998	1994–1996	KGS	5%	0	0		–	
Latvia	02/1999	1994–1996	SDR	SDR 24 million until 2003, 5% thereafter	0	0		–	
Estonia	11/1999	1995–1997	EEK	5%	0	0		–	
Jordan	04/2000	1994–1996	JOD	10%	1.5	1.3	15%	2006	6 years
Georgia	06/2000	1996–1998	GEL	5%	0	0		–	
Albania	09/2000	1996–1998	ALL	5%		0		–	
Oman	11/2000	1994–1996	OMR	10%	0	0		–	
Croatia	11/2000	1996–1998	Euro	5%	167.6	134.1	20%	2004	4 years
Lithuania	05/2001	1995–1997	USD	5%	118.2*	94.6*	20%*	2005	4 years
Moldova	07/2001	1996–1998	SDR	5%	15.9	12.8	19.5%	2004	3 years
China	12/2001	1996–1998	RMB	8.5%	0	0		–	
Chinese Taipei	01/2002	1990–1992	TWD	5%	17.7	14.1	20%	2000	Minus 2 years
Armenia	02/2003	1995–1997	USD	10% until 2008, 5% thereafter	0	0		–	
FYROM	04/2003	1998–2000	Euro	5%	16.3	16.3	0%	at accession	none
Nepal	04/2004	1996–1998	NPR	10%	0	0		–	
Cambodia	10/2004	1998–2000	KHR	10%	0	0		–	
Saudi Arabia	12/2005	2001–2003	SAR	10%	3,711.9	3,218.3	13%	2015	10 years
Viet Nam	01/2007	1999–2001	VND	10%	3,961.59	3,961.59	0%	–	–
Tonga	07/2007	1996/97–1998/99	TOP	10%	0	0		–	

* *de minimis* amount included in the calculation of AMS. 16 percent reduction if *de minimis* is excluded from final total AMS.

Source: WTO document WT/ACC/10/Rev.3, page 26; WTO document WT/ACC/SPEC/VNM/3/Rev.7 and WTO document WT/ACC/ VNM/48/ Add.1.

n.a.: not available.

from the date of accession.[356] This support may have been limited to a handful of agricultural sectors[357] or it may have been available more broadly.[358]

3.3 Services Schedule

This section first examines the format for Services Schedules and then provides an overview of the specific commitments undertaken by applicants that have acceded to the WTO.

Format for Services Schedules

Notes on the drafting of Services Schedules and the format used for such Schedules are contained in Annex 9.

Overview of specific commitments undertaken by new Members

The complexity of the services commitments means that any attempt to summarize them involves radical simplification.

Table 10 below is based on a total of approximately 160 service sub-sectors and shows that there is quite a wide variation in the number of sub-sectors on which acceding Members have made commitments. Among the points that stand out are:

- The Schedules of specific commitments of the first four governments to accede cover a lower number of sectors than subsequent accessions.
- The two LDCs made commitments in 94 and 77 sub-sectors, respectively or approximately 58 percent and 48 percent of all sub-sectors. Tonga made commitments in 90 sub-sectors.
- Apart from the first four governments to accede, LDCs and Tonga, there is a wide spread in the commitments made by the remaining 16 new Members: from 93 sub-sectors in the case of China (about the same number as one of the LDCs) to 147 sub-sectors for Moldova.
- The number of sub-sectors in which commitments were made by these 16 new Members does not appear to correlate with any of the more obvious criteria that might be used to discern a pattern in these results (date of accession, GDP, GDP per capita).

The above analysis does not tell us which sectors were committed. Table 11 below identifies whether the new Members made specific commitments in 26 basic groups of services sectors. This shows that the Schedules of acceders have not only a high sectoral coverage but that they usually made commitments in key sectors.

- The first four countries to accede made specific commitments in 11 to 21 of these sectors. These accessions are little guide to current practice.

[356] I.e. Latvia, Lithuania, FYROM and Viet Nam.
[357] E.g. Latvia, WTO document WT/ACC/LVA/32, para 107; FYROM WT/ACC/807/27, para 187.
[358] E.g. Lithuania, WTO document WT/ACC/LTU/52, para 149.

Table 10 *Specific commitments on services: number of sub-sectors committed*

Note: The number of GATS services sectors with commitments has been estimated by the WTO Secretariat on the basis of available information and in the light of the Services Sectoral Classification List (WTO document MTN.GNS/W/120).
Source: WTO.

- The two LDCs that have acceded made commitments in 19 and 22 sectors, respectively.
- The other 17 governments made commitments in 22 to 26 sectors – on average, 24 of the 26 sectors.

Leaving aside the first four countries to accede, it will be seen that all of the other 19 acceders (including LDCs) made at least some commitments in the following sectors: professional services (legal, accountancy, architectural and engineering); computer and related services; courier services; telecommunications (value-added and basic), financial services (insurance, banking and other); tourism; and air transport.[359] Fewer made commitments in postal services (6); audiovisual services (11); rail transport (13); maritime transport (15); and road transport (16).

A different sort of analysis is necessary to obtain an idea of the quality of the commitments made. It is beyond the scope of this Handbook to enter into a detailed analysis of all the specific commitments undertaken by new Members in their Schedules, but a few points stand out. First, commitments by new Members tend, overall, to have fewer limitations attached to them than those of older Members. Second, sectors committed are more often "unbound" under mode 1 (cross-border

[359] Recall that the GATS coverage of this sector is limited.

Table 11 *Specific services commitments of acceded WTO Members (sector-level)*

Service Sector \ Acceded Member	Ecuador	Bulgaria	Mongolia	Panama	Kyrgyz Republic	Latvia	Estonia	Jordan	Georgia	Albania	Oman	Croatia	Lithuania	Moldova	China	Chinese Taipei	Armenia	FYROM	Nepal (LDC)	Cambodia (LDC)	Saudi Arabia	Viet Nam	Tonga
Professional: - legal	■	■		■	■	■	■	■	■	■	■	■	■	■	■	■	■	■	■	■	■	■	■
- accountancy	■	■	■	■	■	■	■	■	■	■	■	■	■	■	■	■	■	■	■	■	■	■	■
- taxation	■			■	■	■	■	■	■	■	■	■	■	■	■	■	■	■		■	■	■	
- architectural and engineering	■	■	■	■	■	■	■	■	■	■	■	■	■	■	■	■	■	■	■	■	■	■	■
- medical		■			■	■	■	■	■	■	■	■	■	■	■		■			■	■	■	■
Computer and related	■	■		■	■	■	■	■	■	■	■	■	■	■	■	■	■	■	■	■	■	■	■
R&D		■			■	■	■	■	■		■	■	■	■		■	■	■	■		■	■	
Other business	■	■	■	■	■	■	■	■	■	■	■	■	■	■	■	■	■	■	■	■	■	■	■
Communication: Postal			■		■					■				■				■					■
Courier			■		■	■	■	■	■	■	■	■	■	■	■	■	■	■	■	■	■	■	■
Telecom: - valued added	■	■	■	■	■	■	■	■	■	■	■	■	■	■	■	■	■	■	■	■	■	■	■
- basic	■	■			■	■	■	■	■	■	■	■	■	■	■	■	■	■	■	■	■	■	■
Audiovisual[359]				■	■			■	■		■				■	■	■				■	■	■

[359] Audiovisual services commitments have often been reflected in both the specific commitments in this sector and the list of MFN exemptions.

Service Sector / Acceded Member	Ecuador	Bulgaria	Mongolia	Panama	Kyrgyz Republic	Latvia	Estonia	Jordan	Georgia	Albania	Oman	Croatia	Lithuania	Moldova	China	Chinese Taipei	Armenia	FYROM	Nepal (LDC)	Cambodia (LDC)	Saudi Arabia	Viet Nam	Tonga
Construction	■	■	■	■	■	■	■	■	■	■	■	■	■	■	■	■	■	■	■	■	■	■	■
Distribution	■	■	■	■	■	■	■	■	■	■	■	■	■	■	■	■	■	■	■	■	■	■	■
Educational		■		■	■	■	■	■	■	■	■	■	■	■	■	■	■	■	■	■	■	■	■
Environmental	■	■		■	■	■	■	■	■	■	■	■	■	■	■	■	■	■	■	■	■	■	■
Financial: - insurance	■	■	■	■	■	■	■	■	■	■	■	■	■	■	■	■	■	■	■	■	■	■	■
- banking and other	■	■	■	■	■	■	■	■	■	■	■	■	■	■	■	■	■	■	■	■	■	■	■
Health and Social	■	■		■	■	■	■	■	■	■	■	■	■	■		■	■		■	■	■	■	■
Tourism	■	■	■	■	■	■	■	■	■	■	■	■	■	■	■	■	■	■	■	■	■	■	■
Recreational	■	■		■	■	■	■	■	■	■		■	■	■		■	■	■	■	■	■	■	■
Transport : - maritime transport					■	■	■	■	■	■	■	■	■	■	■					■	■	■	■
- air transport	■	■		■	■	■	■	■	■	■	■	■	■	■	■	■	■	■	■	■	■	■	■
- rail transport		■			■		■		■			■	■	■	■	■	■	■			■	■	
- road transport	■	■			■	■	■		■	■		■	■	■	■	■	■	■		■		■	
TOTAL SECTORS 26	18	21	11	18	26	23	24	23	25	23	22	24	24	25	22	23	24	22	19	22	24	25	22

MFN Exemptions: all except Mongolia, Kyrgyz Republic and Omani.

trade) than under other modes, while commitments under mode 2 (consumption abroad) tend to be unrestricted. Third, a relatively higher number of limitations tend to be attached to commitments under modes 3 (commercial presence) and 4 (movement of natural persons). Examples of limitations under mode 3 include foreign equity limits, restrictions on the type of legal entity and limitations on the number of suppliers. Mode 4 commitments are usually set out in the horizontal section of the Schedule. Commitments cover some or all of the following categories of natural persons: intra-corporate transferees in senior management, executive or specialist positions; services salespersons; persons responsible for setting up a commercial presence; contractual service suppliers (employees of juridical persons) and independent professionals. These categories are usually defined in the horizontal section, which also specifies the length of stay permitted and any other market access or national treatment limitations.

While the importance of the different modes varies from sector to sector it has been estimated that mode 1 accounts for about 35 percent of commercial services trade, mode 2 for 10 to 15 percent, mode 3 for about 50 percent and mode 4 for 1–2 percent of such trade.[360]

360 WTO International Trade Statistics, 2005, p. 8.

ANNEXES

Annex 1

STATISTICAL SURVEY

ANNEX 1.1 OVERVIEW

The WTO Membership
Statistical Information (2005)

Category	Total trade (US$, million)	GDP (US$, million)	Population (thousand)
1. Original WTO Members (128)			
Total (absolute)	22,247,651	39,771,400	4,246,640
Total (% world)	85.82%	89.44%	66.67%
2. Acceded WTO Members (23)			
Total (absolute)	2,633,500	3,213,328	1,543,146
Total (% world)	10.16%	7.23%	24.23%
1 + 2 Total WTO Members (151)			
Total (absolute)	24,881,151	42,984,728	5,789,786
Total (% of world)	95.98%	96.67%	90.90%
3. Acceders (32)			
Total (absolute)	1,029,421	1,470,156	538,602
Total (% world)	3.97%	3.31%	8.46%
1 + 2 + 3 Total WTO Members and Acceders (182)			
Total (absolute)	25,910,571	44,454,884	6,328,387
Total (% of world)	99.95%	99.98%	99.35%
4. Other UN Member States (13)			
Total (absolute)	13,547	10,883	41,280
Total (% world)	0.05%	0.03%	0.70%
1 + 2 + 3 + 4 = World (195)			
Total (absolute)	25,924,118	44,465,667	6,369,668
Total (%)	100.00%	100.00%	100.00%

Note: Trade: imports and exports of merchandise and commercial services. Percentages may not sum to 100%, due to rounding. For statistical information, notes, and sources, see Annex 1.2.

ANNEX 1.2 DETAILS

The WTO membership statistical information (2005)

	Category	Trade (US$, million)							
		Merchandise trade		Trade in commercial services					
		Imports	Exports	Imports	Exports	TOTAL	GDP (current US$, million)	Population (thousand)	GDP/capita (US$/capita)
Original WTO Members (128)									
	Total (absolute)	9,302,102	8,663,637	2,063,042	2,218,870	22,247,651	39,771,400	4,246,640	9,504
	Total (% world)	86.7%	82.8%	89.5%	91.5%	85.8%	89.4%	66.7%	
Acceded WTO Members (under Art. XII) (23)									
1	Albania	2,618	658	1,318	1,154	5,748	8,380	3,130	2,678
2	Armenia	1,768	950	377	323	3,418	4,903	3,016	1,625
3	Bulgaria	18,181	11,725	3,457	4,288	37,651	26,648	7,740	3,443
4	Cambodia	3,927	3,140	620	1,052	8,739	6,187	14,071	440
5	China	659,953	761,953	83,173	73,909	1,578,988	2,234,297	1,304,500	1,713
6	Croatia	18,560	8,773	3,349	9,920	40,602	38,506	4,443	8,666
7	Ecuador	10,309	10,100	2,049	940	23,398	36,489	13,228	2,758
8	*Estonia* (EU)*	10,212	7,693	2,132	3,117	23,153	13,101	1,346	9,733
9	FYR Macedonia	3,228	2,041	483	445	6,198	5,766	2,034	2,835
10	Georgia	2,491	867	578	631	4,567	6,395	4,474	1,429
11	Jordan	10,506	4,302	2,465	2,188	19,461	12,712	5,473	2,323
12	Kyrgyz Republic	1,108	672	287	234	2,301	2,441	5,144	475
13	*Latvia* (EU)*	8,697	5,161	1,541	2,137	17,536	15,826	2,301	6,879
14	*Lithuania* (EU)*	15,548	11,807	1,989	3,074	32,419	25,625	3,414	7,505
15	Moldova	2,293	1,091	418	409	4,211	2,917	4,206	694
16	Mongolia	1,184	1,065	495	382	3,127	1,880	2,554	736
17	Nepal	1,860	830	424	271	3,385	7,391	27,133	272
18	Oman	8,816	18,692	3,052	822	31,381	30,834	2,567	12,012

(*cont.*)

19	Panama	4,180	1,018	1,673	3,106	9,977	15,467	3,232	4,786
20	Saudi Arabia	59,409	180,737	14,239	5,916	260,302	309,779	23,119	13,399
21	Chinese Taipei	182,708	198,169	31,420	25,574	437,871	355,063	22,800	15,573
22	Viet Nam	36,978	32,442	5,282	4,176	78,878	52,408	83,119	631
23	Tonga	120	10	33	26	190	214	102	2,090
	Total (absolute)	1,064,655	1,263,896	160,853	144,096	2,633,500	3,213,228	1,543,146	2,082
	Total (% world)	9.9%	12.1%	7.0%	5.9%	10.2%	7.2%	24.2%	
Acceders (32)									
1	Afghanistan	2,520	340	. . .	. . .	2,860	7,308	. . .	. . .
2	Algeria	20,357	46,001	2,997	1,825	71,181	102,256	32,854	3,112
3	Andorra	. . .	. . .	. . .	. . .	. . .	66	. . .	. . .
4	Azerbaijan	4,211	4,347	2,625	625	11,808	12,561	8,388	1,498
5	Bahamas	2,230	562	1,296	2,455	6,542	5,502	323	17,031
6	Belarus	16,708	15,979	1,213	1,942	35,842	29,566	9,776	3,024
7	Bhutan	386	258	57	46	748	844	637	1,325
8	Bosnia and Herzegovina	7,108	2,406	449	1,010	10,972	9,949	3,907	2,546
9	Cape Verde	438	18	201	252	908	983	507	1,940
10	Comoros	95	14	45	39	193	387	600	645
11	Equatorial Guinea	2,109	7,136	1,484	51	10,780	6,416	504	12,742
12	Ethiopia	4,127	903	1,178	789	6,997	11,174	71,256	157
13	Iran, Islamic Rep. of	38,238	56,252	. . .	. . .	94,490	189,784	68,251	2,781
14	Iraq	23,430	24,096	. . .	. . .	47,526	12,602	. . .	. . .
15	Kazakhstan	17,353	27,849	7,404	2,019	54,624	57,124	15,146	3,772
16	Lao, People's Dem. Rep. of	809	506	. . .	. . .	1,315	2,875	5,924	485
17	Lebanon	9,633	2,337	7,838	10,740	30,548	21,944	3,577	6,135
18	Liberia	324	131	. . .	. . .	455	548	3,283	167
19	Libyan Arab Jamahiriya	7,000	30,110	2,128	419	39,657	38,756	5,853	6,621
20	Russian Federation	125,303	243,569	38,465	24,435	431,772	763,720	143,114	5,336
21	Samoa	187	12	51	111	361	404	185	2,184
22	Sao Tomé and Principe	50	3	23	18	93	71	157	451
23, 24	Serbia and Montenegro	11,635	5,065	1,478	1,909	20,088	26,215	8,064	3,251
25	Seychelles	676	340	251	346	1,613	694	84	8,209
26	Sudan	6,757	4,824	1,801	101	13,482	27,542	36,233	760
27	Syrian Arab Republic	9,520	8,708	2,136	2,827	23,191	26,320	19,043	1,382

		Trade (US$, million)							
		Merchandise trade		Trade in commercial services					
	Category	Imports	Exports	Imports	Exports	TOTAL	GDP (current US$, million)	Population (thousand)	GDP/capita (US$/capita)
28	Tajikistan	1,330	909	250	103	2,592	2,312	6,507	355
29	Ukraine	36,136	34,287	6,962	8,913	86,298	82,876	47,075	1,761
30	Uzbekistan	3,666	4,749	425	660	9,500	13,951	26,167	533
31	Vanuatu	140	39	68	104	352	341	211	1,611
32	Yemen	4,865	6,380	1,103	285	12,632	15,066	20,975	718
	Total (absolute)	357,340	528,130	81,929	62,022	1,029,421	1,470,156	538,602	2,708
	Total (% world)	3.3%	5.0%	3.6%	2.6%	4.0%	3.3%	8.4%	
Total WTO Members (151)									
	Total (absolute)	10,366,756	9,927,533	2,223,895	2,362,966	24,881,150	42,984,728	5,789,786	7,424
	Total (% world)	96.6%	94.9%	96.4%	97.4%	96.0%	96.7%	90.9%	
Total WTO and Acceders (183)									
	Total (absolute)	10,724,096	10,455,663	2,305,824	2,424,988	25,910,571	44,454,885	6,328,387	7,025
	Total (% world)	99.9%	99.9%	100.0%	100.0%	99.9%	100.0%	99.3%	
UN Member-States outside the WTO system (13)									
1	Eritrea	495	10	...	...	505	970	4,401	220
2	Kiribati	74	4	...	...	78	76	99	772
3	Korea, Dem. People's Rep. of	2,718	1,338	...	...	4,056	...	22,488	...
4	Marshall Islands	95	16	...	...	111	144	63	2,282
5	Micronesia (Fed. States of)	137	20	...	...	157	232	110	2,097
6	Monaco	...	...	...	...	...	...	33	...
7	Nauru	...	...	...	...	...	...	...	...
8	Palau	98	6	...	...	104	145	20	7,197
9	San Marino	...	...	...	...	...	900	28	31,915
10	Somalia	...	...	...	...	...	...	8,228	...
11	Timor-Leste	...	...	...	...	...	349	976	358
12	Turkmenistan	3,588	4,935	...	...	8,523	8,067	4,833	1,669

(cont.)

13	Tuvalu	13	0	. . .	. . .	13	. . .	. . .	. . .
	Total (absolute)	7,218	6,329	. . .	. . .	13,547	10,883	41,280	827
	Total (% world)	0.1%	0.1%	. . .	. . .	0.1%	0.0%	0.7%	
	WORLD TOTAL	10,731,314	10,461,992	2,305,824	2,424,988	25,924,118	44,465,667	6,369,668	

Source: WTO Secretariat, using the WTO Statistics Database; World Bank, World Development Indicators and National Income Statistics of Chinese Taipei.

Notes: Total merchandise trade is defined according to the general trade definition, which includes trade flows in regard to warehoused and re-exported goods. It covers all types of inward and outward movement of goods through a country or territory including movements through customs warehouses and free zones. Goods include all merchandise that either add to or reduce the stock of material resources of a country or territory by entering (imports) or leaving (exports) the country's economic territory.

The EC(22) total refer to the sum of the individual member States and do not include adjustment for under-recorded intra-EC imports due to the Intrastate system of collecting trade statistics.

Extra-EC(22) is the difference between the total and intra-trade of EC(22).

World (total) is the sum of the above statistics. It is calculated on the basis of total EC trade (intra plus extra) and the import figure is not adjusted for under-recorded intra-EC imports.

Commercial services: In the fifth edition of the Balance of Payments Manual, the current account is subdivided into goods, services (including government services, n.i.e.), income (investment income and compensation of employees), and current transfers. The commercial services category in this report is defined as being equal to services minus government services, n.i.e. Commercial services is further sub-divided into transport, travel, and other commercial services.

GDP (current US$):GDP at purchaser's prices is the sum of gross value added by all resident producers in the economy plus any product taxes and minus any subsidies not included in the value of the products. It is calculated without making deductions for depreciation of fabricated assets or for depletion and degradation of natural resources. Data are in current U.S. dollars. Dollar figures for GDP are converted from domestic currencies using single year official exchange rates. For a few countries where the official exchange rate does not reflect the rate effectively applied to actual foreign exchange transactions, an alternative conversion factor is used.

Population, total: Total population is based on the de facto definition of population, which counts all residents regardless of legal status or citizenship–except for refugees not permanently settled in the country of asylum, who are generally considered part of the population of their country of origin.

Symbols

. . . = not available.

- = not applicable.

Annex 2

WTO PROVISIONS ON ACCESSION

ACCESSION PROVISION OF THE MARRAKESH AGREEMENT

Article XII

Accession

1. Any State or separate customs territory possessing full autonomy in the conduct of its external commercial relations and of the other matters provided for in this Agreement and the Multilateral Trade Agreements may accede to this Agreement, on terms to be agreed between it and the WTO. Such accession shall apply to this Agreement and the Multilateral Trade Agreements annexed thereto.
2. Decisions on accession shall be taken by the Ministerial Conference. The Ministerial Conference shall approve the agreement on the terms of accession by a two-thirds majority of the Members of the WTO.
3. Accession to a Plurilateral Trade Agreement shall be governed by the provisions of that Agreement.

OTHER RELEVANT PROVISIONS OF THE MARRAKESH AGREEMENT

Article IV:2

2. There shall be a General Council composed of representatives of all the Members, which shall meet as appropriate. In the intervals between meetings of the Ministerial Conference, its functions shall be conducted by the General Council. The General Council shall also carry out the functions assigned to it by this Agreement. The General Council shall establish its rules of procedure and approve the rules of procedure for the Committees provided for in paragraph 7.

Article IX [Extract]

Decision-Making

1. The WTO shall continue the practice of decision-making by consensus followed under GATT 1947. Except as otherwise provided, where a decision cannot be arrived at by consensus, the matter at issue shall be decided by voting. At meetings of the Ministerial Conference and the General Council, each Member of

the WTO shall have one vote. Where the European Communities exercise their right to vote, they shall have a number of votes equal to the number of their member States which are Members of the WTO. Decisions of the Ministerial Conference and the General Council shall be taken by a majority of the votes cast, unless otherwise provided in this Agreement or in the relevant Multilateral Trade Agreement.

2. The Ministerial Conference and the General Council shall have the exclusive authority to adopt interpretations of this Agreement and of the Multilateral Trade Agreements. In the case of an interpretation of a Multilateral Trade Agreement in Annex 1, they shall exercise their authority on the basis of a recommendation by the Council overseeing the functioning of that Agreement. The decision to adopt an interpretation shall be taken by a three-fourths majority of the Members. This paragraph shall not be used in a manner that would undermine the amendment provisions in Article X.

Article XIII

Non-Application of Multilateral Trade Agreements between Particular Members

1. This Agreement and the Multilateral Trade Agreements in Annexes 1 and 2 shall not apply as between any Member and any other Member if either of the Members, at the time either becomes a Member, does not consent to such application.

2. Paragraph 1 may be invoked between original Members of the WTO which were contracting parties to GATT 1947 only where Article XXXV of that Agreement had been invoked earlier and was effective as between those contracting parties at the time of entry into force for them of this Agreement.

3. Paragraph 1 shall apply between a Member and another Member which has acceded under Article XII only if the Member not consenting to the application has so notified the Ministerial Conference before the approval of the agreement on the terms of accession by the Ministerial Conference.

4. The Ministerial Conference may review the operation of this Article in particular cases at the request of any Member and make appropriate recommendations.

5. Non-application of a Plurilateral Trade Agreement between parties to that Agreement shall be governed by the provisions of that Agreement.

Article XVI [Extract]

Miscellaneous Provisions

1. Except as otherwise provided under this Agreement or the Multilateral Trade Agreements, the WTO shall be guided by the decisions, procedures and customary practices followed by the CONTRACTING PARTIES to GATT 1947 and the bodies established in the framework of GATT 1947.

OTHER PROVISIONS

WTO document WT/L/93

DECISION-MAKING PROCEDURES UNDER ARTICLES IX AND XII OF THE WTO AGREEMENT

Statement by the Chairman

As agreed by the General Council on 15 November 1995

On occasions when the General Council deals with matters related to requests for waivers or accessions to the WTO under Articles IX or XII of the WTO Agreement respectively, the General Council will seek a decision in accordance with Article IX:1. Except as otherwise provided, where a decision cannot be arrived at by consensus, the matter at issue shall be decided by voting under the relevant provisions of Articles IX or XII.

The above procedure does not preclude a Member from requesting a vote at the time the decision is taken.

Consequently, if any Member has a particular problem with a proposed decision regarding a request for a waiver or an accession to the WTO, it should ensure its presence at the meeting in which this matter will be considered. The absence of a Member will be assumed to imply that it has no comments on or objections to the proposed decision on the matter.

WTO document WT/GC/M/8

WTO decision-making under Articles IX and XII of the WTO Agreement

The Chairman said that there had been some discussion concerning the manner in which the General Council should take decisions in relation to waivers or accessions to the WTO, which had centred on whether the General Council should seek to adopt such decisions by consensus or whether it should proceed automatically to a vote. After prolonged and wide-ranging consultations on this matter, he proposed a short statement by the Chair to clarify this issue, and underlined that the statement referred only to decision-making procedures under Articles IX and XII of the WTO Agreement and did not change in any way the provisions of the WTO Agreement. If this statement was acceptable, a footnote would be added to any item on a General Council agenda relating to waivers or accessions, in order to draw the attention of Members prior to the General Council meeting. He then read out the proposed text as follows: "On occasions when the General Council deals with matters related to requests for waivers or accessions to the WTO under Articles IX or XII of the WTO Agreement respectively, the General Council will seek a decision in accordance with Article IX:1. Except as otherwise provided, where a decision cannot be arrived at by consensus, the matter at issue shall be decided by voting under the relevant provisions of Articles IX or XII. The above procedure does not preclude a Member from requesting a vote at the time the decision is taken. Consequently, if any Member has a particular problem with a proposed decision regarding a request for a waiver or an accession to the WTO, it should ensure its presence at the meeting in which this matter will be considered. The absence of a Member will be assumed to imply that it has no comments on or objections to the proposed decision on the matter".

The representative of India said his delegation would join in a consensus on the statement by the Chairman on an *ad referendum* basis and on the basis of the following understandings: (i) the statement by the Chairman was for the purpose of organizing the General Council's work relating to waivers and accessions smoothly without, at the same time, adversely affecting Members' rights under the WTO Agreement; (ii) the proposed procedure, which was limited to accessions and waivers, would not be extrapolated or used as a precedent for any other situation; (iii) the phrase "except as otherwise provided" in Article IX meant that where a WTO Agreement provided for decision-making only by consensus, that decision had to be taken only by consensus. India noted with satisfaction that the Chairman's proposed statement had reproduced the phrase "except as otherwise provided" as contained in Article IX. In the specific situation at hand, India was proceeding on the basis that the requirement of consensus referred to in footnote 4 of Article IX was not in any manner impaired; (iv) the Secretariat would make special arrangements to ensure that communications regarding meetings which would include in their agenda items relating to accessions and waivers would be sent to non Geneva-based delegations in time so that they could attend the meetings, if they so desired, without difficulty; (v) in the unfortunate event of voting becoming necessary in respect of any waiver or accession matter, the Chairman would devise a system by which non Geneva-based delegations, even if they were not present in that particular meeting, had an opportunity to participate in the voting process.[1]

The General Council took note of the statements and agreed to the procedures regarding decision-making under Articles IX and XII of the WTO Agreement as proposed by the Chairman (WT/L/93).

Annex 3

MINISTERIAL DECLARATIONS (ACCESSION-RELATED PARAGRAPHS)

SINGAPORE MINISTERIAL DECLARATION

WTO document WT/MIN(96)/DEC

Adopted on 13 December 1996

8. It is important that the 28 applicants now negotiating accession contribute to completing the accession process by accepting the WTO rules and by offering meaningful market access commitments. We will work to bring these applicants expeditiously into the WTO system.

GENEVA MINISTERIAL CONFERENCE

WTO document WT/MIN(98)/DEC/1

Adopted on 20 May 1998

7. We welcome the WTO Members who have joined since we met in Singapore: Congo, Democratic Republic of Congo, Mongolia, Niger and Panama. We welcome the progress made with 31 applicants currently negotiating their accession and renew our resolution to ensure that the accession processes proceed as rapidly as possible. We recall that accession to the WTO requires full respect of WTO rules and disciplines as well as meaningful market access commitments on the part of acceding candidates.

DOHA MINISTERIAL CONFERENCE

WTO document WT/MIN(01)/DEC/1

Adopted on 14 November 2001

9. We note with particular satisfaction that this Conference has completed the WTO accession procedures for China and Chinese Taipei. We also welcome the accession as new Members, since our last Session, of Albania, Croatia, Georgia, Jordan, Lithuania, Moldova and Oman, and note the extensive market-access commitments already made by these countries on accession. These accessions will greatly strengthen the multilateral trading system, as will those of the 28 countries now negotiating their accession. We therefore attach great importance to concluding

accession proceedings as quickly as possible. In particular, we are committed to accelerating the accession of least-developed countries.

38. We confirm that technical cooperation and capacity building are core elements of the development dimension of the multilateral trading system, and we welcome and endorse the New Strategy for WTO Technical Cooperation and Capacity Building, Growth and Integration. We instruct the Secretariat, in coordination with other relevant agencies, to support domestic efforts for mainstreaming trade into national plans for economic development and strategies for poverty reduction. The delivery of WTO technical assistance shall be designed to assist developing and least-developed countries in transition to adjust to WTO rules and disciplines, implement obligations and exercise the rights of membership, including drawing on the benefits of an open, rules-based multilateral trading system. Priority shall also be accorded to small, vulnerable, and transition economies, as well as to Members and Observers without representation in Geneva. We reaffirm our support for the valuable work of the International Trade Centre, which should be enhanced.

42. . . . We agree to work to facilitate and accelerate negotiations with acceding LDCs. We instruct the Secretariat to reflect the priority we attach to LDCs' accessions in the annual plans for technical assistance.

CANCÚN MINISTERIAL CONFERENCE

WTO document WT/MIN(03)/20

Adopted on 23 September 2003

2. At this meeting we have welcomed Cambodia and Nepal as the first least-developed countries to accede to the WTO since its establishment.

HONG KONG MINISTERIAL CONFERENCE

WTO document WT/MIN(05)/DEC

Adopted on 22 December 2005

59. We reaffirm our strong commitment to making the WTO truly global in scope and membership. We welcome those new Members who have completed their accession processes since our last Session, namely Nepal, Cambodia and Saudi Arabia. We note with satisfaction that Tonga has completed its accession negotiations to the WTO. These accessions further strengthen the rules-based multilateral trading system. We continue to attach priority to the 29 ongoing accessions with a view to concluding them as rapidly and smoothly as possible. We stress the importance of facilitating and accelerating the accession negotiations of least-developed countries, taking due account of the guidelines on LDC accession adopted by the General Council in December 2002.

Annex 4

GUIDELINES FOR ACCESSION OF LEAST-DEVELOPED COUNTRIES

WTO document WT/L/508 of 20 January 2003

Decision of 10 December 2002

The General Council,

Having regard to paragraph 2 of Article IV and paragraph 1 of Article XII of the Marrakesh Agreement Establishing the World Trade Organization (the "WTO Agreement"), the commitment made by Ministers, in paragraph 42 of the Doha Ministerial Declaration of 14 November 2001, to facilitate and accelerate the accession negotiations with acceding least-developed countries (LDCs), and the Decision-Making Procedures under Article IX and XII of the WTO Agreement agreed by the General Council (WT/L/93);

Considering the relevant provisions of the WTO Multilateral Trade Agreements, as well as Ministerial Decisions, and WTO legal instruments, on special and differential treatment for developing and least-developed countries;

Conducting the function of the Ministerial Conference in the interval between meetings pursuant to paragraph 2 of Article IV of the WTO Agreement;

Recalling that the Director General shall submit a status report to the Fifth Ministerial Conference on the "Implementation of the commitment by Ministers to facilitate and accelerate the accession of LDCs";

Noting with concern that no LDC has acceded to the Organization in accordance with Article XII of the WTO Agreement since 1995;

Recognizing the need to build on recent progress and for further positive efforts designed to assist LDCs to participate in the rules-based multilateral trading system, as embodied by the WTO and its Agreements;

Taking into account the commitments undertaken by LDC WTO Members at similar levels of development;

Also taking into account the statements made on the accession of LDCs to the WTO:

- By Ministers in the Integrated WTO Plan of Action for the LDCs adopted at the Singapore Ministerial Conference on 13 December 1996;
- by WTO Members at the High Level Meeting on Integrated Initiatives for LDCs' Trade Development on 27–28 October 1997; and
- by the Third United Nations Conference on Least-Developed Countries (LDC-III) in the Brussels Declaration and Programme of Action;
- by LDC Ministers in their Zanzibar Declaration of 24 July 2001; and

Pursuant to the follow-up work undertaken by Members with the adoption of the WTO Work Programme for LDCs on 12 February 2002 (WT/COMTD/LDC/11);

Decides that:

Negotiations for the accession of LDCs to the WTO, be facilitated and accelerated through simplified and streamlined accession procedures, with a view to concluding these negotiations as quickly as possible, in accordance with the guidelines set out hereunder:

1. **MARKET ACCESS**
   - WTO Members shall exercise restraint in seeking concessions and commitments on trade in goods and services from acceding LDCs, taking into account the levels of concessions and commitments undertaken by existing WTO LDCs' Members;
   - acceding LDCs shall offer access through reasonable concessions and commitments on trade in goods and services commensurate with their individual development, financial and trade needs, in line with Article XXXVI.8 of GATT 1994, Article 15 of the Agreement on Agriculture, and Articles IV and XIX of the General Agreement on Trade in Services.
2. **WTO RULES**
   - Special and Differential Treatment, as set out in the Multilateral Trade Agreements, Ministerial Decisions, and other relevant WTO legal instruments, shall be applicable to all acceding LDCs, from the date of entry into force of their respective Protocols of Accession;
   - transitional periods/transitional arrangements foreseen under specific WTO Agreements, to enable acceding LDCs to effectively implement commitments and obligations, shall be granted in accession negotiations taking into account individual development, financial and trade needs;
   - transitional periods/arrangements shall be accompanied by Action Plans for compliance with WTO rules. The implementation of the Action Plans shall be supported by Technical Assistance and Capacity Building measures for the acceding LDCs'. Upon the request of an acceding LDC, WTO Members may coordinate efforts to guide that LDC through the implementation process;
   - commitments to accede to any of the Plurilateral Trade Agreements or to participate in other optional sectoral market access initiatives shall not be a precondition for accession to the Multilateral Trade Agreements of the WTO. As provided in paragraph 5 of Article IX and paragraph 3 of Article XII of the WTO Agreement, decisions on the Plurilateral Trade Agreements shall be adopted by the Members of, and governed by the provisions in, those Agreements. WTO Members may seek to ascertain acceding LDCs interests in the Plurilateral Trade Agreements.

3. **PROCESS**
   - The good offices of the Director-General shall be available to assist acceding LDCs and Chairpersons of the LDCs' Accession Working Parties in implementing this decision;
   - efforts shall continue to be made, in line with information technology means and developments, including in LDCs themselves, to expedite documentation exchange and streamline accession procedures for LDCs to make them more effective and efficient, and less onerous. The Secretariat will assist in this regard. Such efforts will, *inter-alia*, be based upon the WTO Reference Centres that are already operational in acceding LDCs;
   - WTO Members may adopt additional measures in their bilateral negotiations to streamline and facilitate the process, e.g., by holding bilateral negotiations in the acceding LDC if so requested;
   - upon request, WTO Members may through coordinated, concentrated and targeted technical assistance from an early stage facilitate the accession of an acceding LDC.
4. **TRADE-RELATED TECHNICAL ASSISTANCE AND CAPACITY BUILDING**
   - Targeted and coordinated technical assistance and capacity building, by WTO and other relevant multilateral, regional and bilateral development partners, including *inter alia* under the Integrated Framework (IF), shall be provided, on a priority basis, to assist acceding LDCs. Assistance shall be accorded with the objective of effectively integrating the acceding LDC into the multilateral trading system;
   - effective and broad-based technical cooperation and capacity building measures shall be provided, on a priority basis, to cover all stages of the accession process, i.e. from the preparation of documentation to the setting up of the legislative infrastructure and enforcement mechanisms, considering the high costs involved and in order to enable the acceding LDC to benefit from and comply with WTO rights and obligations.

The implementation of these guidelines shall be reviewed regularly in the agenda of the Sub-Committee on LDCs. The results of this review shall be included in the Annual Report of the Committee on Trade and Development to the General Council. In pursuance of their commitments on LDCs' accessions in the Doha Ministerial Declaration, Ministers will take stock of the situation at the Fifth Ministerial Conference and, as appropriate, at subsequent Ministerial Conferences.

Annex 5

DOCUMENTATION AND TIMELINE FOR COMPLETED ACCESSIONS

ANNEX 5.1 WORKING PARTY REPORTS – COMPLETED ACCESSIONS

In the order in which these were adopted.

	Working Party Report	Goods Schedule	Services Schedule
1. Ecuador	WT/L/77 & Corr.1	Add.1 & Add.1/Corr.1, 2	Add.2
2. Bulgaria	WT/ACC/BGR/5 & Corr.1	Add.1	Add.2
3. Mongolia	WT/ACC/MNG/9 & Corr.1	Add.1 & Add.1/Corr.1	Add.2
4. Panama	WT/ACC/PAN/19 & Corr.1	Add.1	Add.2
5. Kyrgyz Republic	WT/ACC/KGZ/26 & Corr.1	Add.1	Add.2
6. Latvia	WT/ACC/LVA/32	Add.1 & Add.1/Corr.1	Add.2
7. Estonia	WT/ACC/EST/28	Add.1	Add.2 & Add.2/Corr.1
8. Jordan	WT/ACC/JOR/33 & Corr. 1	Add.1	Add.2
9. Georgia	WT/ACC/GEO/31	Add.1	Add.2
10. Albania	WT/ACC/ALB/51 & Corr.1	Add.1	Add.2 & Add.2/Corr.1, 2
11. Oman	WT/ACC/OMN/26	Add.1	Add.2
12. Croatia	WT/ACC/HRV/59	Add.1	Add.2 & Add.2/ Corr.1, 2
13. Lithuania	WT/ACC/LTU/52	Add.1 & Add.1/Corr.1	Add.2
14. Moldova	WT/ACC/MOL/37 & Corr.1–4	Add.1	Add.2
15. China	WT/ACC/CHN/49 & Corr.1	Add.1	Add.2
	WT/MIN(01)/3	Add.1	Add.2
16. Chinese Taipei	WT/ACC/TPKM/18	Add.1	Add.2
	WT/MIN(01)/4	Add.1	Add.2
17. Armenia	WT/ACC/ARM/23 & Corr.1	Add.1	Add.2
18. FYROM	WT/ACC/807/27	Add.1	Add.2
19. Nepal	WT/ACC/NPL/16	Add.1	Add.2
	WT/MIN(03)/19		
20. Cambodia	WT/ACC/KHM/21	Add.1	Add.2
	WT/MIN(03)/18		
21. Saudi Arabia	WT/ACC/SAU/61	Add.1	Add.2
22. Viet Nam	WT/ACC/VNM/48	Add.1	Add.2
23. Tonga	WT/ACC/TON/17	Add.1	Add.2
	WT/MIN(05)/4		

ANNEX 5.2 TIMELINE FOR COMPLETED ACCESSIONS

In order of date of WTO accession.

	Ecuador		Bulgaria		Mongolia		Panama		Kyrgyz Republic	
	Date	Time Since Memo	Date	Time Since Memo	Date	Time Since Memo	Date	Time Since Memo	Date	Time Since Memo
Application	09/1992		09/1986		07/1991		08/1991		02/1996	
Working Party Established	10/1992		02/1990		10/1991		10/1991		04/1996	
Memorandum	05/1993		07/1993		01/1992		06/1993		08/1996	
1st Meeting of Working Party	07/1993	2 months	07/1993	1 month	06/1993	1 year 5 months	04/1994	10 months	03/1997	7 months
Draft Working Party Report	10/1994	1 year 5 months	05/1994	10 months	12/1994	2 years 11 months	05/1996	2 years 11 months	04/1998	1 year 8 months
Report Adopted by Working Party	07/1995	2 years 2 months	09/1996	2 years 2 months	06/1996	4 years 5 months	09/1996	2 years 3 months	07/1998	1 year 11 months
Report Adopted by Council	07/1995	2 years 2 months	10/1996	3 years 3 months	07/1996	4 years 6 months	10/1996	3 years 4 months	10/1998	2 years 2 months
Membership	01/1996	2 years 8 months	12/1996	3 years 5 months	01/1997	5 years	09/1997	4 years 3 months	12/1998	2 years 4 months
Total Time	**3 years 4 months**		**10 years 3 months**		**5 years 6 months**		**5 years 1 month**		**2 years 10 months**	

	Latvia		Estonia		Jordan		Georgia		Albania	
	Date	Time Since Memo	Date	Time Since Memo	Date	Time Since Memo	Date	Time Since Memo	Date	Time Since Memo
Application	11/1993		03/1994		01/1994		07/1996		11/1992	
Working Party Established	12/1993		03/1994		01/1994		07/1996		12/1992	
Memorandum	08/1994		03/1994		10/1994		07/1997		01/1995	
1st Meeting of Working Party	03/1995	7 months	11/1994	8 months	10/1996	2 years	03/1998	11 months	04/1996	1 years 3 months
Draft Working Party Report	12/1996	2 years 4 months	11/1998	4 years 8 months	04/1999	4 years 6 months	02/1999	1 year 10 months	07/1999	4 years 6 months
Report Adopted by Working Party	09/1998	4 years 1 month	04/1999	5 years 1 month	11/1999	5 years 1 month	10/1999	2 years 6 months	07/2000	5 years 6 months
Report Adopted by Council	10/1998	4 years 2 months	05/1999	5 years 2 months	12/1999	5 years 2 months	10/1999	2 years 6 months	07/2000	5 years 6 months
Membership	02/1999	4 years 6 months	11/1999	5 years 8 months	04/2000	5 years 6 months	06/2000	3 years 2 months	09/2000	5 years 8 months
Total Time	**5 years**	**3 months**	**5 years**	**8 months**	**6 years**	**4 months**	**4 years**	**1 month**	**7 years**	**10 months**

	Oman		Croatia		Lithuania		Moldova		China	
	Date	Time Since Memo	Date	Time Since Memo	Date	Time Since Memo	Date	Time Since Memo	Date	Time Since Memo
Application	04/1996		09/1993		01/1994		11/1993		07/1986	
Working Party Established	06/1996		10/1993		02/1994		12/1993		03/1987	
Memorandum	06/1996		06/1994		12/1994		12/1996		02/1987	
1st Meeting of Working Party	04/1997	10 months	04/1996	1 year 10 months	11/1995	11 months	06/1997	6 months	10/1987	8 months
Draft Working Party Report	03/1999	2 years 9 months	08/1998	2 years 2 months	06/1997	2 years 6 months	07/1999	2 years 7 months	12/1994	7 years 10 months
Report Adopted by Working Party	09/2000	3 years 3 months	06/2000	6 years	10/2000	5 years 10 months	12/2000	4 years	09/2001	14 years 7 months
Report Adopted by Council	10/2000	3 years 4 months	07/2000	6 years 1 month	12/2000	6 years	05/2001	4 years 5 months	11/2001	14 years 9 months
Membership	11/2000	3 years 5 months	11/2000	6 years 5 months	05/2001	6 years 5 months	07/2001	4 years 7 months	12/2001	14 years 10 months
Total Time		**4 years 7 months**		**7 years 2 months**		**7 years 5 months**		**7 years 4 months**		**15 years 5 months**

	Chinese Taipei		Armenia		FYROM		Nepal		Cambodia		Saudi Arabia	
	Date	Time Since Memo	Date	Time Since Memo	Date	Time Since Memo	Date	Time Since Memo	Date	Time Since Memo	Date	Time Since Memo
Application	01/1992		11/1993		12/1994		05/1989		12/1994		06/1993	
Working Party Established	09/1992		12/1993		12/1994		06/1989		12/1994		07/1993	
Memorandum	10/1992		04/1995		04/1999		08/1998		06/1999		07/1994	
1st Meeting of Working Party	11/1992	1 month	01/1996	9 months	07/2000	1 year	05/2000	1 year	05/2001	1 year	05/1996	1 year
Draft Working Party Report	03/1998	5 years	03/1997	1 year	05/2002	3 months 2 years	06/2003	9 months 4 years	03/2003	11 months 3 years	01/2000	10 months 5 years
Report Adopted by Working Party	09/2001	5 months 8 years	11/2002	11 months 6 years	09/2002	11 months 3 years	08/2003	10 months 5 years	07/2003	9 months 4 years	10/2005	6 months 11 years
Report Adopted by Council	11/2001	11 months 9 years	12/2002	7 months 6 years	10/2002	5 months 3 years	09/2003	5 years	09/2003	1 month 4 years	11/2005	3 months 11 years
Membership	01/2002	1 months 9 years 2 months	02/2003	8 months 6 years 10 months	04/2003	6 months 4 years	04/2004	1 month 5 years 8 months	10/2004	3 months 5 years 4 months	12/2005	4 months 11 years 5 months
Total Time		**10 years**		**9 years 3 months**		**8 years 3 months**		**14 years 11 months**		**9 years 10 months**		**12 years 6 months**

	Viet Nam		Tonga	
	Date	Time Since Memo	Date	Time Since Memo
Application	01/1995		06/1995	
Working Party Established	01/1995		11/1995	
Memorandum	09/1996		05/1998	
1st Meeting of Working Party	07/1998	1 year 10 months	04/2001	2 years 11 months
Draft Working Party Report	11/2004	8 years 2 months	03/2003	4 years 10 months
Report Adopted by Working Party	10/2006	10 years 1 month	12/2005	7 years 7 months
Report Adopted by Council	11/2006	10 years 2 months	12/2005	7 years 7 months
Membership	01/2007	10 years 4 months	07/2007	9 years 2 months
Total Time		**12 years**		**12 years 1 month**

Source: WTO

Annex 6

BASIC FACTUAL INFORMATION TO BE SUPPLIED

ANNEX 6.1 OUTLINE FORMAT FOR A MEMORANDUM ON THE FOREIGN TRADE RÉGIME

WTO document WT/ACC/1, Attachment

I. INTRODUCTION

Statement on the general objectives of the Applicant's trade policy regime and their relation with the objectives of the WTO.

II. ECONOMY, ECONOMIC POLICIES AND FOREIGN TRADE

1. Economy:
   (a) general description (territory, population, economic specialization, main economic indicators);
   (b) current economic situation.
2. Economic Policies:
   (a) main directions of the ongoing economic policies, tactical and strategic goals of the economic policies, pricing policy, economic development plans, privatization plans, sectoral priorities, regional development plans, etc;
   (b) monetary and fiscal policies;
   (c) foreign exchange and payments system, relations with International Monetary Fund, application of foreign exchange controls if any;
   (d) foreign and domestic investment policies;
   (e) competition policies.
3. Foreign trade in goods and services: volume and value of trade, exports and imports, foreign trade balance, structure of trade, trade by geographic areas and dynamics of trade, accompanying statistical data and information on publications (Annex 1 refers).
4. Domestic trade in services including value and composition of foreign direct investment.
5. Information on financial movements related to nationals working abroad, remittances, etc.
6. Information on growth in trade in goods and services over recent years and forecasts for years to come.

III. FRAMEWORK FOR MAKING AND ENFORCING POLICIES AFFECTING FOREIGN TRADE IN GOODS AND TRADE IN SERVICES

1. Powers of executive, legislative and judicial branches of government.
2. Government entities responsible for making and implementing policies affecting foreign trade.
3. Division of authority between central and sub-central governments.
4. Any legislative programmes or plans to change the regulatory regime.
5. Laws and Legal Acts (Annex 2 refers).
6. Description of judicial, arbitral or administrative tribunals or procedures, if any.

IV. POLICIES AFFECTING TRADE IN GOODS

1. Import Regulation:
   (a) registration requirements for engaging in importing;
   (b) characteristics of national tariff (the most recent edition of which should be supplied), customs tariff nomenclature (HS), types of duties, general description of the customs tariff structure, weighted average level of duties on main customs tariff groupings; application of m.f.n. tariff rates, tariff preferences;
   (c) tariff quotas, tariff exemptions;
   (d) other duties and charges, specifying any charges for services rendered;
   (e) quantitative import restrictions, including prohibitions, quotas and licensing systems;
   (f) import licensing procedures (Annex 3 refers);
   (g) other border measures, e.g. any other schemes that have border effects similar to those of the measures listed under (e) above;
   (h) customs valuation (WTO Customs Valuation Agreement (Annex 4 refers), the Brussels Definition of Value, or any other system) whether used only for purposes of levying *ad valorem* rates of duty or for other purposes;
   (i) other customs formalities;
   (j) pre-shipment inspection;
   (k) application of internal taxes on imports;
   (l) rules of origin;
   (m) anti-dumping regime;
   (n) countervailing duty regime;
   (o) safeguard regime.
2. Export Regulation:
   (a) registration requirements for engaging in exporting;

(b) customs tariff nomenclature, types of duties, duty rates, weighted averages of rates;
(c) quantitative export restrictions, including prohibitions, quotas and licensing systems;
(d) export licensing procedures;
(e) other measures, e.g. minimum export prices, voluntary export restrictions, orderly marketing arrangements;
(f) export financing, subsidy and promotion policies;
(g) export performance requirements;
(h) import duty drawback schemes.

3. Internal policies affecting foreign trade in goods:
   (a) industrial policy, including subsidy policies;
   (b) technical regulations and standards, including measures taken at the border with respect to imports (Annex 5 refers);
   (c) sanitary and phytosanitary measures, including measures taken with respect to imports;
   (d) trade-related investment measures;
   (e) state trading practices (Annex 6 refers);
   (f) free zones;
   (g) free economic zones;
   (h) trade-related environmental policies;
   (i) mixing regulations;
   (j) government-mandated counter-trade and barter;
   (k) trade agreements leading to country-specific quotas allocation;
   (l) government procurement practices, including general legal regime and procedures for tendering, dealing with tenders and award of contracts;
   (m) regulation of trade in transit.
4. Policies affecting foreign trade in agricultural products:
   (a) imports – i.e. comprehensive description of the types of border protection maintained: customs duties and/or any other border measures;
   (b) exports – i.e. description of, and the budgetary expenditure and any revenue foregone involved in each of the export subsidy measures in place;
   (c) export prohibitions and restrictions;
   (d) export credits, export credit guarantees or insurance programmes;
   (e) internal policies – i.e. description of, and the budgetary expenditure and any revenue foregone involved in each of the domestic support measures in place.

5. Policies affecting foreign trade in other sectors:
   (a) textiles regime;
   (b) policies affecting foreign trade in other major sectors.

V. TRADE-RELATED INTELLECTUAL PROPERTY RÉGIME

1. General:
   (a) intellectual property policy;
   (b) responsible agencies for policy formulation and implementation;
   (c) membership of international intellectual property conventions and of regional or bilateral agreements;
   (d) application of national and m.f.n. treatment to foreign nationals;
   (e) fees and taxes.
2. Substantive standards of protection, including procedures for the acquisition and maintenance of intellectual property rights:
   (a) copyright and related rights, including rights of performers, producers of phonograms and broadcasting organizations;
   (b) trademarks, including service marks;
   (c) geographical indications, including appellations of origin;
   (d) industrial designs;
   (e) patents;
   (f) plant variety protection;
   (g) layout designs of integrated circuits;
   (h) requirements on undisclosed information, including trade secrets and test data;
   (i) any other categories of intellectual property.
3. Measures to control abuse of intellectual property rights.
4. Enforcement:
   (a) civil judicial procedures and remedies;
   (b) provisional measures;
   (c) any administrative procedures and remedies;
   (d) any special border measures;
   (e) criminal procedures.
5. Laws, decrees, regulations and other legal acts relating to the above.
6. Statistical data on applications for and grants of intellectual property rights, as well as any statistical data on their enforcement.

VI. TRADE-RELATED SERVICES RÉGIME

1. General
   General description of the overall market and regulatory structures of the most prominent services sectors (e.g. financial services,

telecommunications, professional services, construction, tourism, transportation). A complete list of services sectors is found in document MTN.GNS/W/120, the "Services Sectoral Classification List" (Annex 7 refers).

2. Policies Affecting Trade in Services
   General reference to main laws, regulations, rules, procedures, decisions, administrative action and other legal instruments and a description of specific measures affecting trade in services. Distinctions based on modes of supply and/or sectors could be made whenever relevant:
   (a) Government departments, agencies, professional associations or other bodies with authority or a role relevant to the conduct of service activities;
   (b) Judicial, arbitral or administrative tribunals or procedures providing for the review of, or remedies in relation to, administrative decisions affecting trade in services;
   (c) Provisions, including those in international agreements, concerning qualification requirements and procedures, technical standards and licensing and/or registration requirements for the supply of services;
   (d) Provisions governing the existence and operation of monopolies or exclusive service suppliers;
   (e) Provisions relating to safeguard measures as they apply to trade in services;
   (f) Provisions relating to international transfers and payments for current transactions of services;
   (g) Provisions relating to capital transactions affecting the supply of services;
   (h) Provisions governing the procurement by governmental agencies of services;
   (i) Provisions concerning any form of aid, grant, domestic subsidy, tax incentive or promotion scheme affecting trade in services.

Market Access and National Treatment

Limitations or conditions applied to market access and national treatment. Please specify, whether applied on a horizontal (e.g. measures relating to foreign investment regime, movement of persons supplying a services, real estate ownership and conditions of establishment) or a sectoral basis:

(a) Limitations on the number of service suppliers;
(b) Limitations on the total value of service transactions or assets;
(c) Limitations on the total number of service operations or on the total quantity of service output;

(d) Limitations on the total number of natural persons that may be employed in a particular service sector;
(e) Restrictions on, or requirements of specific types of legal entity through which a service may be supplied;
(f) Limitations on the participation of foreign capital;
(g) Measures providing for less than the treatment accorded to national services or service suppliers.

Most-Favoured-Nation Treatment

Indicate any existing measures inconsistent with m.f.n. treatment.

VII. INSTITUTIONAL BASE FOR TRADE AND ECONOMIC RELATIONS WITH THIRD COUNTRIES

1. Bilateral or plurilateral agreements relating to foreign trade in goods and trade in services (Annex 8A refers).
2. Economic integration, customs union and free-trade area agreements (Annex 8B refers).
3. Labour markets integration agreements.
4. Multilateral economic cooperation, membership in the multilateral economic organizations, trade-related programmes of other multilateral organizations.

ANNEX 6.2 STATISTICS AND PUBLICATIONS

WT/ACC/1, ANNEX 1

1. Foreign trade statistics for good and services: responsible agencies.
2. Publications related to statistics.
3. Statistical Data:
   (a) main economic indicators:
      (i) GNP;
      (ii) GNP per capita;
      (iii) budget;
      (iv) production and consumption of the basic goods;
      (v) annual changes in prices;
      (vi) employment in different sectors;
      (vii) levels of employment;
      (viii) balance of payments;
      (ix) foreign exchange.

(b) foreign trade statistics:
   (i) foreign trade (aggregates at the two-digit HS level);
   (ii) export statistics;
   (iii) import statistics;
   (iv) imports from main suppliers, preferably at a tariff line level;
   (v) trade by geographic areas (main trade partners).
(c) government procurement statistics:
   (i) volume of government procurement broken down by:
      – central government, sub-central government and other entities, and within each of these headings;
      – supplies, construction and services.

ANNEX 6.3 LIST OF LAWS AND LEGAL ACTS

WT/ACC/1, Annex 2

1. Laws and legal acts regulating the activity of the customs authorities; responsible agencies.
2. Laws and legal acts relating to non-tariff regulation of imports, exports and trade in transit, rules of origin: responsible agencies.
3. Laws and regulations relating to foreign investment: responsible agencies.
4. Other laws and legal acts dealing with economic issues that affect trade: responsible agencies.
5. (a) Existing, laws, regulations or administrative guidelines which significantly affect trade in services.
   (b) Publications or sources of information, concerning measures of general application, of relevance to the GATS.
   (c) Enquiry points, if any, as foreseen in Article III of GATS.

ANNEX 6.4 INFORMATION ON IMPORT LICENSING PROCEDURES

WT/ACC/1, Annex 3

The following is designed to elicit information on import licensing and similar administrative procedures maintained or applied by the Applicant. If different procedures or methods of licensing or similar administrative procedures are applied to different categories of products, to different countries of supply or to different modes of importation, they should be separately described in respect of each question as relevant.

I. OUTLINE OF SYSTEMS

1. Give a brief description of each licensing system as a whole and, with respect to each, reply to the following questions as relevant, placing all of the material with respect to a given system in sequence together, and using cross references as appropriate when elements which have already been described are also present in another system.

II. PURPOSES AND COVERAGE OF LICENSING

1. Identify each licensing system maintained and state what products, appropriately grouped, are covered.
2. The system applies to goods originating in and coming from which countries?
3. Is the licensing intended to restrict the quantity or value of imports, and if not, what are its purposes? Have alternative methods of accomplishing the purposes been considered and if so which? Why have they not been adopted?
4. Cite the law, regulation and/or administrative order under which the licensing is maintained. Is the licensing statutorily required? Does the legislation leave designation of products to be subjected to licensing to administrative discretion? Is it possible for the government (or the executive branch) to abolish the system without legislative approval?

III. PROCEDURES

1. For products under restriction as to the quantity or value of imports (whether applicable globally or to a limited number of countries or whether established bilaterally or unilaterally):
   (a) Is information published, and where, concerning allocation of quotas and formalities of filing applications for licenses? If not, how is it brought to the attention of possible importers? Of governments and export promotion bodies of exporting countries and their trade representatives? Is the overall amount published? The amount allocated to goods from each country? The maximum amount allocated to each importer?
   (b) How is the size of the quotas determined: on a yearly, six-monthly or quarterly basis? Are there cases where the size of quota is determined on a yearly basis but licenses are issued for imports on a six-monthly or quarterly basis? In the latter case, is it necessary for importers to apply for fresh licence on a six-monthly or quarterly basis?
   (c) Are licenses allotted for certain goods partly or only to domestic producers of like goods? What steps are taken to ensure that licenses

allocated are actually used for imports? Are unused allocations added to quotas for a succeeding period? Are the names of importers to whom licenses have been allocated made known to governments and export promotion bodies of exporting countries upon request? If not, for what reason? (Indicate products to which replies relate.)

(d) From the time of announcing the opening of quotas, as indicated in I above, what is the period of time allowed for the submission of applications for licenses?

(e) What are the minimum and maximum lengths of time for processing applications?

(f) How much time remains, at a minimum, between the granting of licenses and the date of opening of the period of importation?

(g) Is consideration of licence applications effected by a single administrative organ? Or must the application be passed on to other organs for visa, note or approval? If so, which? Does the importer have to approach more than one administrative organ?

(h) If the demand for licenses cannot be fully satisfied, on what basis is the allocation to applicants made? First come, first served? Past performance? Is there a maximum amount to be allocated per applicant and, if so, on what basis is it determined? What provision is made for new importers? Are applications examined simultaneously or on receipt?

(i) In the case of bilateral quotas or export restraint arrangements where export permits are issued by exporting countries, are import licenses also required? If so, are licenses issued automatically?

(j) In cases where imports are allowed on the basis of export permits only, how is the importing country informed of the effect given by the exporting countries to the understanding between the two countries?

(k) Are there products for which licenses are issued on condition that goods should be exported and not sold in the domestic market?

2. Where there is no quantitative limit on importation of a product or on imports from a particular country:

(a) How far in advance of importation must application for a licence be made? Can licenses be obtained within a shorter time-limit or for goods arriving at the port without a licence (for example, owing to inadvertency)?

(b) Can a licence be granted immediately on request?

(c) Are there any limitations as to the period of the year during which application for licence and/or importation may be made? If so, explain.

(d) Is consideration of licence applications effected by a single administrative organ? Or must the application be passed on to other organs for visa, note or approval? If so, which? Does the importer have to approach more than one administrative organ?

3. Under what circumstances may an application for a licence be refused other than failure to meet the ordinary criteria? Are the reasons for any refusal given to the applicant? Have applicants a right of appeal in the event of refusal to issue a licence and, if so, to what bodies and under what procedures?

IV. ELIGIBILITY OF IMPORTS TO APPLY FOR LICENCE

1. Are all persons, firms and institutions eligible to apply for licenses:
   (a) under restrictive licensing systems?
   (b) under non-restrictive systems?

If not, is there a system of registration of persons or firms permitted to engage in importation? What persons or firms are eligible? Is there a registration fee? Is there a published list of authorized importers?

V. DOCUMENTATION AND OTHER REQUIREMENTS FOR APPLICATION FOR LICENCE

1. What information is required in applications? Submit a sample form. What documents is the importer required to supply with the application?
2. What documents are required upon actual importation?
3. Is there any licensing fee or administrative charge? If so, what is the amount of the fee or charge?
4. Is there any deposit or advance payment requirement associated with the issue of licenses? If so, state the amount or rate, whether it is refundable, the period of retention and the purpose of the requirement.

VI. CONDITIONS OF LICENSING

1. What is the period of validity of a licence? Can the validity of a licence be extended? How?
2. Is there any penalty for the non-utilization of a licence or a portion of a licence?
3. Are licenses transferable between importers? If so, are any limitations or conditions attached to such transfer?
4. Are any other conditions attached to the issue of a licence:
   (a) for products subject to quantitative restriction?
   (b) for products not subject to quantitative restriction?

VII. OTHER PROCEDURAL REQUIREMENTS

1. Are there any other administrative procedures, apart from import licensing and similar administrative procedures, required prior to importation?
2. Is foreign exchange automatically provided by the banking authorities for goods to be imported? Is a licence required as a condition to obtaining foreign exchange? Is foreign exchange always available to cover licenses issued? What formalities must be fulfilled for obtaining the foreign exchange?

ANNEX 6.5 INFORMATION ON IMPLEMENTATION AND ADMINISTRATION OF THE CUSTOMS VALUATION AGREEMENT

WT/ACC/1, Annex 4

1. Questions concerning Article 1:
   (a) Sales between related persons:
      (i) Are sales between related persons subject to special provisions?
      (ii) Is the fact of intercompany prices prima facie considered as grounds for regarding the respective prices as being influenced?
      (iii) What is the provision for giving the communication of the aforementioned grounds in writing if the importer so requests? (Article 1.2(a))
      (iv) How has Article 1.2(b) been implemented?
   (b) Price of lost or damaged goods:
   Are there any special provisions or practical arrangements concerning the valuation of lost or damaged goods?
2. How has the provision of Article 4 to allow the importer an option to reverse the order of application of Articles 5 and 6 been implemented?
3. How has Article 5.2 been implemented?
4. How has Article 6.2 been implemented?
5. Questions concerning Article 7:
   (a) What provisions have been made for making value determinations pursuant to Article 7?
   (b) What is the provision for informing the importer of the customs value determined under Article 7?
   (c) Are the prohibitions found in Article 7.2 delineated?
6. How have the options found in Article 8.2 been handled? In the case of f.o.b. application, are ex-factory prices also accepted?
7. Where is the rate of exchange published, as required by Article 9.1?
8. What steps have been taken to ensure confidentiality, as required by Article 10?

9. Questions concerning Article 11:
   (a) What rights of appeal are open to the importer or any other person?
   (b) How is he to be informed of his right to further appeal?
10. Provide information on the publication, as required by Article 12, of:
    (a) (i) the relevant national laws;
    (ii) the regulations concerning the application of the Agreement;
    (iii) the judicial decision and administrative rulings of general application relating to the Agreement;
    (iv) general or specific laws being referred to in the rules of implementation or application.
    (b) Is the publication of further rules anticipated? Which topics would they cover?
11. Questions concerning Article 13:
    (a) How is the obligation of Article 13 (last sentence) being dealt with in the respective legislation?
    (b) Have additional explanations been laid down?
12. Questions concerning Article 16:
    (a) Does the respective national legislation contain a provision requiring customs authorities to give an explanation in writing as to how the customs value was determined?
    (b) Are there any further regulations concerning an above-mentioned request?
13. How have the Interpretative Notes of the Agreement been included?
14. How have the provisions of the Decision of 26 April 1984 on the Treatment of Interest Charges in the Customs Value of Imported Goods (Val/6/Rev.1) been implemented?
15. For those countries applying paragraph 2 of the Decision of 24 September 1984 on the Valuation of Carrier Media Bearing Software for Data Processing Equipment (Val/8), how have the provisions of this paragraph been implemented?
    – For all questions listed above, an indication of the reference is requested.

ANNEX 6.6 INFORMATION ON TECHNICAL BARRIERS TO TRADE

WT/ACC/1, Annex 5

1. Description of relevant laws, regulations, administrative orders, etc, relating to implementation and administration of technical barriers to trade. All necessary references should be provided.

2. Information regarding:
   (a) names of publications, if any, on work relating to draft technical regulations or standards and procedures;
   (b) the name and address of the enquiry point(s) foreseen in Articles 10.1 and 10.3 of the WTO Agreement on Technical Barriers to Trade (the Agreement) with an indication as to whether it is/they are fully operational;
   (c) the name and address of the agency dealing with consultations as foreseen in Article 14 of the Agreement;
   (d) the name and address of agencies that are dealing with other specific functions foreseen in the Agreement;
   (e) the scope of responsibility of the central government authorities in the area of notification requirements foreseen in Article 10.11 of the agreement and of individual government authorities, if the responsibility is divided among two or more such authorities;
   (f) measures and arrangements to ensure that national and sub-national authorities preparing new technical regulations or substantial amendments to existing ones, provide early information on their proposals.

ANNEX 6.7 INFORMATION ON STATE TRADING

WT/ACC/1, Annex 6

INFORMATION ON STATE TRADING

Definition of State Trading[1]

Governmental and non-governmental enterprises, including marketing boards, which have been granted exclusive or special rights or privileges, including statutory or constitutional powers, in the exercise of which they influence through their purchases or sales the level or direction of imports or exports.

Questionnaire on State Trading[1]

I. ENUMERATION OF STATE TRADING ENTERPRISES

1. Does your country maintain enterprises covered by the provisions of Article XVII? If so, list the products or groups of products for which State enterprise is maintained or for which an enterprise has exclusive or special privileges.

[1] This is the working definition for the purposes of notification and does not alter substantive disciplines of Article XVII″ – see Understanding on the Interpretation of Article XVII the GATT1994 annexed to the Marrakesh Agreement Establishing the WTO.

II. REASON AND PURPOSE FOR INTRODUCING AND MAINTAINING STATE TRADING ENTERPRISES

1. State for each product the reason and purpose for introducing and maintaining the enterprise (it should be indicated, for example, whether the purpose or the effect of the enterprise is to prevent prices to consumers from exceeding certain maximum limits, or to protect domestic producers by the control of imports and/or the purchase of domestic supplies at above world price levels, or to facilitate export sales, or to make it possible to establish or administer a stabilization arrangement). A description of the legal provisions should be included in so far as this has not been submitted in earlier notifications.

III. DESCRIPTION OF THE FUNCTIONING OF STATE TRADING ENTERPRISES

1. Describe, item by item, the functioning of such enterprises and state in particular:

   Whether the enterprise deals with exports or with imports, or both;

   Whether private traders are allowed to import or export and, if so, on what conditions; Whether there is free competition between private traders and the State trading enterprise;

   The criteria used for determining the quantities to be exported and imported;

   How export prices are determined; How the mark-up on imported products is determined; How export prices and the re-sale prices of imports compare with domestic prices;

   Whether long-term contracts are negotiated by the State trading enterprise; Whether State trading methods are used to fulfil contractual obligations entered into by the government.

IV. STATISTICAL INFORMATION

1. Furnish statistics (where possible by quantity and value) of imports, exports and national production on the products notified, on the following lines:
   (a) the figures should cover the last three available years;
   (b) the figures for the three groups (imports, exports and national production) should be given, whether possible, in a comparable form;
   (c) the figures should be broken down so as to show:
      (i) trade by the enterprise;
      (ii) other trade.

V. REASONS WHY NO FOREIGN TRADE HAS TAKEN PLACE (IF THIS IS THE CASE) IN PRODUCTS AFFECTED

1. In cases where no foreign trade has taken place in the products affected, state the reasons.

VI. ADDITIONAL INFORMATION

1. Provide any additional information that may be appropriate.

ANNEX 6.8 SERVICES SECTORAL CLASSIFICATION LIST

WTO document MTN.GNS/W/120, also appended to the scheduling guidelines contained in WTO document S/L/92

SERVICES SECTORAL CLASSIFICATION LIST

SECTORS AND SUB-SECTORS		CORRESPONDING CPC
1.	BUSINESS SERVICES	Section B
A.	Professional Services	
a.	Legal Services	861
b.	Accounting, auditing and bookkeeping services	862
c.	Taxation services	863
d.	Architectural services	8671
e.	Engineering services	8672
f.	Integrated engineering services	8673
g.	Urban planning and landscape architectural services	8674
h.	Medical and dental services	9312
i.	Veterinary services	932
j.	Services provided by midwives, nurses, physiotherapists and para-medical personnel	93191
k.	Other	
B.	Computer and Related Services	
a.	Consultancy services related to the installation of computer hardware	841
b.	Software implementation services	842
c.	Data processing services	843
d.	Data base services	844
e.	Other	845+849
C.	Research and Development Services	
a.	R&D services on natural sciences	851

b.	R&D services on social sciences and humanities	852
c.	Interdisciplinary R&D services	853
D.	<u>Real Estate Services</u>	
a.	Involving own or leased property	821
b.	On a fee or contract basis	822
E.	<u>Rental/Leasing Services without Operators</u>	
a.	Relating to ships	83103
b.	Relating to aircraft	83104
c.	Relating to other transport equipment	83101+83102+83105
d.	Relating to other machinery and equipment	83106–83109
e.	Other	832
F.	<u>Other Business Services</u>	
a.	Advertising services	871
b.	Market research and public opinion polling services	864
c.	Management consulting service	865
d.	Services related to man. consulting	866
e.	Technical testing and analysis serv.	8676
f.	Services incidental to agriculture, hunting and forestry	881
g.	Services incidental to fishing	882
h.	Services incidental to mining	883+5115
i.	Services incidental to manufacturing (except for 88442)	884+885
j.	Services incidental to energy distribution	887
k.	Placement and supply services of Personnel	872
l.	Investigation and security	873
m.	Related scientific and technical consulting services	8675
n.	Maintenance and repair of equipment (not including maritime vessels, aircraft or other transport equipment)	633+8861−8866
o.	Building-cleaning services	874
p.	Photographic services	875
q.	Packaging services	876
r.	Printing, publishing	88442
s.	Convention services	87909*
t.	Other	8790
2.	<u>COMMUNICATION SERVICES</u>	
A.	<u>Postal services</u>	7511
B.	<u>Courier services</u>	7512

* The (*) indicates that the service specified is a component of a more aggregated CPC item specified elsewhere in this classification list.

C.	Telecommunication services	
a.	Voice telephone services	7521
b.	Packet-switched data transmission services	7523
c.	Circuit-switched data transmission services	7523**
d.	Telex services	7523**
e.	Telegraph services	7522
f.	Facsimile services	7521**+7529**
g.	Private leased circuit services	7522**+7523**
h.	Electronic mail	7523**
i.	Voice mail	7523**
j.	On-line information and data base retrieval	7523**
k.	electronic data interchange (EDI)	7523**
l.	enhanced/value-added facsimile services, incl. store and forward, store and retrieve	7523**
m.	code and Protocol conversion	n.a.
n.	on-line information and/or data processing (incl.transaction processing)	843**
o.	other	
D.	Audiovisual services	
a.	Motion picture and video tape production and distribution services	9611
b.	Motion picture projection service	9612
c.	Radio and television services	9613
d.	Radio and television transmission services	7524
e.	Sound recording	n.a.
f.	Other	
E.	Other	
3.	CONSTRUCTION AND RELATED ENGINEERING SERVICES	
A.	General construction work for buildings	512
B.	General construction work for civil engineering	513
C.	Installation and assembly work	514+516
D.	Building completion and finishing work	517
E.	Other	511+515+518
4.	DISTRIBUTION SERVICES	
A.	Commission agents' services	621
B.	Wholesale trade services	622
C.	Retailing services	631+632 6111+6113+6121
D.	Franchising	8929

** The (**) indicates that the service specified constitutes only a part of the total range of activities covered by the CPC concordance (e.g. voice mail is only a component of CPC item 7523).

E.	Other	
5.	EDUCATIONAL SERVICES	
A.	Primary education services	921
B.	Secondary education services	922
C.	Higher education services	923
D.	Adult education	924
E.	Other education services	929
6.	ENVIRONMENTAL SERVICES	
A.	Sewage services	9401
B.	Refuse disposal services	9402
C.	Sanitation and similar services	9403
D.	Other	
7.	FINANCIAL SERVICES	
A.	All insurance and insurance-related services	812**
a.	Life, accident and health insurance services	8121
b.	Non-life insurance services	8129
c.	Reinsurance and retrocession	81299*
d.	Services auxiliary to insurance (including broking and agency services)	8140
B.	Banking and other financial services (excl. insurance)	
a.	Acceptance of deposits and other repayable funds from the public	81115–81119
b.	Lending of all types, incl., inter alia, consumer credit, mortgage credit, factoring and financing of commercial transaction	8113
c.	Financial leasing	8112
d.	All payment and money transmission services	81339**
e.	Guarantees and commitments	81199**
f.	Trading for own account or for account of customers, whether on an exchange, in an over-the-counter market or otherwise, the following:	
	– money market instruments (cheques, bills, certificate of deposits, etc.)	81339**
	– foreign exchange	81333
	– derivative products incl., but not limited to, futures and options	81339**
	– exchange rate and interest rate instruments, inclu. products such as swaps, forward rate agreements, etc.	81339**
	– transferable securities	81321*

	– other negotiable instruments and financial assets, incl. bullion	81339**
g.	Participation in issues of all kinds of securities, incl. under-writing and placement as agent (whether publicly or privately) and provision of service related to such issues	8132
h.	Money broking	81339** i.
	Asset management, such as cash or portfolio management, all forms of collective investment management, pension fund management, custodial depository and trust services	8119+** 81323*
j.	Settlement and clearing services for financial assets, incl. securities, derivative products, or and other negotiable instruments	81339** 81319**
k.	Advisory and other auxiliary financial services on all the activities listed in or Article 1B of MTN.TNC/W/50, incl. credit reference and analysis, investment and portfolio research and advice, advice on acquisitions and on corporate restructuring and strategy	8131 8133
l.	Provision and transfer of financial information, and financial data processing and related software by providers of other financial services	8131
C.	<u>Other</u>	
8.	<u>HEALTH RELATED AND SOCIAL SERVICES</u> (other than those listed under 1.A.h-j.)	
A.	<u>Hospital services</u>	9311
B.	<u>Other Human Health Services</u>	9319 (other than 93191)
C.	<u>Social Services</u>	933
D.	<u>Other</u>	
9.	<u>TOURISM AND TRAVEL RELATED SERVICES</u>	
A.	<u>Hotels and restaurants (incl. catering)</u>	641–643
B.	<u>Travel agencies and tour operators services</u>	7471
C.	<u>Tourist guides services</u>	7472
D.	<u>Other</u>	
10.	<u>RECREATIONAL, CULTURAL AND SPORTING SERVICES</u> (other than audiovisual services)	
A.	<u>Entertainment services</u> (including theatre, live bands and circus services)	9619
B.	<u>News agency services</u>	962

C.	Libraries, archives, museums and other cultural services	963
D.	Sporting and other recreational services	964
E.	Other	
11.	TRANSPORT SERVICES	
A.	Maritime Transport Services	
a.	Passenger transportation	7211
b.	Freight transportation	7212
c.	Rental of vessels with crew	7213
d.	Maintenance and repair of vessels	8868**
e.	Pushing and towing services	7214
f.	Supporting services for maritime transport	745**
B.	Internal Waterways Transport	
a.	Passenger transportation	7221
b.	Freight transportation	7222
c.	Rental of vessels with crew	7223
d.	Maintenance and repair of vessels	8868**
e.	Pushing and towing services	7224
f.	Supporting services for internal waterway transport	745**
C.	Air Transport Services	
a.	Passenger transportation	731
b.	Freight transportation	732
c.	Rental of aircraft with crew	734
d.	Maintenance and repair of aircraft	8868**
e.	Supporting services for air transport	746
D.	Space Transport	733
E.	Rail Transport Services	
a.	Passenger transportation	7111
b.	Freight transportation	7112
c.	Pushing and towing services	7113
d.	Maintenance and repair of rail transport equipment	8868**
e.	Supporting services for rail transport services	743
F.	Road Transport Services	
a.	Passenger transportation	7121+7122
b.	Freight transportation	7123
c.	Rental of commercial vehicles with operator	7124
d.	Maintenance and repair of road transport equipment	6112+8867
e.	Supporting services for road transport services	744
G.	Pipeline Transport	
a.	Transportation of fuels	7131
b.	Transportation of other goods	7139

H.	Services auxiliary to all modes of transport	
a.	Cargo-handling services	741
b.	Storage and warehouse services	742
c.	Freight transport agency services	748
d.	Other	749
I.	Other Transport Services	
12.	OTHER SERVICES NOT INCLUDED ELSEWHERE	95+97+98+99

ANNEX 6.9 LISTS OF FOREIGN TRADE AGREEMENTS

WTO document WT/ACC/1, Annex 8

A. List of Foreign Trade Agreements.

B. List of Trade Agreements or parts of them which contain preferential trade provisions, indicating by HS (2 digit) the tariff lines involved, the margin of preference granted, reciprocity provisions and details of any other preferential treatment.

Annex 7

SUPPLEMENTARY FACTUAL INFORMATION

ANNEX 7.1 CHECKLIST OF ILLUSTRATIVE SPS AND TBT ISSUES

WTO document WT/ACC/8
15 November 1999

TECHNICAL NOTE ON THE ACCESSION PROCESS

Note by the Secretariat

Checklist of Illustrative SPS and TBT Issues for Consideration in Accessions

This document has been prepared in consultation with WTO members and reflects the development of "standard form" questionnaires in recent accession Working Parties. It should assist acceding governments in the provision of information which will facilitate discussion in their Working Party on accession, focussing on SPS and TBT issues.

Checklist of Illustrative SPS Issues for Consideration in Accessions

Commitments (by the time of accession)	WTO Reference
1. Standstill: the introduction of new standards, animal health regulations and food safety regulations shall conform to SPS Agreement principles.	1. Generally agreed principle in WTO accession negotiations.
2. Establishment and operation of a single Contact Point for Information ("enquiry point").	2. Article 7 and Annex B.3.
3. Transparency: notification and access to documentation:	3. Articles 7 and Annex B, Also G/SPS/7.
(a) identification of authority responsible for making notifications to the WTO and ensuring transparency obligations are met on an ongoing basis;	(a) Annex B.5.(b) and Annex B.10.

Commitments (by the time of accession)	WTO Reference
(b) establish guidance or law requiring publication of proposed measures at an early stage for comment;	(b) Annex B.5(a).
(c) provision in law or administrative procedure to provide copies of proposed measures to WTO Members; and	(c) Annex B.5.(c).
(d) require in law or administrative procedure, a reasonable period of time for comment from Members and the public, and establishment of a process to take comments into account without discrimination.	(d) Annex B.5(d).
4. Necessity: measures are applied only to the extent necessary to protect human, animal or plant health.	4. Article 2.2.
5. Regulations Based on Science: regulations governing animal and plant health and food safety shall be based on scientific evidence.	5. Articles 2.2, 3.3 and 5.2.
6. Harmonization: to the extent possible, members shall follow international standards, guidelines, and recommendations in establishing SPS measures.	6. Articles 3.1, 3.3 and 3.4.
7. Equivalence: members shall recognize different measures that achieve the same level of protection.	7. Article 4.
8. Risk Assessment: developing scientific evidence and conducting risk assessments to ensure that measures are based on science and applied only to the extent necessary to protect health.	8. Article 5.1, 5.2 and 5.3.
9. Regional conditions: measures take into account the regional characteristics both of the areas from which products originate and the areas for which they are destined.	9. Article 6 and Annexes A.6 and A.7.

Commitments (by the time of accession)	WTO Reference
10. Non-discrimination: measures do not arbitrarily or unjustifiably discriminate between different members or between domestic and foreign suppliers.	10. Article 2.3, and Annex C.1(a) and (d).
11. Control, inspection and approval procedures: ensure that procedures, including systems for approval of the use of additives or for establishing tolerances for contaminants in foods, beverages or feedstuffs comply with the Agreement.	11. Article 8 and Annex C.

Checklist of Illustrative TBT Issues for Consideration in Accessions

Commitments (by the time of accession)	WTO Reference
1. Standstill: the introduction of new standards, technical regulations and conformity assessment procedures should be fully compatible with the TBT Agreement	1. Generally agreed principle in WTO accession negotiations
2. Submission of Statement on Implementation	2. Article 15.2 and TBT Committee Decision (WTO document G/TBT/1)
3. Establishment and operation of a single Contact Point for Information ("inquiry point")	3. Article 10
4. Identification of authority responsible for notifications, publications and other internal procedures to ensure transparency obligations are met on an ongoing basis:	4. Articles 2, 3, 5, 7, 10, 15.2, Annex 3 and WTO document G/TBT/1
(a) identification of publication where notices of proposed technical regulations and conformity assessment procedures will appear;	(a) Articles 2.9.1, 3.1, 5.6.1, 7.1, 10.1.5

Commitments (by the time of accession)	WTO Reference
(b) identification of authority responsible for making notifications to the WTO;	(b) Article 2.9.2, 2.10.1, 3.2, 3.3, 5.6.2, 5.7.1, 7.2, 7.3, 10.7, 10.10
(c) guidance/law to ensure regulatory authorities afford non-discriminatory consideration of comments in the preparation of a final regulation;	(c) Articles 2.9.4, 2.10.3, 3.15 3.3, 5.6.4, 5.7.3, 7.1, 7.3
(d) guidance/law to ensure regulatory authorities allow a reasonable period of time between the final publication of a technical regulation and conformity assessment procedure and its entry into force so that suppliers can adapt;	(d) Articles 2.11, 2.12, 3.1, 5.8, 5.9, 7.1
(e) publication and notification of work programme for standards and non-governmental conformity assessment procedures, including publication of notices of draft standards and an opportunity for public comment.	(e) Article 4, Annex 3 (J, K, L, N, 0); Article 8.1
5. Development and Application of Technical Regulations and Conformity Assessment Procedures: Existence of legal and/or administrative underpinnings (or reasonable measures" as appropriate) to ensure ongoing compliance with provisions of the agreement concerning, in particular:	5. Articles 2, 3, 5, 6, 7
(a) non-discrimination with respect to the treatment of products;	(a) Articles 2.1, 3.1, 5.1, 5.2, 7.1
(b) the prohibition of unnecessary obstacles to international trade and the consideration of less trade-restrictive alternatives to fulfilling legitimate objectives;	(b) Articles 2.2, 3.1, 5.1, 5.2, 7.1
(c) the ongoing review of technical regulations to ensure they are appropriate to achieve the desired legitimate objective;	(c) Article 2.3, 3.1, 7.1

Commitments (by the time of accession)	WTO Reference
(d) the consideration of appropriate international standards, guides and recommendations as a basis for technical regulations and conformity assessment procedures;	(d) Article 2.4, 3.1, 5.4, 7.1
(e) the consideration of equivalent technical regulations of other Members;	(e) Article 2.7, 3.1, 7.1
(f) the acceptance of the results of conformity assessment procedures conducted by bodies in an exporting Member country;	(f) Article 6, 7.1
(g) non-discriminatory and cost-based fee structure.	(g) Article 5.2, 7.1, 10.4
6. Development and Application of Standards and Conformity Assessment Procedures: Existence of legal and/or administrative underpinnings (or "reasonable measures" as appropriate) to ensure ongoing compliance with provisions of the agreement concerning, in particular:	6. Article 4 and Annex 3, Article 8
(a) non-discrimination with respect to the treatment of products;	(a) Annex 3 (D), Article 8.1
(b) the prohibition of unnecessary obstacles to international trade;	(b) Annex 3 (E), Article 8.1
(c) the consideration of appropriate international standards, guides and recommendations as a basis for standards;	(c) Annex 3 (F), Article 8.1
(d) non-discriminatory and cost-based fee structure.	(d) Annex 3 (M), Annex 3 (P), Articles 8.1, 10.4

ANNEX 7.2 INFORMATION TO BE PROVIDED ON DOMESTIC SUPPORT AND EXPORT SUBSIDIES IN AGRICULTURE

WTO document WT/ACC/4 of 18 March 1996

ACCESSION TO THE WORLD TRADE ORGANIZATION

Information to be Provided on Domestic Support and Export Subsidies in Agriculture

Technical Note by the Secretariat

1) The purpose of this technical note is to allow acceding governments to present factual information on their domestic support and export subsidy measures actually in place in agriculture, as required under Section IV, 4(b) and (e) of the Outline Format for a Memorandum on the Foreign Trade Régime (WT/ACC/1), in a manner consistent with the notification requirements of the Agreement on Agriculture. To this end, the following paragraphs are designed to identify agricultural policy measures in the area of domestic support and export subsidies under the Agreement on Agriculture on which such information is required. (The definition of products covered by the Agreement on Agriculture is contained in Annex of the Agreement).

2) To present the information in the prescribed form, the formats used by WTO Members to notify their current measures are proposed as the basis for collection (G/AG/2). Accordingly, the description of any measures maintained by acceding governments should be sufficiently detailed to enable Members to make a judgement as to the relationship between each of the measures in question and the relevant criteria of the Agreement on Agriculture.

3) The information to be provided in this context is without prejudice to any additional information which Members may wish to request from acceding governments on any other aspects of their trade regime on agriculture. In this regard, it should be noted that information on border measures affecting foreign trade in agricultural products should be provided under Section IV, 4 (a) and (c) of the Outline Format.

Domestic Support

4) The Agreement on Agriculture prohibits the use of domestic support in favour of agricultural producers in excess of commitment levels specified in Schedules (Article 3:2 and Article 6) with the exception of support granted by means of three groups of policies:

(i) measures that have no, or at most minimal, trade distortion effects or effects on production and which meet basic and policy-specific criteria and other conditions as set out in Annex 2 of the Agreement on Agriculture; these are known as "green box" measures;

(ii) some measures of assistance, whether direct or indirect, to encourage agricultural and rural development and which are an integral part of the development programmes of developing countries (Article 6:2); and

(iii) direct payments under production-limiting programmes (Article 6:5).

5) The types of measures in operation that may fall into the "green box" include those in the following categories, provided they meet basic and policy specific criteria and conditions as set out in Annex 2 of the Agreement on Agriculture:

General government services; research; pest and disease control; training services; extension and advisory services; inspection services; marketing and promotion services; infrastructural services; public stockholding for food security purposes; domestic food aid; and other similar types of measure.

Direct payments to producers; decoupled income support; income insurance and safety-net programmes; natural disaster relief; producer and resource retirement programmes; investment aids; environmental programmes; regional assistance programmes; and other similar types of measure.

6) Such measures should be listed as set out in Supporting Table DS:1 (attached). In order to do this, the following information is required:

- a description of each measure with reference to the criteria in the relevant section of Annex 2 of the Agreement on Agriculture;
- the monetary value and any revenue foregone involved with each measure, normally using the average of the most recent 3 year period;
- data sources of the above information.

7) For developing countries, the following types of measures may fall into the category of development measures which are also exempt from commitments to be specified in Schedules:

- investment subsidies which are generally available to agriculture;
- agricultural input subsidies, generally available to low-income or resource-poor producers;
- domestic support to producers to encourage diversification from growing illicit narcotic crops.

8) Such measures should be listed as set out on Supporting Table DS:2 (attached). In order to do this, the following information is required:

- a description of each measure with reference to the criteria in Article 6:2 of the Agreement on Agriculture;
- the monetary value and any revenue foregone involved with each measure, normally using the average of the most recent 3 year period;

- data sources of the above information.

9) Direct payments under production-limiting programmes may be exempt from commitments to be specified in Schedules, if they:

(i) are based on fixed area and yields; or
(ii) are made on 85 percent or less of the base level of production; or
(iii) are livestock payments made on a fixed number of head.

10) Such measures should be listed as set out on Supporting Table DS:3 (attached). In order to do this, the following information is required:

- a description of each measure with reference to the criteria in Article 6:5 of the Agreement on Agriculture;
- the monetary value and any revenue foregone involved with each measure, normally using the average of the most recent 3 year period;
- data sources of the above information.

Other Domestic Support Measures

11) As noted above, any other domestic support in favour of agricultural producers is subject to commitments to be specified in Schedules. Under the Agreement on Agriculture the commitments are to be made on the basis of a "Total Aggregate Measurement of Support (Total AMS)" which is an aggregation of support measures provided on a product-specific basis for those measures that affect only one or a limited number of products, and support measures provided on a non-product-specific basis for other measures. The Total AMS, including the Base Total AMS and the Current Total AMS, is defined in Article 1(h) of the Agreement on Agriculture. The AMS is defined in Article 1(a) of the Agreement on Agriculture.

Product-specific AMS measures

12) A product-specific AMS should be calculated for any agricultural product that has any form of administered price operating, for example, as part of a programme to stabilize prices, trigger public intervention, trigger direct payments (e.g. deficiency payments) or provide minimum income levels, etc. In addition, any other type of product-specific measure (such as product-specific fertilizer or transport subsidies) should also be included in the product-specific AMS.

13) An AMS should be calculated for each basic agricultural product, as close as practicable to the point of first sale of the product concerned, on which these measures operate, including support at both the national and the sub-national level. The calculation of the product-specific AMS is described in Annex of the Agreement on Agriculture[1].

[1] It may not be practicable to calculate the AMS however, if, for example, an appropriate world price for the product in question cannot be established (c.f. paragraph 15 below). If this is the case, an "equivalent measurement of support" may need to be established as set out in Annex of the Agreement on Agriculture (Supporting Table DS:8 attached).

14) In order to calculate a product-specific AMS for these products, relevant tables from Supporting Tables DS:5 to DS:7 (attached) should be used.
15) The information required in these tables is, for each product covered, the following:

- for any domestic support measure that affects the producer price (normally for each of the last three years:
- the applied administered price;
- an external reference price, e.g. an estimate of the world price such as the c.i.f. price or f.o.b. price. This price should be adjusted to a similar stage of processing as the administered price. (For deficiency payments, the reference price should be that used for determining payments);
- the amount of eligible production that receives the administered price;
- the budgetary cost of price-related non-exempt direct payments (where this is the option used under paragraph 10 of Annex 3 of the Agreement on Agriculture);
- the value of any associated fees or levies.
- for other measures (for the same period):
- the budgetary expenditures and any revenue foregone involved with the measure for each product;
- the value of any associated fees or levies.
- data sources of the above information.

16) For any measure which affects the producer price, Supporting Table DS:5 should be used unless the measure in question involves direct payments from the government to producers, in which case Supporting Table DS:6 should be used. The results of the calculations in Supporting Tables DS:5 and DS:6 should, along with the budgetary cost (or revenue foregone) of other measures, be entered in Supporting Table DS:7 which allows all product-specific AMS to be totalled. For more details on the calculation methodology of the product-specific AMS, see Annex of the Agreement on Agriculture.
17) Note, however, that the Agreement on Agriculture (Article 6:4) provides for a "de minimis" level of 5 percent (developed countries) or 10 percent (developing countries) of the value of production of the product concerned. If the information provided shows that product-specific AMS represents less than the "de minimis" percentage, the product-specific AMS may be exempted from the commitments to be included in Schedules.

The non-product-specific AMS

18) For measures not included in the product-specific AMS, a non-product-specific AMS should be calculated by aggregating the value of any non-exempt non-product-specific measures such as input subsidies (e.g. fertilizer or transport subsidies) and credit and other financial input assistance.

19) In order to calculate this AMS as shown in Supporting Table DS:9 (attached), the following information is required, normally for each of the three most recent years:

- the budgetary outlays and any revenue foregone involved with each measure;
- the value of any associated fees and levies;
- date sources of the above information.

20) As with the product-specific AMS, if the information provided shows that the value of the non-product-specific AMS does not exceed 5 percent (developed) or 10 percent (developing) of the total value of agricultural production, the de minimis provision may apply (Article 6:4).

Aggregating AMS commitments

21) As commitments to be included in Schedules under the Agreement on Agriculture are made on the Total AMS (the aggregate of all individual AMS and any equivalent measurements of support) Supporting Table DS:4 (attached) can be used to get an aggregate figure. This need only include AMS that are over the relevant de minimis level (if any).

Export Subsidies

22) The Agreement on Agriculture prohibits the use of those export subsidies listed in Article 9:1 with the exception of those that apply to products explicitly specified in Schedules (Article 3:3). Such subsidies include (for more precision, see Article 9:1):

(a) direct subsidies contingent on export performance;
(b) the sale or disposal for export of non-commercial stocks at a price lower than that in the domestic market;
(c) payments on exports financed by virtue of governmental action including those financed from the proceeds of a levy on producers;
(d) subsidies to reduce the costs of marketing exports (other than widely available export promotion and advisory services) including handling, upgrading and other processing costs, and the costs of international transport and freight;
(e) internal transport charges on export shipments on terms more favourable than for domestic shipments; and,
(f) subsidies on agricultural products contingent on their incorporation in exported products.

23) Developing countries may not be required, during the implementation period of the Agreement on Agriculture, to take commitments on subsidies in categories (d) and (e) listed in paragraph 19 (Article 9:4).

24) Acceding governments should provide information on the amount of subsidy and the quantity of subsidized product exported, if any, for each category of export subsidy. In order to do this, Supporting Table ES:1 (attached) should be used which requires the following data, normally for each of the last three years:

- the budgetary expenditures and any revenue foregone involved with each measure for each product;
- the quantity of product exported that received such subsidies and a detailed description of the product including tariff line references at least the six-digit level;
- data sources of the above information.

25) For the purposes of Supporting Table ES:1, the following level of product aggregation should be used:

(i) Wheat and wheat flour
(ii) Coarse grains
(iii) Rice
(iv) Oilseeds
(v) Vegetable oils
(vi) Oilcakes
(vii) Sugar
(viii) Butter and butter oil
(ix) Skim milk powder
(x) Cheese
(xi) Other milk products
(xii) Bovine Meat
(xiii) Pigmeat
(xiv) Poultry meat
(xv) Sheepmeat
(xvi) Live animals
(xvii) Eggs
(xviii) Wine
(xix) Fruit
(xx) Vegetables
(xxi) Tobacco
(xxii) Cotton

26) In the case of subsidies on agricultural products contingent on their incorporation in exported products, aggregate budgetary outlays only should be listed in Supporting Table ES:1.

27) If the acceding government does not maintain, at present, any export subsidy listed in Article 9:1 of the Agreement on Agriculture, a statement to this effect should be included in lieu of Supporting Table ES:1.

Supporting Table DS:1

DOMESTIC SUPPORT:
REPORTING PERIOD: calendar year, marketing year, etc.
Measures exempt from the reduction commitment – "Green Box"

Measure type	Name and description of measure with reference to criteria in Annex 2 of the Agreement on Agriculture	Monetary value of measure in year in question	Data sources
1	2	3	4
(a) "general services"			
(b) "public stockholding for food security purposes"			
(c) "domestic food aid"			
(d) "decoupled income support"			
(e) "income insurance and income safety-net programmes"			
(f) "payments for relief from natural disasters"			
(g) "structural adjustment assistance provided through producer retirement programmes"			
(h) "structural adjustment assistance provided through resource retirement programmes"			
(i) "structural adjustment assistance provided through investment aids"			
(j) "environmental programmes"			
(k) "regional assistance programmes"			
(l) "other"			

Supporting Table DS:2

DOMESTIC SUPPORT:
REPORTING PERIOD: calendar year, marketing year, etc.

Measures exempt from the reduction commitment – Special and Differential Treatment – "Development Programmes"

Measure type	Name and description of measure with reference to criteria in Article 6:2 of the Agreement on Agriculture	Monetary value of measure in year in question	Data sources
1	2	3	4
(a) "investment subsidies generally available to agriculture" (b) "input subsidies generally available to low-income or resource-poor producers" (c) "support to encourage diversification from growing illicit narcotic crops"			

Supporting Table DS:3

DOMESTIC SUPPORT:

REPORTING PERIOD: calendar year, marketing year, etc.

Measures exempt from the reduction commitment – Direct Payments under Production-Limiting Programmes – "Exempt Direct Payments"

Measure type	Name and description of measure with reference to criteria in Article 6:5 of the Agreement on Agriculture	Monetary value of measure in year in question	Data sources
1	2	3	4
(a) "payments based on fixed area and yields" (b) "payments based on 85 percent or less of the base level of production" (c) "livestock payments made on a fixed number of head"			

Supporting Table DS:4

DOMESTIC SUPPORT:
REPORTING PERIOD: calendar year, marketing year, etc.
Calculation of the Total Aggregate Measurement of Support

Description of basic products (including non-product specific AMS)	Product-specific AMS (from Supporting Tables DS:5 to DS:7 below)	Product-specific measurements of support (from Supporting Table DS:8 below)	Current Total AMS (aggregate)
1	2	3	4
Product A			Total Product A
Product B			Total Product B
Product C			Total Product C
. . .			. . .
Non-product-specific AMS			Total Non-product-specific AMS (from Supporting Table DS:9 below)
			TOTAL: Current Total AMS

Supporting Table DS:5

DOMESTIC SUPPORT:
REPORTING PERIOD: calendar year, marketing year, etc.
Product-Specific Aggregate Measurements of Support: Market Price Support

Description of basic products	Calendar / marketing year beginning . . .	Measure type(s)	Applied administered price	External reference price	Eligible production	Associated fees/levies	Total market price support	Data sources
1	2	3	4	5	6	7	8 (4–5*6)–7	9

Supporting Table DS:6

DOMESTIC SUPPORT:
REPORTING PERIOD: calendar year, marketing year, etc.

Product-Specific Aggregate Measurements of Support: Non-Exempt Direct Payments

Description of basic product	Calendar / marketing year beginning . . .	Measure type(s)	Applied administered price	External reference price	Eligible production	Total price-related direct payments	Other non-exempt direct payments	Associated fees/levies	Total direct payments	Data sources
1	2	3	4	5	6	7 ((4−5)*6)	8	9	10 (7+8−9)	11

Supporting Table DS:7

DOMESTIC SUPPORT:
REPORTING PERIOD: calendar year, marketing year, etc.

Product-Specific Aggregate Measurements of Support: Other Product-Specific Support and Total Product-Specific AMS

Description of basic product	Calendar / marketing year beginning . . .	Measure type(s)	Other product-specific budgetary outlays	Other product specific support (include calculation details)	Associated fees/levies	Total other product-specific support	Market price support (Supporting Table DS:5)	Non-exempt direct payments (Supporting Table DS:6)	Total AMS	Data sources
1	2	3	4	5	6	7 (4+5–6)	8	9	10 (7+8+9)	11

Supporting Table DS:8

DOMESTIC SUPPORT:
REPORTING PERIOD: calendar year, marketing year, etc.
Product-Specific Equivalent Measurements of Support

Description of basic products	Calendar / marketing year beginning . . .	Measure type(s)	Applied administered price	Production eligible to receive the applied adminis-tered price	Market price support budgetary outlays	Equivalent measure-ment of support (include calculation details)	Non-exempt direct pay-ments	Other product-specific support	Associated fees/levies	Total monetary value of equiva-lent commit-ment	Data sources
1	2	3	4	5	6	7	8	9	10	11 (7+8+ 9–10)	12

Supporting Table DS:9

DOMESTIC SUPPORT:
REPORTING PERIOD: calendar year, marketing year, etc.
Non-Product-Specific AMS

Measure type(s)	Calendar / marketing year beginning . . .	Non-product-specific budgetary outlays	Other non-product-specific support (include calculation details)	Associated fees/levies	Total non-product-specific support	Data sources
1	2	3	4	5	6 (3+4–5)	7

Supporting Table ES:1

EXPORT SUBSIDIES:

REPORTING PERIOD: calendar year, marketing year, etc.

Export Subsidies: Outlay and Quantity

Description of products	Direct export subsidies	Sales of stocks	Producer financed subsidies	Cost reduction measures	Internal transport subsidies	Total product specific export subsidies	Quantity of subsidized exports	Data source
1	2	3	4	5	6	7	8	9

ANNEX 7.3 INFORMATION TO BE PROVIDED ON POLICY MEASURES AFFECTING TRADE IN SERVICES

This Annex reproduces the text of WTO document WT/ACC/5, excluding its Annex 1 containing the Services Sectoral Classification List which is reproduced in Annex 6.8 above.

Information to be Provided on Policy Measures Affecting Trade in Services

Technical Note by the Secretariat

I. The purpose of this technical note is to assist acceding governments in submitting factual information on their policies affecting trade in services sectors relevant to their economy as required under Sections VI.1 and VI.2 of the Outline Format for a Memorandum on the Foreign Trade Régime (WT/ACC/1). To this end, the following paragraphs and the annexed tables are designed to facilitate the description of policy measures[2] maintained by acceding governments and which are relevant to the provisions of the General Agreement on Trade in Services (GATS). A general description of the overall market and regulatory structures of the most prominent services sectors in the acceding governments must be provided separately under Section VI.1 of the Memorandum on the Foreign Trade Régime.

II. It should be noted that there are two sorts of provisions under the GATS. The first are general obligations, some of which apply to all services sectors (e.g. MFN, transparency, etc.) and some only to those under scheduled commitments. The second are specific commitments which are negotiated undertakings particular to each Member. To guide the submission of information in a manner which would also facilitate subsequent work, notably the tabling of specific commitments during the bilateral market access negotiations in this area between acceding governments and Members, the present note is based on the extensive technical work undertaken on the scheduling of initial commitments in trade in services (MTN.GNS/W/164 and Add.1).

III. The information to be provided in this context is without prejudice to any additional information which Members may wish to request from acceding governments on any other aspects of their trade regime in services. A complete list of services sectors – the "Services Sectoral Classification List" – is reproduced in Annex I.

[2] Measures refer to any measures taken by: (i) central, regional or local government, and authorities; and (ii) non-governmental bodies in the exercise of powers delegated by central, regional or local governments or authorities (Article I.3 of GATS).

Measures Relating to Market Access: Table 1

Modes of Supply (Col 1)

IV. For each of the measures to be listed in column 2, an indication should be provided on its relevant mode(s) of supply, in accordance with the scope of the GATS as set out in Article I.2. The modes are essentially defined on the basis of the origin of the service supplier and consumer, and the degree and type of the territorial presence which they have at the moment the service is delivered.

V. The following provides a common understanding on what each mode covers:

(a) Cross-border supply: The service supplier is typically not present within the territory of the government where the service is delivered. Examples are international transport, the supply of a service through telecommunications or mail, and services embodied in exported goods (e.g. a computer diskette, or drawings).

(b) Consumption abroad: This mode of supply is often referred to as "movement of the consumer". The essential feature of this mode is that the service is delivered outside the territory of the government concerned. It typically includes crossing of the border by the consumer as, for example, in tourism services. However, activities such as ship repair abroad, where only the property of the consumer moves, or is situated abroad, are also covered.

(c) Commercial presence: This mode covers not only the presence of juridical persons in the strict legal sense, but also that of legal entities which share some of the same characteristics. It thus includes, inter alia, corporations, joint ventures, partnership, representative offices and branches.

(d) Presence of natural persons: This mode covers natural persons who are themselves service suppliers, as well as natural persons who are employees of service suppliers.

(e) Relationship between modes of supply: Where a service transaction requires in practical terms the use of more than one mode of supply, coverage of the transaction is only ensured when each relevant mode of supply is noted.

Description of Measures (Col 2)

VI. For each of the modes of supply listed in column 1, a detailed description[3] should be provided on any existing measures maintained by the acceding

[3] The description of any reported measure should be sufficiently detailed to enable Members to make a judgement as to the relationship of the measure in question and the relevant types of measures ((a) through (f)) under Article XVI of the GATS.

government which may limit market access horizontally or to any specific service sector. Such measures may include:

(a) limitations[4] on the number of service suppliers (e.g. ceiling on the total number of banks, a licence for a new restaurant based on an economic needs test; quotas on foreign medical practitioners; government or privately owned monopoly for labour exchange agency services; nationality requirements for suppliers of services);
(b) limitations on the total value of transactions or assets (e.g. foreign bank subsidiaries limited to × percent of total domestic assets of all banks);
(c) limitations on the total number of services operations or on the total quantity of service output (e.g. restrictions on broadcasting time available for foreign films);
(d) limitations on the total number of natural persons (in particular non-nationals) that may be employed in the sector (or the share of wages paid to foreign labour);
(e) restrictions on, or requirements of, specific types of legal entity through which that service may be supplied (e.g. commercial presence excludes representative offices, foreign companies required to established subsidiaries, commercial presence must take the form of a partnership);
(f) limitations on the participation of foreign capital (e.g. foreign equity ceiling of × percent for a particular form of commercial presence);

Relevant Laws and Regulations (Col 3)

VII. A reference to the laws or regulations relevant to each of the measures listed in column 2 should be listed in column 3 as appropriate. Where relevant, a cross-reference to laws or regulations separately noted under the section describing horizontal provisions and those relating to any specific service sector should also be introduced.

Measures Relating to National Treatment: Table 2

Modes of Supply (Col 1)

VIII. See paragraphs 4–5.

[4] "Limitations" refer to the "terms", "conditions", "limitations" and "qualifications" as used in Articles XVI and XVII of the GATS.

Description of Measure (Col 2)

IX. For each of the modes of supply listed in column 1, a detailed description[5] should be provided on any existing measures which may limit the provision of national treatment to foreign suppliers of services horizontally or those of any specific service sector. In each case, such measures include any measures providing, whether *de jure* or *de facto*, less favourable treatment than that accorded to domestic suppliers (e.g. domestic broadcasters are given preference in the allocation of transmission frequencies within the national territory, a measure stipulates that prior residency is required for the issuing of a licence to supply the service).

Relevant Laws and Regulations (Col 3)

X. See paragraph 7.

Measures Relating to Most-Favoured-Nation Treatment: Table 3

Description of Measure (Col 1)

XI. An indication should be provided of any existing measures which may be applied, whether horizontally or to any specific service sector, by the acceding government on a non-MFN basis (e.g. measures resulting from bilateral or other preferential agreements or reciprocity requirements under domestic law).

Relevant Laws and Regulations (Col 2)

XII. See paragraph 7.

Other Measures: Table 4

Description of Measure (Col 1)

XIII. List any other measures, including subsidy programmes, whether applied horizontally or to any specific service sector, which may be relevant to gain a full understanding on the market conditions in the acceding government, with a reference to whether and how such measures are relevant to the provisions of Articles V, VI, VII and VIII of the GATS.[6]

Relevant Laws and Regulations (Col 2)

XIV. See paragraph 7.

[5] The description of any reported measure should be sufficiently detailed to enable Members to make a judgement as to the relationship of the measure in question and the relevant description under Article XVII of the GATS.

[6] With respect to information affected by Article VI of the GATS, it should be borne in mind that licensing requirements do not require scheduling as reservations unless they are not consistent with Articles XVI or XVII of the GATS, or otherwise may not meet the criteria under Article VI referred to above.

Other Laws, Regulations and Other Legal Instruments: Table 5

XV. List all laws, regulations or other legal instruments, not already cited in Tables 1 to 4, which are related to the implementation of the specific regulatory structure and modus operandi, whether applied horizontally or to any specific service sector, particularly with respect to the Articles listed in paragraph 13 above as they affect foreign services suppliers.

ACCEDING GOVERNMENT

INFORMATION TO BE PROVIDED ON POLICY MEASURES AFFECTING TRADE IN SERVICES

Table 1: Measures Relating to Market Access

A. HORIZONTAL

Mode(s) of Supply	Measures	Relevant Laws and Regulations
(1) Cross-border supply	(1)	
(2) Consumption abroad	(2)	
(3) Commercial presence	(3)	
(4) Presence of natural persons	(4)	
(5) Relationship between modes of supply	(5)	

B. SPECIFIC SERVICE SECTOR OR SUB-SECTOR

Mode(s) of Supply	Measures	Relevant Laws and Regulations
(1) Cross-border supply	(1)	
(2) Consumption abroad	(2)	
(3) Commercial presence	(3)	
(4) Presence of natural persons	(4)	
(5) Relationship between modes of supply	(5)	

Table 2 *Measures Relating to National Treatment*

A. HORIZONTAL		
Mode(s) of Supply	Measures	Relevant Laws and Regulations
(1) Cross-border supply	(1)	
(2) Consumption abroad	(2)	
(3) Commercial presence	(3)	
(4) Presence of natural persons	(4)	
(5) Relationship between modes of supply	(5)	

B. SPECIFIC SERVICE SECTOR OR SUB-SECTOR		
Mode(s) of Supply	Measures	Relevant Laws and Regulations
(1) Cross-border supply	(1)	
(2) Consumption abroad	(2)	
(3) Commercial presence	(3)	
(4) Presence of natural persons	(4)	
(5) Relationship between modes of supply	(5)	

Table 3 *Measures Relating to Most-Favoured-Nation Treatment (MFN)*

A. HORIZONTAL	
Measures[7]	Relevant Laws and Regulations
B. SPECIFIC SERVICE SECTOR OR SUB-SECTOR	
Measures[7]	Relevant Laws and Regulations

[7] An indication of mode(s) of supply should be provided, if relevant.

Table 4 *Other Measures*

A. HORIZONTAL	
Measures[7]	Relevant Laws and Regulations
B. SPECIFIC SERVICE SECTOR OR SUB-SECTOR	
Measures[7]	Relevant Laws and Regulations

Table 5 *Other Laws, Regulations and Other Legal Instruments*

A. HORIZONTAL
B. SPECIFIC SERVICE SECTOR OR SUB-SECTOR

ANNEX 7.4 IMPLEMENTATION OF THE WTO AGREEMENT ON TRADE-RELATED ASPECTS OF INTELLECTUAL PROPERTY RIGHTS (TRIPS)

WTO document WT/ACC/9 of 15 November 1999 and Corr. 1.

Implementation of the WTO Agreement on
Trade-related Aspects of Intellectual Property Rights (TRIPS)

Note by the Secretariat

This document has been prepared in consultation with WTO members and reflects the development of "standard form" questionnaires in recent accession Working Parties. It should assist acceding governments in the provision of information which will facilitate discussion in their Working Party on accession, focussing on TRIPS issues.

Country
Implementation of the WTO Agreement
on Trade-Related Aspects of Intellectual Property Rights (TRIPS)

TRIPS Agreement	Country
General Obligations	**IP Agreements to which the country adheres**
Compliance with Articles 1 through 12 and Article 19 of the Paris Convention for the Protection of Industrial Property in respect of Parts II, III, and IV of the TRIPS Agreement. TRIPS Article 2.	
Under Paris, Article 1(2), industrial property has as its object patents, utility models, industrial designs, trademarks, service marks, trade names, indications of source or appellations of origin, and the repression of unfair competition.	
In Paris. Article 1(3), industrial property applies not only to industry and commerce proper, but to agricultural and extractive industries and to all manufactured or natural products, e.g., wines, grain, tobacco leaf, fruit, cattle, minerals, mineral waters, beer, flowers, and flour.	
Under Paris, Article 2, nationals of Members are to enjoy in other Members the advantages that their respective laws grant to nationals, and shall have the same protection and the same legal remedy against any infringement of their rights if they conform to the conditions and formalities imposed upon the Member's nationals.	
Paris. Article 3, requires that nationals of non-Member countries domiciles or that have "real and effective" industrial or commercial establishments in a Member country be treated as nationals of a Member country.	
Under Paris, Article 4.a right of priority is to be given an applicant for a patent, for registration of a utility model, an industrial design, or of a trademark who has filed the equivalent of a regular national filing under the domestic legislation of a Member country. The periods of priority are to be 12 months for patents and utility models, and 6 months for industrial designs and trademarks. The Article discusses the technical details of granting priority in depth.	

TRIPS Agreement	Country
Article 4bis states that patents obtained for the same invention in various members of the Paris Union are independent of each other.	
Article 4ter requires that inventors have the right to be named as such in the patent.	
Under Article 4quater restrictions or limitations on the sale of a patented product or a product produced by a patented process cannot be the grounds for refusing a patent or invalidating one already issued. Under Article 5(A)(1), importation of a patented product manufactured in a Paris Union country cannot be the basis of forfeiture of the patent. Article 5(A)(2) and (3) authorize countries to use compulsory licensing as a means to prevent abuses, such as the failure to work, but they may not forfeit a patent unless the grant of a compulsory license would not be sufficient to prevent the abuse. Proceedings for forfeiture or revocation cannot be institute until two years after the grant of the first compulsory license.	
Article 5(A)(4) prohibits application for a compulsory license for failure to work until four years have passed since tile application was filed or three years from date of grant and no compulsory license is to be granted if the patentee justifies the failure to work. Licenses are to be non-exclusive, and may not be transferred except with the enterprise or goodwill that exploits the license. Article 5(B) prohibits forfeiture of industrial designs for failure to work or for importing articles corresponding to those that are protected.	
Article 5(C) prohibits cancellation of a mark for unjustified non-use before a reasonable period of time has passed and permits the proprietor to use differing elements that do not diminish the distinctive character of a mark without invalidating the registration or diminishing the protection granted the mark. Concurrent use of the mark by co-proprietors is permitted so long as the public is not mislead.	

TRIPS **Agreement**	**Country**
Under Article 5(D), protection of patents, registered trademarks, and industrial designs cannot be conditioned upon indication or mention of such patent, trademark registration, or industrial design protection.	
Article 5bis requires that a grace period of at least six months be provided for the payment of maintenance fees for industrial property, but a surcharge is permissible. countries are authorized to restore patents that lapsed for non-payment of fees.	
Article 5ter prohibits a Paris Member from making use of patented devices aboard a vessel, aircraft, of land vehicle temporarily or accidentally in the territory or the Member.	
Article 5quater requires that process patent owners have all the rights against an imported product produced by the patent process that they would have with respect to products manufactured at home.	
Article 5quinquies requires that Paris Members protect industrial designs.	
Article 6 makes the conditions for filing and registration of trademarks subject to domestic legislation but also makes filing and registration independent of those in other countries, including the country of origin.	
Article 6bis requires parties, ex officio if legally possible or at the request of an interested party, to refuse to register or, for a period of at least 5 years, to cancel the registration of a trademark confusingly similar to a well-known mark. No time limit is placed on a mark used in bad faith.	

TRIPS Agreement	Country
Article 6ter requires Members to refuse to register or to invalidate the registration that includes, without authorization, armorial bearings, flags, state emblems, official signs and hallmarks, etc. An exception is provided for owners of rights acquired in good faith before the Convention entered into force for that country.	
Article 6quater makes the assignment of a mark valid if the portion of the business or goodwill of the business together with the exclusive right to manufacture and sell the goods bearing the mark are also transferred.	
Article 6quinquies requires that trademarks duly registered in a Member be accepted for filing in other Members, with certain reservations, and establishes the conditions under which a trademark may be denied registration or may be invalidated.	
Article 6sexties states that Paris Members undertake" to protect service marks without being required to provide for their registration.	
Article 6septies requires that trademark owners be able to oppose or request cancellation of a registration of their trademarks applied for by their agent or representative without their authorization "unless the agent or representative justifies his action.	
Article 7 states that the nature of the goods to which a trademark is applied may in no case be an obstacle to the registration of the trademark. (Duplicate language is in TRIPS Article 15.4.)	
Article 7bis requires that Members permit registration of collective marks belonging to associations the existence of which is not contrary to the law of the country of origin, even where the association is not established in the country where protection is being sought.	

TRIPS Agreement	Country
Article 8 requires that trade names be protected by Members without the necessity of registration, whether or not the names are part of a trademark.	
Article 9 requires seizure on importation or exclusion or goods bearing a trademark or trade name without authorization, unless a country's laws provide for neither remedy, in which case domestic actions and remedies must be available.	
Article 10 applies the obligation of Article 9 to the direct or indirect use of false indications of source of goods, or false indication of the producer, manufacturer, or merchant of such goods.	
Article 10bis requires Members to provide protection against unfair competition, including against acts that create confusion of various kinds about the goods or activities of a competitor, that consist of false allegations about a competitor, or that are apt to mislead the public regarding a competitor's goods.	
Article 10ter requires that Members undertake to assure to foreign nationals effective legal remedies to repress actions referred to in Articles 9, 10 and 10bis, and to allow federations and associations representing foreign businesses, on the basis of reciprocity, to take action in court and before administrative authorities to repress such acts.	
Article 11 requires that temporary protection. consistent with domestic legislation, be afforded to patentable inventions, utility models, industrial designs and trademarks in respect of goods exhibited at official or officially recognized international exhibitions held in their territory.	
Article 12 requires Members to establish industrial property offices for patents. utility models, industrial designs and trademarks for the communication to the public through publication of a periodic journal of the names of patent owners with a brief designation of their inventions, and the reproduction of trademarks.	

TRIPS Agreement	**Country**
Article 19 authorizes Members to enter into separate and special industrial property agreements among themselves, so long as those agreements do not contravene the provisions of Paris.	
National treatment, with exceptions allowed in the Paris, Berne and Rome Conventions. Article 3.	
Most-Favoured-Nation treatment, with enumerated exceptions. Article 4.	
Copyright and Neighbouring Rights	**Citation to copyright and related laws**
Compliance with Articles I through 21 of the Berne Convention with the exception of Article 6bis, Article 9.1.	
Article 2 defines "literary and artistic works" as "every production in the literary, scientific and artistic domain whatever may be the mode or form of its expression," giving examples. Limitations related to speeches are provided in Article 2bis.	
Article 3 requires that protection be provided to the works of authors who are nationals of Berne Union members and to works of nationals of non-Union countries if those works are published in a Union member simultaneously with publication in the non-Union country.	
Article 4 requires that protection be provided cinematographic works not falling under Article 3 if the maker has a headquarters or habitual residence in a Union member and to works of architecture or artistic works incorporated into a building or structure in a Union member.	
Article 5 requires that authors enjoy the rights required by Berne and any other rights a country provides works on a national treatment basis without being subject to any formalities.	

TRIPS Agreement	Country
Article 7 requires that the term of protection for copyright be 50 years following the death of the author. Special terms are authorized for cinematographic works, anonymous or pseudonymous works, photographic works and works of applied art. Article 8 gives authors of protected works the exclusive right to make or authorize the making of translations of the work.	
Article 9 requires that authors be given the exclusive right to authorize reproduction of the work in any manner or form with only limited exceptions that do not conflict with the normal exploitation of the work and do not unreasonably prejudice the legitimate interests of the author.	
Articles 10 and 10bis define certain authorized "free uses of works".	
Articles 11, 11bis, and 11ter require that authors of dramatic, dramatico-musical and musical works and any translation thereof and authors of literary and artistic works, the exclusive right to authorize the public performance of their works, including by broadcast, public recitation and any communication to the public.	
Article 12 requires that authors of literary or artistic works have the exclusive right to authorize adaptations, arrangements and other alterations of their works.	
Article 13 authorizes countries to impose reservations and conditions on the exclusive right granted authors of musical works or written works that are recorded.	
Articles 14 requires that authors of literary and artistic works have the exclusive right to authorize the cinematographic adaptation and reproduction of their works and the distribution, public performance and communication to the public of the adaptation or reproduction, without the limitations authorized under Article 13(1).	

TRIPS Agreement	Country
Article 14bis specifies that a cinematographic work is to be protected as an original work without prejudice to any work that is adapted or reproduced and the author of the cinematographic work is to enjoy the same rights as the author of any other work.	
Article 14ter requires "droit de suite" in connection with subsequent sales works of art and manuscripts.	
Article 15 requires that ownership of a work, for purposes of litigation, be presumed to be that which appears on the work in the usual manner.	
Article 16 requires that infringing copies of a work be subject to seizure whether domestically produced or imported.	
Article 18 requires that copyright protection be applied to all works which, at the moment Berne becomes effective, have not fallen into the public domain in the country of origin through the expiry of the term of protection.	
Article 19 authorizes Union members to provide greater protection than that required by the Convention.	
Article 20 authorizes Union members to enter into special agreements among themselves to provide more extensive rights than those provided by Berne.	
Protect computer programs, whether in source or object code, as literary works under the Berne Convention. Protect compilations of data, whether in machine readable or other form are to be protected as intellectual creations if they constitute such. Article 10.	
Provide rental rights at least for computer programs and cinematographic works with certain exceptions. Article 11.	

TRIPS Agreement	Country
Provide a term of protection of fifty years from the death of tile author (Berne Article 7.1 and TRIPS Article 9.1) or, for works the term of which is not measured by the life of the author, a term of 50 years from the end of the calendar year of authorized publication, or, if not published within fifty years from making, fifty years from the end of the calendar year of making. Article 12.	
Confine limitations and exceptions to exclusive rights to certain special cases which do not conflict with a normal exploitation of the work and do not unreasonably prejudice the right holder's legitimate interests. Article 13.	
Provide performers with the right for 50 years from the date of a performance to prevent unauthorized fixation of their unfixed performances and of reproductions of such fixations and to prevent the unauthorized broadcast by wireless means and communication to the public of their live performances. Article 14.1 and 5.	
Provide phonogram producers with the right for 50 years from the date of first authorized fixation to prohibit unauthorized reproduction of their phonograms, directly or indirectly, and to prohibit rental of copies of their phonograms once sold or otherwise distributed. Article 14.2,.4, and.5.	
Providing broadcasting organizations with the exclusive rights for 20 years of fixation, reproduction of fixations, and rebroadcasting by wireless means of their broadcasts and the communication to the public of broadcasts of their broadcasts or provide to the owners of the copyright in the material broadcast the possibility of exercising such rights. Article 14.3 and 5.	

TRIPS Agreement	**Country**
Trademarks	**Citation to appropriate law**
Provide trademark or service mark protection for any sign, or combination of signs capable of distinguishing the goods or services of one undertaking from those of other undertakings. Article 15.1.	
Not deny registration for a mark based solely on the nature of the goods or services to which a trademark is to be applied. Article 15.4.	
Trademarks must be published before or shortly after registration to permit opposition or opportunity to apply for cancellation. Article 15.5.	
Provide trademark owners the exclusive right to prevent unauthorized use identical or similar marks for similar goods or services of other parties if confusion is likely to result. Article 16.1.	
Presume confusion where an identical mark is used without authorization on identical goods or services. Article 16.1.	
Provide protection for well know trademarks and service marks in accordance with Article 6bis, of the Paris Convention, even where use is on goods or services which are not similar to those in respect of which a trademark is registered if the latter use would imply a connection with the right holder or would be likely to damage the right holder's interests. Article 16.2 and.3.	
Allow only limited exceptions to the rights conferred by a trademark such as fair use of descriptive terms. Article 17.	
Provide a period of protection for registration of at least seven years, renewable indefinitely. Article 18.	

TRIPS Agreement	**Country**
Allow cancellation for non-use only after a period of three years of uninterrupted non-use unless valid reasons exist for the non-use, including government interference with use. Article 19.1.	
No encumbering of the use of a trademark by special requirements. Article 20.	
May establish conditions for licensing but compulsory licensing not permitted and owner of registered mark must be able to assign it with or without transfer of business. Article 21.	
Geographical Indications	**Citation to appropriate law or laws**
Provide means to prevent deceptive use of Geographical indications identifying location where a given quality, reputation or other characteristic of a good is attributable to its location. Article 22.1 and 2. Refuse to register or invalidate registrations of trademarks containing geographical indications except in instances in which such marks have been used continuously for at least 10 years or in good faith before 15 April 1994. Article 22.3	
Protect against use of geographical indications even when literally true but which falsely represent that the goods originate in another territory. Article 22.4	
Protect, with certain exceptions, appellations or origin for wines and spirits even against use accompanied by expressions such	
Protect, with certain exceptions, appellations or origin for wines and spirits even against use accompanied by expressions such as "kind", "type", "style", etc. Articles 23.1 and 24.	
Refuse or invalidate, with certain exceptions trademark registrations containing geographical indications for wines and spirits if they do not originate in the place named. Articles 23.2 and 24.	

TRIPS Agreement	Country
Industrial Designs	**Citation to appropriate law**
Provide, with certain exceptions, protection for new or original, independently created industrial designs. Article 25.1.	
Ensure that requirements for securing protection for textile designs are not prohibitive of such protection. Article 25.2.	
Protection should last at least 10 years.	
Patents	**Citation to appropriate law**
Provide patents for any inventions, whether products or processes, in all fields of technology if they are new, involve an inventive step and are industrially applicable. Exceptions are permitted for plants and animals, except for microorganisms and non-biological and microbiological processes. Exemptions are also permitted for reasons of ordre public and morality. Article 27.	
Provide patent owners with the right to prevent others from making, using, offering for sale, selling or importing a patented product or from using a patent process or using, offering for sale, selling or importing a product produced directly using such process. Article 28.1.	
Give patent owners the right to assign the rights in the patent, or transfer the rights by succession, or license them. Article 28.2.	
Require applicants to disclose the invention so that one skilled in the art can carry it out and may require indication of the best mode and information on corresponding foreign applications. Article 29.	

TRIPS Agreement	**Country**
Ensure that any exceptions to exclusive patent rights do not unreasonably conflict with normal exploitation of the patent and do not unreasonably prejudice the legitimate interests of the patent owner, taking third party interests into account. Article 30.	
Compulsory licenses can be issued only when enumerated conditions are met, including such things as notice, remuneration, limitations on use and transfer of the license, etc. Article 31.	
Provide an opportunity for judicial review of decisions to revoke or forfeit a patent. Article 32.	
Provide a patent term of at least 20 years from the filing date. Article 33.	
Shift the burden of proof in process patent infringement actions to the defendant in instances in which tile product produced by the process is new or where it is substantially likely that the identical product was made using the process, and the patent owner has been unable through reasonable efforts to determine the process used. Article 34.	
Integrated-Circuit Layout Designs	**Citation to appropriate law**
Provide protection for original layout designs of integrated circuits that are registered or have been commercially exploited anywhere in the world. Articles 3, 4, 5 and 7 of the Washington Treaty as incorporated into TRIPS by Article 35.	
Make unlawful, except in certain circumstances, the reproduction, importation, sale or other distribution of a protected layout design or an integrated circuit embodying such design or an article containing such a microcircuit. Article 6 of Washington and Article 36 of TRIPS.	

TRIPS Agreement	**Country**
Provide such protection for a term of 10 years from the films, of an application for registration or from first commercial exploitation. Article 38.	
Undisclosed Information	**Citation to appropriate law or laws**
Provide protection for undisclosed information that is secret (not generally known or readily ascertainable); has commercial value because of its secrecy., and has been subject to reasonable steps to keep it secret. Article 39.2.	
Protect data submitted to obtain marketing approval for pharmaceutical or agricultural chemicals utilizing a new chemical entity. Article 39.3.	
Enforcement	**Citation to appropriate law or laws**
–General Provisions	
Provide for effective action against infringement of intellectual property rights without creating barriers to legitimate trade or opportunities for abuse. Article 41.1.	
Provide enforcement procedures that are fair and equitable and are not unnecessarily complicated or costly and do not entail unreasonable time-limits or unwarranted delays. Article 41.2.	
Provide decisions on the merits based upon the evidence presented in the case to the parties, preferably in writing with the reasons explained. Article 41.3.	
Provide for appeals to judicial bodies of final administrative decisions and of at least the legal aspects of initial judicial decisions on the merits of a case. Article 41.4.	

TRIPS Agreement	**Country**
Civil and Administrative Procedures and Remedies	
Provide a procedure that allows plaintiffs to bring an action for infringement; requires that defendants be notified; permits both side to present evidence in support of their position; and protects confidential information. Article 42.	
Authorize judges to order production of evidence necessary to substantiate a party's claims where that party has been unable to obtain such evidence from the opposing party. Article 43.1.	
Authorize judges to enjoin a defendant, except the government, from infringing intellectual property rights. Article 44.1.	
Authorize judges to order the payment of monetary damages adequate to compensate for the injury done by the infringement. Article 45.1.	
Authorize judges to order infringer to pay right holders enforcement costs and recovery of profits and/or statutory damages. Article 45.2.	
Authorize additional remedies including seizure of infringing goods, and the materials and implements the predominant use of which is infringement. Article 46.	
Authorize indemnification of defendant, including attorneys' fees in the event of abuse by plaintiffs. Article 48.1.	
Exempt public authorities and officials from liability in connection with the administration of intellectual property laws only where the actions are taken or intended in good faith within the scope of tile relevant authority. Article 48.2.	

TRIPS Agreement	Country
Ensure that administrative remedies conform to the principles in the preceding Articles. Article 49.	
–Provisional Measures	
Authorize judges to grant temporary restraining orders and provisional relief to prevent infringement and to preserve evidence. Article 50.1.	
Authorize judges to require the complaining party to indemnify the defending party against harm if the decision on the merits finds the provisional relief unjustified. Article 50.3.	
Provide for notice, for formal action by the plaintiff after temporary restraining orders, etc. Article 50.4.	
–Border Measures	
Provide for suspension of release by customs authorities of goods suspected of bearing a counterfeit trademark or of being a piratical copyrighted work, either at the request of a right holder. Members are authorized to extend such protection to holders of other forms of intellectual property, Article 51.	
Require right holders initiating border measures to provide evidence of a prima facie infringement and a description of tile goods sufficient for customs authorities to recognize them. The right holder must be notified within a reasonable time is action will be taken on his behalf. Article 52.	
Authorize authorities to require the right holder requesting border measures to post a bond sufficient to protect the defendant and to prevent abuse. Article 53.	
Requires prompt notification of the right holder and the importer when action under Article 51 is taken. Article 54.	

TRIPS Agreement	**Country**
Requires that customs authorities be notified within a maximum of 20 days of the receipt of notice that proceedings on the merits have begun or the suspension is to be revoked. Article 55.	
Authorities must be authorized to require the right holder to compensate the importer or owner of the goods subject to border measures if goods were wrongfully detained or if proceedings leading to a decision on the merits are not begun within tile allotted time. Article 56.	
Right holders must be allowed to inspect the detained goods in order to substantiate the right holder's claims. Importers must be given similar authority. Members may give the right holder the names and addresses of those involved in the importation when infringement is found to exist. Article 57.	
Establishes the conditions that must be in place if customs authorities are authorized to act ex officio, including the ability to ask the right holder for information at any time; the requirement to notify the importer promptly of the suspension; and the requirement that public officials be liable if they act in bad faith. Article 58.	
Competent authorities must be able to order destruction or disposal other than by re-export of infringing goods where appropriate. Article 59.	
Members are authorized to except from border measures small quantities of infringing goods of a non-commercial nature carried in personal luggage or shipped in small consignments. Article 60.	

TRIPS Agreement	Country
–Criminal Procedures	
Provide criminal procedures and penalties, sufficient to act as a deterrent, for wilful trademark counterfeiting or copyright piracy on a commercial scale. Authorizes extension of criminal actions to other forms of intellectual property where infringements are willful and on a commercial scale. Article 61.	

Annex 8

FORMATS FOR INITIAL TARIFF OFFER AND FOR SCHEDULE OF CONCESSIONS AND COMMITMENTS ON GOODS

ANNEX 8.1 FORMAT FOR INITIAL TARIFF OFFER

The format for initial offers on tariffs is a simplified version of the Schedule containing the results of the negotiations. It has not been formally standardized but experience shows that at a minimum initial offers should contain the information indicated in the Table below.

As negotiations proceed, implementation periods for the reduction of tariff bindings can be negotiated and additional columns "final bound rate" and "implementation period" can be added (after column 4) as part of revised offer(s).

Format for Tariff Offers

HS Number (National Nomenclature of the Applicant) (1)	Description of Each Product (2)	Currently Applied Rate* (3)	Proposed Bound Rate at Accession (4)	Other Duties and Charges (ODC) (5)

* While these will not appear in the final Schedule, the currently applied rates of duty need to be supplied, particularly as some WTO Members expect these to provide a reference point for the negotiations. This can be done either in a column in the initial offer as indicated above or in a separate communication.

Preferential tariffs and non-tariff measures may be bound but, as a rule, initial offers only contain offers of MFN tariff concessions.

Items in the offer are arranged by the headings of the Harmonized System nomenclature. This was revised in 1992, 1996, 2002 and 2007. The Schedules of three out of the four countries that were the first to accede to the WTO used HS 1992, while three out of the four to accede most recently used HS 2002. Initial offers and Schedules should normally be prepared in the version of the nomenclature applied by the acceding government at the time the document is prepared.

As noted above, rates of other duties and charges also need to be inserted in Column 5 and an offer made on these ('zero' if no ODCs are applied). To anticipate the discussion on the results of the negotiations below, Members generally expect these to be bound at zero.

ANNEX 8.2 FORMAT FOR BILATERAL TARIFF AGREEMENTS

Negotiations for the Accession of *COUNTRY 1 (APPLICANT)* to the WTO

The Permanent Mission of *country 1* and the Permanent Mission of *country 2 (WTO Member)* hereby inform the Director-General of the World Trade Organization that they have concluded their bilateral market access negotiations in the context of the accession of *country 1* to the WTO.

They accordingly attach hereto the original of the list of concessions on goods which *country 1* grants to *country 2* (Attachment 1).

Country 1 also grants to *country 2* Initial Negotiating Rights for goods negotiated with *country 2* as identified in Column [. . .] of the attached list of concessions at the rate which *country 1* binds in its Schedule.

The specific commitments on services that *country 1* will grant to *country 2* will be those contained in [WTO document WT/ACC/SPEC/ of [date], as modified in] Attachment 2 hereto.

For *country 2*	For *country 1*
Ambassador	Head of the Delegation

Done in Geneva, *date*

In 3 exemplars

Attachment 1

HS Number	Description	Bound Rate at Date of Accession	Final Bound Rate	Implementation Period	Interim [rate (over . . . years)]	ODC	INRs

ANNEX 8.3 FORMAT FOR TARIFF SCHEDULE

Part I, Section I-A: MFN tariff concessions on agricultural products

Schedule [Number] – [Name of Member]

This Schedule is authentic only in the [English] [French] [Spanish] language

PART I – MOST FAVOURED-NATION TARIFF

SECTION I – Agricultural Products

SECTION I – A Tariffs

Notes:

1	2	3	4	5	6	7	8	9	10
Harmonized System No.	Description	Bound rate at date of accession	Final bound rate	Implementation	Present concession established	INR	Concession first incorporated in a GATT Schedule	Earlier INRs	ODCs

The format above may be varied when necessary, e.g. to introduce an additional column for agricultural special safeguards (SSG). Only one new Member has negotiated special safeguard clauses.[1]

- Headnotes. Contain general obligations or obligations that do not find their place elsewhere in the standard format.

The practice followed in a few of the earlier accessions[2], of binding all agricultural products not individually scheduled at a single rate in a headnote has not been followed recently. In all recent accessions all products in the new Member's tariff have been listed and bound individually, as described below.

Recent accession Schedules have all included headnotes on the following subjects:

- Staging of reductions in the bound rate. In the most straightforward cases, the obligation is expressed thus: "Where there is a rate indicated in the "Final bound rate" column, the tariff reduction for that tariff line shall be implemented in equal annual stages beginning from the date of accession of [X] to the WTO. Successive reductions shall be implemented as of 1 January each year until the final bound rate is reached as indicated in the "Implementation" column. The reduced rate will in each stage be rounded off to the first decimal". If this is not the case, this is also specified here.[3]
- Certain products to be treated no less favourably than other products. One such obligation reads: "[X] shall maintain its applied rate, including other duties and charges, for HS 1205 (rape or colza (canola) seeds, whether or not broken, at a level no higher than for HS 1201 (soya beans, whether or not broken)".[4] The aim of these provisions is presumably to safeguard Members' right, under the MFN provision in Article I:1 of GATT 1994, to receive no less a favourable treatment than that accorded to like products.

Sometimes the headnotes have also been used to spell out commitments regarding: the relationship between the tariff rates on a raw material and the processed product (barley and malt) and advance notice of changes in tariff rates (barley)[5]; tariff headings and sub-headings for, e.g. special quality beef', rice[6] and fish species[7]; ODCs[8]; and TRQs.[9]

Exceptionally, headnotes have contained the sort of provisions that are normally the subject of Protocol commitments in the text of the Working Party Report[10].

- Column 1. Harmonized System number.

[1] Chinese Taipei (32 tariff lines at the 8 digit level). [2] Mongolia, Panama and Latvia.
[3] Viet Nam, Saudi Arabia, Nepal, Cambodia, FYROM.
[4] Viet Nam, Saudi Arabia, Nepal, Cambodia, FYROM, China. [5] China, Note 2 d) and e).
[6] Chinese Taipei, Notes 3 and 4. [7] China Endnote 1, page 438. [8] FYROM, Note 3.
[9] Chinese Taipei. [10] China, Notes 3 and 4.

Schedules are usually prepared in the version of the World Customs Organization HS nomenclature applied at the time of accession. While the HS nomenclature is at the 6-digit level, Schedules are usually prepared on the basis of the national nomenclature of the acceding government, which can be at the 8 or 10-digit level, or more.

- Column 2. Description of each product as they appear in the tariff nomenclature of the Member.
- Column 3. Bound rate at date of accession.

Maximum rate of duty that the Member is permitted to charge under WTO rules on the product concerned at the date of accession.

- Column 4. Final bound rate.

This column is left blank if the bound rate is to come into force from the date of accession. If a phasing-in period has been negotiated, this column shows the final bound rate.

- Column 5. Implementation

This column notes the date on which the final bound rate comes into force. If all the tariff reductions indicated in the previous columns are to be implemented in equal annual stages, this fact can be indicated in a Headnote and any deviations from equal annual reductions in this column. Deviations, if they take the form of a single interim rate, are normally indicated in a separate "interim" column. When there is more than one deviation per tariff line, a staging matrix is annexed to the Schedule.

- Column 6. Present concession established.

Not relevant for acceders.

- Column 7. INR (initial negotiating rights).

This column notes the Members that have been granted such rights. WTO Members wishing to renegotiate the level of their bindings on a specific item (or items) must follow the procedures in Article XXVIII of GATT 1994 as modified by the Understanding on the Interpretation of that Article[11]. These require that compensation be offered to each Member holding negotiating rights as a principle supplier, a substantial supplier or an initial negotiator of the concession. The amount of the compensation is related to the level of trade between the two countries concerned in the item at the time of the renegotiation. If the initial negotiator is neither a principal supplier nor a substantial supplier, the amount of compensation required is therefore likely to be small.

[11] See Results of the Uruguay Round of Multilateral Trade Negotiations.

– Column 8. Concession first incorporated in a GATT Schedule.

Not relevant for acceders.

– Column 9. Earlier INRs.

Not relevant for acceders.

– Column 10. ODCs (other duties and charges).

This column indicates the rate at which ODCs are to be bound. Members generally expect acceders to bind all ODCs at zero but 2 bound some ODCs.[12]

[12] Saudi Arabia, Chinese Taipei. Nepal bound ODCs at zero in Part I of its Schedule with a staging matrix for the elimination of existing ODCs.

Part I, Section I-B: MFN tariff quotas on agricultural products

Schedule [Number] – [Name of country] PART I – MOST FAVOURED-NATION TARIFF SECTION I – B Tariff Quotas						
Notes						
1	2	3	4	5	6	7
Description of products	Tariff item number	Initial quota quantity and in-quota tariff rate	Final quota quantity and in-quota tariff rate	Implementation period	Initial negotiating right	Other terms and conditions

9 new Members have negotiated agricultural tariff quotas. In some cases these will be phased out during an implementation period.[13]

[13] Viet Nam, FYROM, Chinese Taipei, China, Lithuania, Latvia, Panama, Bulgaria, Ecuador.

Part I, Section II: MFN tariff concessions on other (i.e. non-agricultural) products

The format for this is identical to the format for MFN tariff bindings on agricultural products, and similar comments apply.

Part II: Concessions on preferential tariffs

Schedule [Number] – [Name of Member]

This Schedule is authentic only in the [English] [French] [Spanish] language

PART II – PREFERENTIAL TARIFF

This Part was originally included in Schedules to GATT 1947 to record any bindings of the historical preferences permitted by Article I:2 to 4 of GATT 1947. Very few bindings of preferential rates have ever been made and there are no such bindings in the Schedules of countries that have acceded to WTO.

PART III – NON-TARIFF CONCESSIONS

Schedule [Number] – [Name of Member]

This Schedule is authentic only in the [English] [French] [Spanish] language

PART III – NON-TARIFF CONCESSIONS

Tariff Item Number	Description of Products	Concessions

This Part is not found in the Goods Schedules of Original Members as non-tariff measures are subject to the rules of general application contained in its various Agreements rather than concessions on individual products. It defines the products concerned and lists the concession on each product. Four of the last nine applicants to accede to WTO have agreed to commitments in Part III. In two of these cases, bindings provide for the phasing-out of tariff quotas on specified non-agricultural products.[14] In the third case this Part provides for: tariff quotas on specified non-agricultural products during an implementation period, at the end of which the quota quantities will be the subject of further negotiation; for a commitment to eliminate licenses on certain agricultural and non-agricultural products on the date of accession; and a tariff-only regime on some other products.[15] In the fourth case, this Part notes that none of the agricultural products that it lists are subject to quantitative restrictions.[16]

[14] Viet Nam, Chinese Taipei. [15] China, Note 3, p. 441. [16] Saudi Arabia.

Annex 9

DRAFTING A SERVICES SCHEDULE

The basic reference document that WTO Members and governments under accession use to draft their commitments is the "Guidelines for the Scheduling of Specific Commitments under the General Agreement on Trade in Services (GATS)".[1] Certain other documents that serve as reference material for the drafting of commitments are attached to these Guidelines. In addition, governments should consult the United Nations Provisional Central Product Classification, 1991 Version (UN CPC 1991). This section presents a brief summary of the scheduling guidelines.

The General Agreement on Trade in Services consists of the framework agreement – the Articles of the Agreement, its Annexes, and the attached Schedules of specific commitments and the lists of exemptions from MFN. The Schedules and the exemption lists are integral parts of the Agreement.

It is only by reference to a Member's Schedule, and (where relevant) its MFN exemption list, that it can be seen to which services sectors and under what conditions the basic principles of the GATS -market access, national treatment and MFN treatment – apply within that Member's jurisdiction. In its Schedule, each Member identifies the service sectors to which it will apply the market access and national treatment obligations under the GATS, and specifies any exceptions from those obligations it wishes to maintain. The commitments and limitations are in every case entered with respect to each of the four modes of supply which constitute the definition of trade in services in Article I of the GATS:

1. **Cross-border supply** – the possibility for non-resident service suppliers to supply services cross-border into the Member's territory.
2. **Consumption abroad** – the freedom for the Member's residents to purchase services in the territory of another Member.
3. **Commercial presence** – the opportunities for foreign service suppliers to establish, operate or expand a commercial presence in the Member's territory, such as a branch, agency, or wholly-owned subsidiary.
4. **Presence of natural persons** – the possibilities offered for the entry and temporary stay in the Member's territory of foreign individuals in order to supply a service.

In order to determine the level of market access guaranteed by a given Schedule, it is therefore necessary to examine the range of activities covered in each service

[1] S/L/92, adopted by the Council for Trade in Services on 23 March 2001.

sector and the limitations on market access and national treatment pertaining to the different modes of supply. In addition, in cases where a Member has also tabled a list of MFN exemptions, this must be examined in order to assess the extent to which the Member gives preferential treatment to one or more of its trading partners.

A specific commitment in a services Schedule is an undertaking to provide market access and national treatment for the service activity in question on the terms and conditions specified in the Schedule. When making a commitment, a government binds the specified level of market access and national treatment and undertakes not to impose any new measures that would restrict entry into the market or the operation of the service. Specific commitments thus have an effect similar to a tariff binding – they are a guarantee to economic operators in other Members that the conditions of entry and operation in the market will not be changed to their disadvantage. Commitments can only be withdrawn or modified after the agreement of compensatory adjustments with affected Members, as specified in Article XXI of the GATS. Such modifications of commitments may not affect the application of Most-Favoured-Nation (MFN) treatment. Commitments can however be added or improved at any time.

The Schedules all conform to a standard format. For each service sector or sub-sector that is offered, the Schedule must indicate, with respect to each of the four modes of supply, any limitations on market access or national treatment which are to be maintained. A commitment therefore consists of eight entries which indicate the presence or absence of market access or national treatment limitations with respect to each mode of supply. The first column in the standard format contains the sector or subsector which is the subject of the commitment; the second column contains limitations on market access; the third column contains limitations on national treatment. In the fourth column governments may enter any additional commitments which are not subject to scheduling under market access or national treatment.

Commitments are split into two sections: First, "horizontal" commitments which stipulate limitations that apply to all of the sectors included in the Schedule; these often refer to a particular mode of supply, notably commercial presence and the presence of natural persons. Any evaluation of sector-specific commitments must therefore take the horizontal entries into account. In the second section of the Schedule, commitments which apply to trade in services in a particular sector or subsector are listed.

The terminology used in Schedules has also been standardized wherever possible. What follows is a description of the information which has to be inscribed in each column of the Schedules and a summary of the terminology used.

- **The information that is entered in the columns**
  - Sector or sub-sector column: this column contains a clear definition of the sector, subsector or activity that is the subject of the specific commitment. Members are free, subject to the results of their negotiations with other participants, to identify which sectors, subsectors or activities they will list

in their Schedules, and it is only to these that the commitments apply. Committed sectors are sometimes very broad, as in "banking and other financial services" and sometimes very narrow, as in "noise abatement services".

In the great majority of Schedules the order in which the sectors are listed corresponds to the Services Sectoral Classification List[2] which lists twelve broad sectors as follows: 1. Business; 2. Communication; 3. Construction and Engineering; 4. Distribution; 5. Education; 6. Environment; 7. Financial; 8. Health; 9. Tourism and Travel; 10. Recreation, Cultural, and Sporting; 11. Transport; 12. Other. Furthermore, in most cases, the sectoral entries are accompanied by numerical references to the United Nations Central Product Classification (1991), which gives a detailed explanation of the services activities covered by each listed sector or subsector, and on which the sectoral listing is based. Where this was not possible, listings are to provide a sufficiently detailed definition to avoid any ambiguity as to the scope of the commitment. The Annex on Financial Services to the GATS is sometimes used for the scheduling of commitments in this sector. For telecom, the Notes for Scheduling Basic Telecom Services Commitments[3] is often used as a reference along with the Services Sectoral Classification List (Annex 6.8).

- Market access column: When a Member undertakes a commitment in a sector or subsector it must indicate for each mode of supply what limitations, if any, it maintains on market access. Article XVI:2 of the GATS lists six categories of restriction which may not be adopted or maintained unless they are specified in the Schedule. All limitations in Schedules therefore fall into one of these categories. They comprise four types of quantitative restriction plus limitations on types of legal entity and on foreign equity participation.
- National Treatment column: The national treatment obligation under Article XVII of the GATS is to accord to the services and service suppliers of any other Member treatment no less favourable than is accorded to domestic services and service suppliers. A Member wishing to maintain any limitations on national treatment – that is any measures which result in less-favourable treatment of foreign services or service suppliers – must indicate these limitations in the third column of its Schedule.
- Additional commitments column: Entries in this column are not obligatory but a Member may decide in a given sector to make additional commitments relating to measures other than those subject to scheduling under Articles XVI and XVII, for example qualifications, standards and licensing matters. This column is to be used to indicate positive undertakings, not the listing of additional limitations or restrictions.

[2] Contained in document MTN.GNS/W/120, and also appended to the Scheduling Guidelines that are contained in document S/L/92.

[3] S/GBT/W/2/Rev.1.

- **How commitments are recorded in Schedules**

In essence, the entries which constitute a legally binding commitment in a Member's Schedule indicate the presence or absence of limitations on market access and national treatment in relation to each of the four modes of supply for a listed sector, sub-sector or activity. In the following cases the entries use uniform terminology:

- Where there are no limitations on market access or national treatment in a given sector and mode of supply, the entry reads NONE. When the term NONE is used in the second or sector-specific part of the Schedule it means that there are no limitations specific to this sector: it must be borne in mind that, as noted above, there may be relevant horizontal limitations in the first part of the Schedule.
- All commitments in a Schedule are bound unless otherwise specified. In such a case, where a Member wishes to remain free in a given sector and mode of supply to introduce or maintain measures inconsistent with market access or national treatment, the Member has entered in the appropriate space the term UNBOUND.
- In some situations a particular mode of supply – such as the cross-border supply of bridge-building services – may not be technically possible or feasible. In such cases the term UNBOUND has been used, usually in conjunction with an explanatory footnote stating "Unbound due to lack of technical feasibility".

In many cases it will be seen that there are textual descriptions of bound commitments which indicate limitations on market access or national treatment. Such entries, which vary in length considerably, do not use uniform terminology but are based on one of two common approaches:

- The entry describes in the appropriate space the nature of the limitation, indicating the elements which make it inconsistent with Articles XVI and XVII of the GATS.
- In some cases, Members have chosen to indicate a limited commitment by describing what they are offering rather than the limitations they are maintaining. Such an approach is often used to indicate the market access opportunities for the entry of certain categories of foreign natural persons who supply services.

- **Drafting a List of Article II (Most Favoured-Nation) Exemptions**

Most-Favoured-Nation treatment is a general obligation that applies to all measures affecting trade in services. However, it has been agreed that particular measures inconsistent with the MFN obligation can be maintained – in principle for not more than ten years and subject to review after not more than five years. Such measures must have been specified in a list of MFN Exemptions submitted by the end of the Uruguay Round of Multilateral Trade Negotiations or as part of the Protocol of Accession by governments acceding to the WTO. Subsequently, requests for exemptions from Article II (MFN) can only be granted under the waiver procedures of the Marrakesh Agreement.

These lists are largely self-explanatory and are structured in a straightforward manner. In order to ensure a complete and precise listing of a Member's MFN exemptions, each Member is required to provide five types of information for each exemption:

(i) Description of the sector or sectors in which the exemption applies;
(ii) Description of the measure, indicating why it is inconsistent with Article II;
(iii) The country or countries to which the measure applies;
(iv) The intended duration of the exemption;
(v) The conditions creating the need for the exemption.

It is a basic principle of the Agreement that specific commitments are applied on an MFN basis. Where commitments are entered, therefore, the effect of an MFN exemption can only be to permit more favourable treatment to be given to the country to which the exemption applies than is given to all other Members. Where there are no commitments, however, an MFN exemption may also permit less favourable treatment to be given. It is not necessary to list measures providing for preferential liberalization of trade in services among Members of economic integration agreements, such as Free Trade Areas; such preferential treatment is permitted under Article V of the GATS and must meet the criteria laid down in that Article.

Annex 10

TEXT OF DECISIONS ON ACCESSION AND ACCESSION PROTOCOLS

WTO document WT/ACC/10/Rev.3 of 28 November 2005

ANNEX 10.1 GENERAL COUNCIL DECISIONS

The following text has been used until January 2001:

> "The General Council,
>
> Having regard to the results of the negotiations directed towards the establishment of the terms of accession of [name of applicant] to the Agreement Establishing the World Trade Organization and having prepared a Protocol for the Accession of [name of applicant].
>
> Decides, in accordance with Article XII of the Agreement Establishing the World Trade Organization, that [name of applicant] may accede to the Agreement Establishing the World Trade Organization on the terms set out in the said Protocol".

The text has been amended to be in line with other decision documents and from the accession of China onwards has read as follows:

> "The General Council,
>
> *Having regard to* paragraph 2 of Article XII and paragraph 1 of Article IX of the Marrakesh Agreement Establishing the World Trade Organization, and the Decision-Making Procedures under Articles IX and XII of the Marrakesh Agreement Establishing the World Trade Organization agreed by the General Council (WT/L/93),
>
> *Taking note* of the application of [name of applicant] for accession to the Marrakesh Agreement Establishing the World Trade Organization dated 7 December 1995,
>
> *Noting* the results of the negotiations directed toward the establishment of the terms of accession of [name of applicant] to the Marrakesh Agreement Establishing the World Trade Organization and having prepared a Protocol on the Accession [name of applicant] (WT/ACC/. . . /. . .),

Decides as follows:

[name of applicant] may accede to the Marrakesh Agreement Establishing the World Trade Organization on the terms and conditions set out in the Protocol annexed to this Decision.

ANNEX 10.2 ACCESSION PROTOCOLS

The following text is common to all Protocols of applicants that have acceded to WTO. Some Protocols contain additional provisions.

Protocol of Accession of [Name of Applicant]

to the Marrakesh Agreement Establishing

the World Trade Organization

"The World Trade Organization (hereinafter referred to as the "WTO"), pursuant to the approval of the General Council of the WTO accorded under Article XII of the Marrakesh Agreement Establishing the World Trade Organization (hereinafter referred to as "WTO Agreement"), and the Republic of . . . [name of applicant] . . . (hereinafter referred to as "[short form of name]"),

Taking note of the Report of the Working Party on the Accession of . . . [name of applicant] . . . to the WTO in document WT/ACC/[. . .] (hereinafter referred to as the "Working Party Report"),

Having regard to the results of the negotiations on the accession of . . . [name of applicant] . . . to the WTO,

Agree as follows:

Part I – General

1. Upon entry into force of this Protocol, . . . [name of applicant] . . . accedes to the WTO Agreement pursuant to Article XII of that Agreement and thereby becomes a Member of the WTO.

2. The WTO Agreement to which . . . [name of applicant] . . . accedes shall be the WTO Agreement as rectified, amended or otherwise modified by such legal instruments as may have entered into force before the date of entry into force of this Protocol. This Protocol, which shall comprise the commitments referred to in paragraph . . . [list of relevant commitment paragraph numbers] . . . of the Working Party Report, shall be an integral part of the WTO Agreement.

3. Except as otherwise provided for in the paragraphs referred to in paragraph . . . [list of relevant paragraphs numbers] . . . of the Working Party Report, those obligations in the Multilateral Trade Agreements annexed to the WTO Agreement that are to be implemented over a period of time starting with the entry into

force of that Agreement shall be implemented by . . . [name of applicant] . . . as if it had accepted that Agreement on the date of its entry into force.

Part II – Schedules

4. The Schedules annexed to this Protocol shall become the Schedule of Concessions and Commitments annexed to the General Agreement on Tariffs and Trade 1994 (hereinafter referred to as the "GATT 1994") and the Schedule of Specific Commitments annexed to the General Agreement on Trade in Services (hereinafter referred to as "GATS") relating to . . . [name of applicant] . . . The staging of the concessions and commitments listed in the Schedules shall be implemented as specified in the relevant parts of the respective Schedules.

5. For the purpose of the reference in paragraph 6(a) of Article II of the GATT 1994 to the date of that Agreement, the applicable date in respect of the Schedules of Concessions and Commitments annexed to this Protocol shall be the date of entry into force of this Protocol.

Part III – Final Provisions

6. This Protocol shall be open for acceptance, by signature or otherwise, by . . . [name of applicant] . . . until . . . [date] . . .

7. This Protocol shall enter into force on the thirtieth day following the day of its acceptance.

8. This Protocol shall be deposited with the Director-General of the WTO. The Director-General of the WTO shall promptly furnish a certified copy of this Protocol and a notification of acceptance thereto pursuant to paragraph 7 to each Member of the WTO and to . . . [name of applicant] . . .

9. This Protocol shall be registered in accordance with the provisions of Article 102 of the Charter of the United Nations.

Done at Geneva this . . . day of . . . [date] . . ., in a single copy in the English, French and Spanish languages each text being authentic, except that a Schedule annexed hereto may specify that it is authentic in only one or more of these languages".

Annex 11

LIST OF WTO AGREEMENTS AND ASSOCIATED LEGAL INSTRUMENTS

This Annex reproduces the table of contents of the Marrakesh Agreement Establishing the World Trade Organization, listing the major WTO Agreements. For related Decisions and Declarations, see The Results of the Uruguay Round of Multilateral Trade Negotiations – The Legal Texts.

AGREEMENT ESTABLISHING THE WORLD TRADE ORGANIZATION

ANNEX I

Annex 1A Multilateral Agreements on Trade in Goods

- **GATT 1994**

  Other duties and charges (GATT Art.II:l[b]), Understanding
  State trading enterprises (GATT Art.XVII), Understanding
  Balance-of-payments, Understanding
  Regional trade agreements (GATT Art.XXIV)
  Waivers of Obligations, Understanding Concession withdrawal (GATT Art.XXVIII), Understanding Marrakesh Protocol to the GATT 1994

- **Agriculture**
- **Sanitary and Phytosanitary Measures**
- **Textiles and Clothing**
- **Technical Barriers to Trade**
- **Trade-Related Investment Measures** (TRIMs)
- **Anti-Dumping** (Article VI of GATT 1994)
- **Customs valuation** (Article VII of GATT 1994)
- **Preshipment Inspection**
- **Rules of Origin**
- **Import Licensing**
- **Subsidies and Countervailing Measures**
- **Safeguards**

Annex 1B General Agreement on Trade in Services (GATS)

Annex 1C Trade-Related Aspects of Intellectual Property Rights (TRIPS)

Annex 2 Dispute Settlement Understanding

Annex 3 Trade Policy Review Mechanism

Annex 4 Plurilateral Trade Agreements

- Annex 4(a) Agreement on Trade in Civil Aircraft
- Annex 4(b) Agreement on Government Procurement
- Annex 4(c) International Dairy Agreement
- Annex 4(d) International Bovine Meat Agreement

Annex 12

OVERVIEW OF PROTOCOL COMMITMENTS

This table indicates the main subjects on which new Members have undertaken Protocol commitments. These are either set out in the body of the Report and incorporated by reference in the Protocol, or in the text of the Protocol itself. The new Members are arranged in the order in which they acceded.

	Ecuador	Bulgaria	Mongolia	Panama	Kyrgyz Republic	Latvia	Estonia	Jordan	Georgia	Albania	Oman	Croatia	Lithuania	Moldova	China	Chinese Taipei	Armenia	FYROM	Nepal	Cambodia	Saudi Arabia	Viet Nam	Tonga
Economic Policies																							
Monetary and Fiscal	■						■																
Foreign Exchange															■	■						■	
Balance of Payments Measures		■					■		■	■				■	■				■	■			■
Investment															■						■	■	■
State Ownership, Privatization		■	■		■	■	■		■	■		■	■	■	■	■	■	■		■	■	■	
Pricing	■	■		■	■	■	■	■	■	■	■	■	■	■	■	■	■	■	■	■	■	■	■
Competition																							
Policy Framework																							
Executive, Legislative, Judicial Branches						■	■	■							■		■					■	
Judicial Review					■				■		■	■			■		■		■	■	■	■	■
Sub-Central, Uniform Administration					■	■	■	■	■	■		■	■	■	■	■	■					■	■

	Ecuador	Bulgaria	Mongolia	Panama	Kyrgyz Republic	Latvia	Estonia	Jordan	Georgia	Albania	Oman	Croatia	Lithuania	Moldova	China	Chinese Taipei	Armenia	FYROM	Nepal	Cambodia	Saudi Arabia	Viet Nam	Tonga
Trade in Goods																							
Trading Rights																							
Trade in Goods - Imports																							
Customs Duties																							
Other Duties and Charges (ODCs)																							
Tariff Rate Quotas																							
Tariff Exemptions																							
Fees and Charges for Services Rendered																							
Internal Taxes																							
Quantitative Restrictions, Licensing																							
Customs Valuation																							

	Ecuador	Bulgaria	Mongolia	Panama	Kyrgyz Republic	Latvia	Estonia	Jordan	Georgia	Albania	Oman	Croatia	Lithuania	Moldova	China	Chinese Taipei	Armenia	FYROM	Nepal	Cambodia	Saudi Arabia	Viet Nam	Tonga
Rules of Origin		■			■		■	■	■	■	■	■	■	■	■	■	■	■	■	■	■	■	■
Other Formalities													■							■	■		
Preshipment Inspection	■		■	■	■			■	■	■				■	■	■	■		■	■	■	■	■
Anti-dumping, Countervailing Duties, Safeguards	■	■		■	■	■	■	■	■	■	■	■	■	■	■	■	■	■	■	■	■	■	■
Trade in Goods - Exports																							
Export Duties, Taxes		■	■			■	■		■			■			■			■	■	■	■	■	■
Export Restrictions	■		■	■	■		■	■	■	■	■	■	■	■	■		■		■	■	■	■	■
Export Subsidies	■	■	■	■	■	■	■	■	■	■	■	■	■	■	■	■	■	■		■	■	■	

	Ecuador	Bulgaria	Mongolia	Panama	Kyrgyz Republic	Latvia	Estonia	Jordan	Georgia	Albania	Oman	Croatia	Lithuania	Moldova	China	Chinese Taipei	Armenia	FYROM	Nepal	Cambodia	Saudi Arabia	Viet Nam	Tonga
Trade in Goods – Internal																							
Subsidies																							
Technical Barriers to Trade																							
Sanitary and Phytosanitary Measures																							
Trade-Related Investment Measures																							
State Trading Entities																							
Free Zones																							
Barter																							
Government Procurement																							
Transit																							
Trade in Goods - Sectors																							
Agriculture																							
Civil Aircraft																							

	Ecuador	Bulgaria	Mongolia	Panama	Kyrgyz Republic	Latvia	Estonia	Jordan	Georgia	Albania	Oman	Croatia	Lithuania	Moldova	China	Chinese Taipei	Armenia	FYROM	Nepal	Cambodia	Saudi Arabia	Viet Nam	Tonga
Textiles and Clothing																							
Trade-Related Intellectual Property Rights																							
TRIPS																							
Trade in Services																							
Services																							
Transparency																							
Publication																							
Notifications																							
Trade Agreements																							
Trade Agreements																							

Note 1. TBT China: Paragraphs 177,178,180,182, 184, 185, 187, 190, 191, 192, 193, 194, 195, 196, 197. Protocol I 13.
Note 2. SPS Saudi Arabia: Paragraphs 207, 208, 210, 212, 215, 216, 218, 222, 223, 224.
Note 3. TRIPS China: 49, 252, 256, 259, 263, 265, 270, 275, 284, 286, 288, 291, 292, 296, 299, 302, 304, 305,. Protocol VI.
Note 4. Services China: 307, 308, 309, 310, 312, 313, 314, 315, 316, 317, 318, 320.
Note 5. Services Viet Nam: 479, 480, 483, 484, 485, 488, 489, 491, 494, 496, 498, 499, 502, 503, 506, 507, 508.

Annex 13

SUGGESTED FORMATS FOR LEGISLATIVE ACTION PLANS

ANNEX 13.1 SUGGESTED FORMAT FOR COMPREHENSIVE LEGISLATIVE ACTION PLAN

Legislative Action Plan

Legislation	Purpose of Legislation	Status	Time Period
List each piece of legislation to be introduced or modified, starting with horizontal legislation and continuing with legislation relating to individual WTO Agreements.		E.g. being drafted, passed first reading in Parliament, adopted.	Remaining steps, with dates.

ANNEX 13.2 SUGGESTED FORMAT FOR LEGISLATIVE ACTION PLAN ON SPECIFIC SUBJECTS

Action Plan for the Implementation of Individual Agreement

Article of the Agreement	Obligations under the Article	Details of the extent to which the applicant is already in compliance	Further action required for full conformity	Deadline	Technical assistance needs

Annex 14

AGRICULTURAL TARIFF RATE QUOTAS AND SPECIAL SAFEGUARDS

	Number of Tariff Rate Quotas	Number of Tariff Lines with Tariff Rate Quotas	Tariff Lines with Special Safeguards
Ecuador	14	17 (HS 6 and 8 digit level)	0
Bulgaria	73	90 (HS 8 digit level)	21 (HS 6 and 8 digit level)
Mongolia	0	0	0
Panama	19	57 (HS 8 digit level)	6 (HS 8 digit level)
Kyrgyz Republic	0	0	0
Latvia	4	4 (HS 4, 6, 8 digit level)	0
Estonia	0	0	0
Jordan	0	0	0
Georgia	0	0	0
Albania	0	0	0
Oman	0	0	0
Croatia	9	9 (HS 4, 6, 8 digit level)	0
Lithuania	4	4 (HS 4, 6, 8 digit level)	0
Moldova	0	0	0
China	10	46 (HS 8 digit level)	0
Chinese Taipei	22	117 (HS 8 digit level)	32 (HS 8 digit level)
Armenia	0	0	0
FYROM	1	1 (HS 10 digit level)	0
Nepal	0	0	0
Cambodia	0	0	0
Saudi Arabia	0	0	0
Viet Nam	3	21	0
Tonga	0	0	0

Source: WTO document WT/ACC/10 and its Revisions.

Annex 15

SECTORAL INITIATIVES

PRODUCT COVERAGE OF SUCCESSFUL PLURILATERAL SECTORAL NEGOTIATIONS DURING THE URUGUAY ROUND

This Annex reproduces the text of Annex 5 of WTO document TN/MA/S/13. This notes that it is "based on non-official documents. The WTO Secretariat did not provide assistance to the Participants in negotiating these plurilateral sectoral initiatives and it cannot, therefore, guarantee that the product coverage described herein is entirely accurate. This Annex should be considered of an indicative nature only."

Please note that while the items listed below are defined in the HS 1992 nomenclature, the results of accession market access negotiations are normally consolidated in the HS nomenclature in force at the time of accession.

It may also be noted that the product coverage of some of these initiatives is being renegotiated as part of the Doha Round and that further sectoral initiatives are being discussed.

HS92 item	Product description
1. Agricultural Equipment (Tariff elimination)	
8432	Agricultural, horticultural, or forestry machinery for soil preparation or cultivation; lawn or sports-ground rollers; parts thereof
8433	Harvesting or threshing machinery, including straw or fodder balers; grass or hay mowers; machines for cleaning, sorting or grading eggs, fruit or other agricultural produce, other than machinery of heading 8437, parts thereof
8434	Machinery for sorting, screening, separating, washing, crushing, grinding, mixing, or kneading earth, stone, ores or other mineral substances, in solid (including powder or paste) form; machinery for agglomerating, shaping or molding solid mineral fuels, ceramic paste, unhardened cements, plastering materials or other mineral products in powder or paste form; machines for forming foundry molds of sand; parts thereof
ex8701.90	Agricultural tractors

2. Beer (Tariff elimination)

2203	Beer

3. Chemicals (Harmonization)

Chapters 28–39 of the Harmonized System	Product coverage does not include HS items contained in Annex 1 of the Agreement on Agriculture.

5. Construction Equipment (Tariff elimination)

8425	Pulley tackle and hoists other than skip hoists; winches and capstans
8426	Derricks; cranes, including cable cranes, mobile lifting frames, straddle carriers and works trucks fitted with a crane
8428	Other lifting, handling, loading or unloading machinery (For example, elevators, escalators, conveyors, teleferics)
8429	Self-propelled bulldozers, angledozers, graders, levelers, scrapers, mechanical shovels, excavators, shovel loaders, tamping machines and rollers
8430	Other moving, grading, leveling, scraping, excavating, tamping, compacting, extracting or boring machinery, for earth, minerals or ores; pile-drivers and pile-excavators; snow-ploughs and snow-blowers
Ex 8431	Parts suitable for the use solely or principally with the machinery of headings 8425 to 8430, except 8431.2.0 (parts for 8427 fork lift trucks)
8479.10	Machinery for public works, building or the like
8701.30	Track-laying tractors
8704.10	Dumpers designed for off-highway use

6. Distilled Spirits (Brown) (Tariff elimination)

2208.20	Brandy
2208.30	Whiskey
2208.90	Fruit brandy

7. Furniture (Tariff elimination)

ex9401.10	Seats for aircraft, not already covered by the civil aircraft code
9401.30	Swivel seats with variable height adjustment
9401.40	Seats other than garden seats or camping equipment, convertible into beds
9401.50	Seats of cane, osier bamboo or similar materials
9401.61	Other seats with wooden frames, upholstered
9401.69	Other seats with wooden frames, not upholstered
9401.71	Other seats with metal frames, upholstered
9401.79	Other seats with metal frames, not upholstered

9401.80	Other seats
9401.90	Parts
9403.10	Metal furniture for offices
9403.20	Other metal furniture
9403.30	Wooden furniture for offices
9403.50	Wooden furniture for kitchens
9403.60	Other wooden furniture
9403.70	Furniture of plastics
9403.80	Furniture of other materials including cane, osier bamboo and similar materials
9403.90	Parts

8. Medical equipment (Tariff elimination)

2844.40	Radioactive elements and isotopes and compounds
3822	Composite diagnostic or laboratory reagents other than those of heading 3002 or 3006
8419.20	Medical, surgical or laboratory sterilizers
ex8419.90	(Parts for 8419.20)
ex8543.80	(Electrical nerve stimulation – t.e.n.s.)
8713	Invalid carriages, whether or not motorized or otherwise mechanically propelled
8714.20	Parts and accessories of vehicles of headings 8711 to 8713: of invalid carriages
9018	Instruments and appliances used in medical, surgical, dental or veterinary sciences, including scintigraphic apparatus, other electro-medical apparatus and sight-testing instruments; parts and accessories thereof
9019	Mechano-therapy appliances; massage apparatus; psychological aptitude-testing apparatus; ozone therapy, oxygen therapy, aerosol therapy, artificial respiration or other therapeutic respiration apparatus; parts and accessories thereof
9021	Orthopedic appliances; splints; artificial parts of the body; hearing aids; parts and accessories thereof
9022.11	X-ray machines for medical, surgical, dental or veterinary uses
9022.19	X-ray machines for other uses
9022.21	Alpha, beta or- gamma ray machines for medical, dental, surgical or veterinary uses
Ex9025.11	Clinical or veterinary thermometers
9402	Medical, surgical, dental or veterinary furniture; parts thereof

9. Paper (Tariff elimination)

Chapters 47, 48, and 49	**Note: No further description was provided**

10. Steel (Tariff elimination)

7206.10	**Note: No further description was provided**
7207	
7208	
7209	
7210	
7211	
7212	
7213	
7214	
7215	
7216	
7217	
7218	
7219	
7220	
7221	
7222	
7223	
7224	
7225	
7226	
7227	
7228	
7229	
7301	
7302	Excluding 7302.30.00
7303	
7304	
7305	
7306	
ex7307.22	Couplings
ex7307.92	Couplings
7308	
7312	
7313	
7314	
7317	

11. Toys (Tariff elimination)

9501	**Note: No further description was provided**
9502	
9503	
9504	
9505	

12. Pharmaceuticals (Note: Partial description of the coverage)[1]

Chapter 30	
2936	Except dihydrostreptomycin and salts, esters, and hydrates thereof
2937	Except dihydrostreptomycin and salts, esters, and hydrates thereof
2939	Except dihydrostreptomycin and salts, esters, and hydrates thereof
2941	Except dihydrostreptomycin and salts, esters, and hydrates thereof

Information Technology Agreement (ITA)

The product coverage of the ITA, as contained in the Annex to document WT/MIN(96)/16, has subsequently been clarified in the Committee of Participants on the Expansion of Trade in Information Technology Products. Please refer to documents G/IT/W/6/Rev.3 and Job(07)/96.

Agreement on Trade in Civil Aircraft

The product coverage is contained in document TCA/4.

[1] The complete product coverage of the Sectoral on Pharmaceuticals can be found in GATT WTO document L/7430 and in WTO document G/MA/W/10. It includes all active ingredients which bear an international non-proprietary name (INN) from the World Health Organization; plus other products described in 4 Annexes, which includes products used for the production and manufacture of finished pharmaceuticals.

INDEX